# DIONYSUS
# MYTH AND CULT

Dionysus. Detail from a wine cup attributed to Pheidippos (ca. 520-510 B.C.). The Metropolitan Museum of Art, Rogers Fund, 1941. (Acc. No. 41.162.8)

# Walter F. Otto

---

𝔢

# DIONYSUS

## MYTH AND CULT

*Translated*
*with an Introduction*
*by* ROBERT B. PALMER

*Indiana University Press*
BLOOMINGTON AND LONDON

*D. M. S.*

*Walterus Otto*
*summarum artium liberalium*
*litterarum studiis utriusque linguae*
*perfecte eruditus,*
*musarum semper amator,*
*v. a. LXXXIV. h.s.e.*
*Te di manes tui*
*ut quietam patiantur*
*atque ita tueantur*
*optamus.*

# Contents

INTRODUCTION, by Robert B. Palmer      ix

FOREWORD, by Walter F. Otto      3

## I. MYTH AND *CULTUS*      7

## II. DIONYSUS

1. *Preface*      49
2. *The Birthplace of the Cult of Dionysus*      52
3. *The Son of Zeus and Semele*      65
4. *The Myths of His Epiphany*      74
5. *The God Who Comes*      79
6. *The Symbol of the Mask*      86
7. *Pandemonium and Silence*      92
8. *The World Bewitched*      95
9. *The Somber Madness*      103
10. *Modern Theories*      120
11. *The Mad God*      133
12. *The Vine*      143
13. *Dionysus Revealed in Vegetative Nature*      152
14. *Dionysus and the Element of Moisture*      160
15. *Dionysus and the Women*      171
16. *Ariadne*      181

17.  *The Fate of Dionysus*                          189

18.  *Dionysus and Apollo*                            202

19.  *Concluding Remarks on Tragedy*                  209


NOTES                                                211

INDEX                                                237

# *Plates*

*Frontispiece*   Dionysus.  Detail from a wine cup.

*Plate No.*                                    *facing page*

 1.  Maenads in ecstasy before Dionysus column.        54

 2.  Maenads ladling out wine before Dionysus column.  55

 3.  Maenads dancing at the festival of Dionysus.      55

 4.  An altar to Semele and her sisters.               68

 5.  Maenad dancing before Dionysus mask.              88

 6.  Maenad with *thyrsus* and leopard cup.            94

 7.  Hermes bringing new-born Dionysus to nymphs.     102

 8.  The panther of Dionysus.                         112

 9.  A maenad dancing.                                134

10.  Dionysus as seafarer. The Exekias cup.           156

11.  Dionysus in a ship with bow shaped like an ass's head. 170

12.  Dionysus and Ariadne accompanied by satyrs.      182

13.  Dionysus and a satyr.                            198

# Introduction

Gods of Hellas, gods of Hellas,
Can ye listen in your silence?
Can your mystic voices tell us
Where ye hide? In floating islands,
With a wind that evermore
Keeps you out of sight of shore?
Pan, Pan is dead.

ELIZABETH BARRETT BROWNING
*The Dead Pan*

WHEN Elizabeth Barrett Browning wrote these lines which sound so pessimistic and so limited to any lover of the beauty and truth of Greek mythology, she had in mind a famous passage out of Plutarch's *De Oraculorum defectu* (*Mor.* 419 A-E) in which it was reported on good authority that Pan had died.

But let Plutarch tell the story (Philip is speaking):

As for death among such beings [*i.e.*, deities], I have heard the words of a man who was not a fool nor an impostor. The father of Aemilianus the orator, to whom some of you have listened, was Epitherses, who lived in our town and was my teacher in grammar. He said that once upon a time, in making a voyage to Italy, he embarked on a ship carrying freight and many passengers. It was already evening when, near the Echinades Islands, the wind dropped, and the ship drifted near Paxi.[1] Almost everybody was awake, and a good many

1. The name is given to either of two small islands between Corcyra and Leucas off the west coast of the Greek Peloponnesus.

had not finished their after-dinner wine. Suddenly from the island of Paxi was heard the voice of someone loudly calling Thamus, so that all were amazed. Thamus was an Egyptian pilot, not known by name even to many on board. Twice he was called and made no reply, but the third time he answered; and the caller, raising his voice, said, "When you come opposite to Palodes, announce that Great Pan is dead." On hearing this, all, said Epitherses, were astonished and reasoned among themselves whether it was better to carry out the order or to refuse to meddle and let the matter go. Under the circumstances Thamus made up his mind that if there should be a breeze, he would sail past and keep quiet, but with no wind and a smooth sea about the place, he would announce what he had heard. So, when he came opposite Palodes, and there was neither wind nor wave, Thamus, from the stern, looking toward the land, said the words as he had heard them: "Great Pan is dead." Even before he had finished, there was a great cry of lamentation, not of one person, but of many, mingled with exclamations of amazement.[2]

This event occurred supposedly in the first century A.D., during the reign of Tiberius, in a Roman world in which the rationalistic and evolutionistic approach to religion had already done much to bring death not only to Pan but to many of the other greater and lesser gods of the Greek pantheon. Later, however, Christian legend[3] was to suggest that Pan had died on the very day when Christ had mounted the cross. It is this later tradition which leads to the hymn of triumph with which Mrs. Browning's poem ends:

> Oh brave poets, keep back nothing,
> Nor mix falsehood with the whole!

2. The translation is by Frank C. Babbitt (LCL, London, 1936), pp. 401-402.

3. The sources seem to follow two traditions: (1) Pan = demons (Eusebius, *Praeparatio Ev.* 5. 17), or (2) Pan = Christ (Voss, *Harmon. Evangel.* 2. 9, section 23). For this, see G.C. Wagner, "Examen historiae de morte magni Panis," *Miscellanea Lipsiensia*, Vol. IV (Leipzig, 1717), pp.143-163.

> Look up Godward; speak the truth in
> Worthy song from earnest soul;
> Hold, in high poetic duty,
> Truest Truth the fairest Beauty!
> Pan, Pan is dead.

One god had been substituted for another, but the world of godhead remained inviolate.

It is far different today in what has been called "The Post-Christian Era." Since the time of Elizabeth Barrett Browning, three great revolutions have occurred which have changed the world into a *mundus saecularis*. These are the revolutions in thought led by Darwin, Marx, and Freud—the revolutions which came with the exploitation of the concepts of the theory of evolution, of the social nature of man, and of the unconscious. Twentieth-century intellectual man has increasingly divorced himself from his former identity as *homo religiosus* and has embraced instead a philosophy of the non-transcendent. The non-religious man (the term would mean almost nothing in the ancient world) has become a reality. Mircea Eliade has done much to characterize him:

> The non-religious man refuses transcendence, accepts the relativity of "reality" and may even come to doubt the meaning of existence. . . . Modern non-religious man assumes a new existential situation; he regards himself solely as the subject and agent of history, and he refuses all appeal to transcendence. In other words, he accepts no model for humanity outside the human condition as it can be seen by the various historical situations. Man *makes himself*, and he only makes himself completely in proportion as he desacralizes himself and the world. The sacred is the prime obstacle to his freedom. He will become himself only when he is totally demysticized. He will not be truly free until he has killed the last god.[4]

4. Mircea Eliade, *The Sacred and Profane*, W.R. Trask, tr. (New York, 1959), pp.202 f.

It takes a long time to kill gods, both ancient and modern (there are some queer ones who say they have seen Pan since the first century A.D.), but when the last worshipper passes on to the Isles of the Blest, a whole *Weltanschauung* passes along with him, a vision which speaks of *Das Andere*, of otherness, of the unique finality of *Dinge an sich*.

It would be idle to deny that the scholarship devoted to the history of religions has escaped the effect of the gradual disappearance of this vision. To be sure, the first religions to be affected were the "nature" religions of primitive society which existed without a dogma of revelation. The presuppositions inherent in the evolutionary thesis which argued for a progression from the simple and the naive, from unicellular structures to more complex catena-like structures, had already discredited the ethical values to be found in these earlier religions, and had left them to the mercy of the rather crude experiments in interpretation to which they were now subjected. "We kill to dissect" is the way Canon Sanday expressed himself over a century ago as the study of comparative religions burst into the field of Biblical scholarship.[5] To certain scholars, however, who saw in the nature religions only *Urdummheit*[6] or worse, the nature religions were to need little killing. Approached in a rationalistic way, they were subjected to the animistic theories of the great Tylor, the pre-animistic theories of Codrington and Marett, the Durkheimean social theories which believed society had deified itself. In fact, with Durkheim, society had finally become God.

But the most devastating attack on the mythic awareness of the world of the Thou was to come from the psycho-

5. Quoted by R.R. Goodenough, "Religionswissenschaft," *Numen* 6 (1959), p.79. Canon Sanday must have been thinking of Wordsworth's "We murder to dissect," *The Tables Turned* 28.

6. The thesis of Th. Preuss.

analytic theories which were prepared to eliminate the objective existence or external reality of deity completely. Anthropologists and sociologists had from the beginning recognized the force of the *tremendum* which primitive man had placed outside of himself and over against himself in a vital confrontation. But the psychologists with Freud in the lead were to attempt to prove the Kantian view "that God was not an external substance but only a moral condition within us." In fact, Freud made a valiant effort to show how God was invented in the process of the discovery of the totem. The passage, so often repeated in his works since *Totem and Taboo* (1912-1913), makes rather quaint reading today, in spite of the devastating influence it has had. Take, for example, one of Freud's final works, *Moses and Monotheism* (1939), which is quite typical of his addiction to "hypothesis building," regardless of the nature of the source. In it he had said: [7]

> From Darwin I borrowed the hypothesis that man originally lived in small hordes, each of the hordes stood under the rule of an older male, who governed by brute force, appropriated all the females, and belabored or killed all the young males, including his own sons. From Atkinson I received the suggestion that this patriarchal system came to an end through the rebellion of the sons, who united against the father, overpowered him, and together consumed his body. Following Robertson Smith's totem theory I suggested that the horde, previously ruled by the father, was followed by a totemistic brother clan. In order to be able to live in peace with one another the victorious brothers renounced the women for whose sake they had killed the father, and agreed to practice exogamy. The power of the father was broken and the families were regulated by matriarchy. The ambivalence of the sons toward the father remained in force

7. Sigmund Freud, *Moses and Monotheism*, Katharine Jones, tr. (Vintage Books, New York, 1955), pp.168 f.

during the whole further development. Instead of a father, a certain animal was declared the totem; it stood for their ancestor and protecting spirit, and no one was allowed to hurt or kill it. Once a year, however, the whole clan assembled for a feast at which the otherwise revered totem was torn to pieces and eaten. No one was permitted to abstain from this feast; it was the solemn repetition of the father-murder, in which *social order, moral laws, and religion had their beginnings.*[8]

Religion, in short, was the indirect result of a traumatic accident out of which man invented a "god" to meet his "needs." But why had man continued to cling stubbornly to this delusion? It was because he "remained infantile and needed protection even when he was fully grown; he felt he could not relinquish the support of his god."[9] Thus, "god" developed slowly and painfully out of totemism with its worship of a father substitute and its "institution of laws" and "basic moral restrictions." As for myths—they were to Freud "the echo of that occurrence [*i.e.,* the death of the father of the horde] which threw its shadow over the whole development of mankind."[10]

God, therefore, to the Freudians would be an invention of a traumatized psyche (collective or no) and could have no external reality beyond that which He had been given by a psyche which clung to Him because of an infantile "need." "We kill in order to dissect."

Not all of the followers of Freud, however, could accept the master's hypothesis on the origins of religion. Somehow or other, the rich tapestry of mythic occurrences and the mystical experiences of mankind seemed inexplicable if they were subjected to rational explanations of this type. As a

8. My italics.
9. Freud, cited, p. 165.
10. Freud, preface to Theodore Reik, *Ritual: Psychoanalytic Studies* (New York, 1946).

consequence, Jung, much to Freud's sorrow, turned to a study of myths in various cultures, both Eastern and Western, and invented the theory of the "collective unconscious."

According to this theory, the mind contains, among other elements, "fantasy pictures of an impersonal nature which cannot be reduced to experiences in the individual's past, and these cannot be explained as something individually acquired. These fantasy pictures undoubtedly have their closest analogies in mythological types. We must, therefore, assume that they correspond to certain *collective* (and not personal) structural elements of the human psyche in general and, like the morphological elements of the human body, are inherited."[11] These "pre-existent forms of apprehension" or "congenital conditions of intuition" Jung called "archetypes" or "primordial images." Among them is to be found the archetype of the self or the god-image, perhaps the most dynamic and terrifying of all archetypes.

All archetypes are, however, "manifestations of processes in the collective unconscious," and do not refer to anything "that is or has been conscious, but to something *essentially unconscious*. In the last analysis, therefore, *it is impossible to say what they refer to*."[12]

Jung's thesis, although it is far better equipped to explain the striking similarities which exist in the image-making minds of men who have been subject to wildly diverse cultural patterns, is thus basically a product of its age and an extension of Freud's general thesis. It has, however, adopted certain of the methods and much of the vocabulary of theology and, therefore, appeals more often to the theologian than to the clinical psychologist. Fundamentally, however, it re-

11. C.G. Jung, C. Kerényi, *Essays on a Science of Mythology*, Bollingen Series 22 (New York, 1949), pp.102 f.
12. Ibid.

mains solipsistic in nature, in spite of its emphasis on the collective unconscious, with the soul creating its mystical experience out of itself as it reacts to internal stimuli. In any case, the "god-image" remains firmly ensconced in the archetype of the self which is, in turn, to be found somewhere in the Jungian collective unconscious. God, therefore, remains an "idea," an archetype with no guarantee of external reality.

Archetypes, moreover, are somehow inherited like "the morphological elements of the human body." The solipsistic chain must be broken in one way or another. Such a thesis can lead only to Lamarckianism and the genetical heresy that acquired qualities can be transmitted to future generations, a heresy to which Freud had been converted by the need he had to see in modern man "memory traces of the archaic heritage of mankind." That this heresy made few converts among modern geneticists seemed to bother neither psychologist. Thus theology, biology, and psychology were blended forcibly and synthetically to produce a twilight zone which seemed strangely at odds with the basic tenets of any one of the three fields from which it had been created.

It is to this same twilight zone that many classicists would relegate the work of Walter F. Otto which follows. Otto is accused by his detractors of pursuing the method of the theologian and not the pragmatic approach of the scholar— of writing prophecy, not history.

In the field of Greek religion, at least, the scholar-theologian has received short shrift from the philologist. One of the first to try to infiltrate the sacred precinct was Creuzer in 1810.[13] But Creuzer, who was an incurable Romantic in nature, let his enthusiasm for parallels between the East and

13. Georg F. Creuzer, *Symbolik und Mythologie der alten Völker* (Leipzig, Darmstadt, 1810-1812). Creuzer was preceded by C.G. Heyne, who in 1764 had already suggested that myths contained insights into reality. Creuzer, however, received the brunt of the attack.

the West becloud his better judgments to the point where he began to ignore the uniqueness of his source materials. Creuzer had his Lobeck.[14] With the appearance of the two volumes entitled *Aglaophamus*, the theological approach to Greek religion was dealt a stunning setback, and the "rationalists" took over. Nietzsche for a short period attempted to break their stranglehold, but Nietzsche had his Wilamowitz. Consequently, the study of Greek religion in the first half of the twentieth century was dominated by two men, both committed to the philologist's approach with its painstaking appeal to ancient and indigenous source materials. These were Ulrich von Wilamowitz-Moellendorf and Martin P. Nilsson. In spite of Wilamowitz' proud statement that he would only "think Greek," it was Nilsson, the great Swedish historian of religion, who was the least susceptible to outside influences. Wilamowitz began his final work on Greek religion, *Der Glaube der Hellenen*, with the thesis: "Die Götter sind da!" a thesis to which he honestly attempted to adhere, although, as Otto points out in *Dionysus*, the old rational presuppositions were too firmly entrenched in him to be abandoned completely. As for Nilsson, he has stuck to his guns, and it is he who has resisted the approach of Walter F. Otto to the end.[15]

Otto apparently had committed the unpardonable sin of heresy. Using all of the paraphernalia of scholarship: a precise and careful knowledge of the sources, a fine store of

14. And his Hermann, it might be added. See C.A. Lobeck, *Aglaophamus* (Königsberg, 1829); G. Hermann, *Ueber das Wesen und die Behandlung der Mythologie: ein Brief zu Herrn Hofrath Creuzer* (Leipzig, 1819).

15. See Martin P. Nilsson, "Letters to Professor Nock on Some Fundamental Concepts of the Science of Religion," written in 1947 and reprinted in *Opuscula Selecta*, Vol. III (Lund, 1960), pp.345-382. For Nilsson's views on Otto as a prophet and theologian, see *Gnomon* 11 (1938), pp.177 f.

critical acumen, a broad and catholic knowledge of ancient civilization in all of its facets, he had written what Guthrie correctly calls "a testament of Dionysiac worship."[16] To do this he had adopted a method and a pattern which would have been perfectly understood by many of the pre-Socratics with their concern with primal forms. He had insisted upon thinking theologically about a cult which had hitherto been approached historically.

Like the pre-Socratics, he had asked not so much *cur* or *quam ob rem* but *unde, quomodo*, and *qualis*—especially *qualis*. If the question *cur* was asked, moreover, it was asked in the form of *cur in hoc loco* rather than *cur denique*. At the heart of Otto's thesis lay the imminence of the god Dionysus, *in illo tempore*, to use Eliade's term. But the *why* of his imminence was not questioned so much as the *whence* of his appearance, and the how of this appearance, whenever and wherever it occurred.

It is Otto's commitment to these questions which leads him to use his sources as he does, culling his information—to the despair of the evolutionists—not only from the earlier centuries of Greece but from all the centuries intervening between the first manifestations of Dionysus and the later traces of him to be found, for example, in the *Dionysiaca* of Nonnus 5th c. A.D.). If a god appears, so he seems to imply, all of his manifestations must be studied whether early or late. This is not to deny the importance of their earliness or lateness, but the numinal awareness of a late source (i.e., Nonnus) can bear witness to the true essence of the god as well—or perhaps, at times, even better than the rather muted account to be found in Homer, one of our earliest, and apparently one of our more biased, literary sources.

16. W.K.C. Guthrie, *The Greeks and Their Gods* (London, 1950), p.146.

As for Otto's rejection of the psychological and anthropological approach to religion, the reasons seem clear enough. Most psychologists and most anthropologists, with the exception of Pater Schmidt, Jung, and William James, have carefully limited their investigations to a descriptive analysis of man's psyche and his social institutions. As a result, they have little to say about *Urformen*—in fact, they would consider the pursuit of "primaeval" forms a fruitless undertaking. Both, moreover, are captives of their method. The psychologists, who would put God into the soul and imprison Him there, can not have much to say about an external deity like Dionysus. The comparative anthropologists,[17] moreover, by the very fact that they have to find certain common denominators for man in society, are ill prepared to deal with the particular or unique occurrence—precisely those occurrences which characterize the epiphany of the god Dionysus. Otto, on the other hand, stresses always the uniqueness and the externality of "the god who appears."

There is, in addition, a basic principle of modern scientific scholarship which Otto's theological approach permits him to realize. Baldly stated, it is that "things or objects to be known exist independently of the knowledge we have of them."[18] Applied to religion, this principle could easily echo Tersteegen's statement: "Ein begriffener Gott ist kein Gott" (A god who is understood is no god). Dionysus, as Otto so clearly illustrates, is a god of paradox. Any study of him will inevitably lead to a statement of paradox and a realization that there will always be something beyond, which can never be explained adequately in any language other than the

17. The same can be said for the phenomenological approach to religion.

18. So once again, among others, J. Maritain in "Freudianism and Psychoanalysis," in *Freud and the 20th Century*, ed. B. Nelson (New York, 1959), p.232.

symbolic—and yet concrete—language of poetry or myth.

It is this which leads Otto to write at times in what can only be characterized as an apocalyptic style, "to speak with tongues," as it were. That this may embarrass Otto's philological critics is understandable since it forces them to meet him on two fronts: that of scholarship and that of poetry. But then we have long seen that the poet-theologian[19] and the poet-philosopher[20] find it impossible to live completely—or even partially—within the narrow limits of the disciplines to which they have made their major commitments.

F. Dümmler, in a review of W. H. Roscher's magisterial work, *Ausführliches Lexikon der griechischen und römischen Mythologie*, once said that "it is well known and quite understandable that the preoccupation with mythology has something intoxicating about it, and the man who does research in myth must always become to a certain degree a poet of theogonies."

Such is the case with Otto. If his Dionysus is read together with his *Die Götter Griechenlands*,[21] as it should be, a new theogony of the early world of Greece is created, a theogony which seems truer and closer to the real meaning of Greek myth as spoken *Wahrheit*[22] than we have had from the pens of most of Otto's great contemporaries.[23]

The mysterious voice heard off the islands of Paxi may

---

19. Consider for a moment Homer, Aeschylus, Hesiod, Virgil, Blake, Milton, Dante, Goethe, Hopkins, etc.; the list is almost endless.

20. Plato, Lucretius, Empedocles come to mind immediately in the ancient world.

21. W.F. Otto, *Die Götter Griechenlands*[2] (Frankfurt am Main, 1947), translated into English by Moses Hadas as *The Gods of Homer* (London, 1954).

22. That Otto's method has given us a new insight into Greek religion goes without saying. But that one of his insights should be vindicated so soon after his death in 1958 is particularly gratifying. Otto had insisted that Dionysus was an early god of the Greek pantheon. In this few scholars were willing to follow him. Now we read in Linear B

have been right about the death of Pan or the ancient gods, Hölderlin notwithstanding, but the world of Dionysus speaks to us again across the centuries through the words of what at times seems to be one of the last scions of the house of Thebes. Let no man arrogate to himself the right to say that a god has died until the echo which remains after the departure of the last of his worshippers has been dispelled.

ROBERT B. PALMER

*Scripps College*

script in a Pylos fragment (Xa O6) the word di-wo-nu-so-jo, growing evidence of the fact that we shall be forced to revise our concepts of the religious picture of the Mycenaean period given us by Nilsson and others. See J. Puhvel, "Eleuthêr and Oinoâtis," *Mycenaean Studies,* E.L. Bennett, Jr., ed. (Madison, 1964), pp.161-170.

23. This should in no way be interpreted as an attack on the value of Nilsson's *Geschichte der Griechischen Religion*, probably the greatest work of an encyclopaedic nature on Greek religion in the twentieth century. But Nilsson is, as he, himself, states, creating a reference work or handbook in which each god has been neatly and effectively tucked away in a huge filing cabinet. Such a method is hostile to theogonies and to statements of faith, as Nilsson clearly understood—hence his books, *Greek Religion* (1940) and *Greek Piety* (1948).

# DIONYSUS
## MYTH AND CULT

# Foreword

Dionysus had to be omitted from my book on *The Gods of Greece* (1929) because he does not belong to the circle of the true Olympians to which it was dedicated. Now he becomes the subject of a book of his own.

The way in which things are seen here diverges significantly from the norm. Usually one expects a study of ancient beliefs in deity to trace an evolution which starts with the crudity of first beginnings and ends with the splendor and dignity of the classical forms of deity. Here, on the contrary, the critical moment of original genius is moved back to the beginning which is prior to the activity of individual poets and artists. In fact, their activity would be quite unthinkable without this powerful impetus. Compared to this primal creation, the more recent brush strokes applied to the picture, however significant they may be in and of themselves, must appear trifling. Whoever calls this way of thinking unhistorical places strictures on the concept "historical" by presupposing that wherever greatness exists, the most critical and most remarkable phase is not inauguration and inception but the developmental process which gradually causes the jejune, that which has arisen out of pure need, to become significant and alive. This assumption runs counter to the unanimous testimony and transcendental apperception of all religions. But that is not all: it is irreconcilable with the nature and destiny of creativity in general—no matter where and how this may make its appearance in the world. It is clear how great a need there is for a new foundation for the study of the forms of deity.

Hence, this book begins with the problems of myth and *cultus* in general and only then proceeds to a study of Dionysus.

I am quite aware of the risk involved in talking about a Greek god who has been a holy name and an eternal symbol to our noblest minds. May these pages which I dedicate to the memory of these great men not prove wholly unworthy of their memory.

W. F. OTTO

*Frankfurt am Main,*
   *August, 1933*

### TRANSLATOR'S NOTE

The term *Kultus*, as Otto uses it throughout the book, is best understood in the light of Joachim Wach's definition: "All actions which flow from and are determined by religious experiences are to be regarded as practical expressions or *cultus*. In a narrower sense, however, we call *cultus* the act or acts of the *homo religiosus:* worship" (J. Wach, *Sociology of Religion* [Chicago, 1944], p.25). In any case, *Kultus* does not mean "ritual," which is only *one* of the acts of *cultus*.

# I

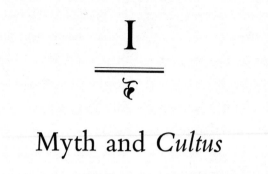

# Myth and *Cultus*

THE more recent efforts to understand ancient Greek religion are divided into two opposing schools of thought, the first of which can be characterized as anthropological in nature, the second philological. Both seek to work their way back to the beginnings of religious belief in order to understand, in terms of these beginnings, the elements which evolved later.

The followers of the anthropological approach are convinced that the original content of this belief must be similar to the naive ideas found today (or supposedly found today) among primitive peoples and in remote rural areas of Europe. There must have been a time, so the argument goes, when the basic perspectives of all peoples, relatively speaking, must have been determined by simple needs and good common sense. The religious concepts of the Greeks are to be traced back to this early period, the general nature of which can supposedly be established by a study of the primitive cultures we have with us today. Thus, what is "useful"—and "useful" in its simplest state of being—becomes the area of investigation into which a search is made for the original meaning of each form in which deity appears, and complete satisfaction is reached if one of these deities can be characterized as a "Vegetation deity."

These theorists, who derive their principles from anthropology and ethno-psychology, are opposed by the philologists, who subscribe to the basic principle that one should: "limit oneself to the Greeks and think 'Greek' about everything Greek." This is how it was expressed recently by Wilamowitz, who has become the philologists' leading spokesman with the publication of his remarkable final work, *Der Glaube der Hellenen*. His attacks on the views and methods of the "anthropologists" were so sharp and, indeed, frequently so bitterly scornful that we had the right to expect to find in his own presentation an entirely different answer to the basic questions involved. But we were disappointed. It became clear that the philological school, for which he could speak as a legitimate representative, actually agrees completely—in all its crucial points—with its opponents. Both apply the biological concept of evolution in exactly the same way.

Just as biology thought it was justified in believing that a line of constant development leads from the lowest to the highest organisms, so these two schools also place so-called "simple" concepts at the beginning of an evolution of religious thought out of which are to grow, through gradual change, the forms which the great deities assume at their peak. To be sure, in the course of time biology itself had to become a little more modest and had to acknowledge sudden new creations where it had formerly seen only continuous processes. Yet this is not the crucial objection to the methods used in our study of religion. When biology talked of evolution, it always put an *organism* at the beginning—an organism which still had to have, in every instance, no matter how simple it was thought to be, the main characteristic of an organism: it had to be a self-established whole. Only that which is alive is capable of developing. But in the dialectic advanced by the study of religion, evolution does not proceed from a simple form of life to a more complex and higher form but from the

Lifeless to the Alive. For the elements of faith which this study considers primal are nothing but conceptual systems from which life is completely lacking.

This can be demonstrated quite clearly in the observations which Wilamowitz devotes to the historical formation of the gods. He indignantly rejects the opinions of scholars who take their orientation from exotic cultures. But an examination of his own ideas of the nature of the primal forms of religious concepts reveals that his conclusions are not really so different. An example will make this evident. In origin, the god Hermes[1] is supposed to have been nothing more than a protector, and the stone pillars and heaps of stones in front of farm houses and along roads point to his presence. But all of the features which define his character: the paradox of his guiding and his leading astray, the sudden giving and taking away, the wisdom and cunning, the spirit of propitious love, the witchery of twilight, the weirdness of night and death— this diverse whole, which is inexhaustible and yet nowhere denies the unity of its being, is supposed to be only a complex of ideas which had gradually developed from the way of life of the worshippers, from their wishes and inclinations, ideas enriched by the love of story telling.

For the primal and solely true belief, there is left, according to Wilamowitz, only the thought of a protecting and helping god, in short, the idea of an X which lends assistance but has no other properties—except, perhaps, the power necessary for help.

At the beginning of the process called evolution there is, then, a mere Nothingness, and the concept of evolution has, consequently, lost its meaning. For a god like the one assumed here has no real substance, and that which has no essence is nothing. Wilamowitz's precept, which he repeated so often and with such earnestness: "The Gods are there" (i.e., belief

must above all be sure of the gods' existence before imagination can concern itself with them), this basic principle, remains an empty phrase. That which should be respected as
the most sacred object of belief turns out to be "not there"
the first time it is tested, and the objection which Wilamowitz himself justly raised against Usener's theory—"no man
prays to a concept"—applies to Wilamowitz's theory as well.
The protecting, helping god is nothing but an abstraction. It
would have occurred to no one had not the idea of "God,"
as the one almighty being whose Allness precludes form and
character, already been supplied to us by education and religion. It is only the dogmatic concept of a Being to which
all qualities accrue which has led to the mistaken idea that a
something which has only one quality (and that as abstract
a one as "protector") can be not "The God" but at least a
god. That which is presented to us, then, as the substance of
primal belief is actually a later idea emptied of all content.
Wherever belief became directly and unquestionably aware
of a god, there it could only have thought of him as a living
being, not as a mere capability or a power.

If, however, the primal substance of belief was a Something
having a real existence, a living Whole, we may well ask with
surprise why the *character* which it had to have as a living
entity should not have been precisely that character which is
revealed to us in the various reflections of myth. This would
not in any sense preclude the idea of an evolution but, instead, would return to it its logical meaning. Only where
there is a Being can there be an evolution or development.

These observations are directed against the work of a distinguished scholar only because he is the uncontested master
of the research which has been done up to this time; and
hence, the lack of clarity of its fundamentals manifests itself

most in his work. For the mistake of those others, whose views he fought so vehemently, is exactly the same as his.

As for the "Vegetation deity," the "Death God," and similar generalities into which we now like to dissipate living deities as if we had in them the primal concepts of religious consciousness—these, too, are nothing but lifeless ideas. How could they ever have fulfilled the demands of devotion, lifted up the spirit, elicited the powerful forms of *cultus*? No life proceeds from a concept, and if the great forms of the gods, which could motivate the creative spirit of a culture of highest genius, are to be understood historically, then there would be no more unproductive application imaginable than this.

*Cultus*, itself, in whose evidence we place our greatest trust, could teach us that fertility and death did not belong to two separate realms in the belief of early antiquity. Further investigation would finally have to lead to those greater realms of Being out of which godhead has spoken to living faith. Of course, to do this we would have to broaden and elevate our own thinking instead of resigning ourselves condescendingly to banalities. For our fragmented, mechanistic thinking knows nothing of such realms of Being, nothing of their unity. How, then, should it understand their divinity? It examines belief in deity with an astounding naiveté, dissipating its forms only to place them together again artificially to fit the pattern of a historical process. The assurance it needs it gets from ethno-psychology, which assumes that it must be the poverty-stricken concept of "the powerful" which plays the dominant role in primitive world views under the name of Mana, Orenda, etc. We shall leave this so-called primitive way of thinking to the future judgments of anthropologists. That it is suspiciously like our dynamic way of thought is a serious charge against it, not to speak of other objections which could be raised. Still, whatever the anthropologists may some day decide, no thoughtful person should be ignorant of the fact that the road to the gods never starts from "powers," whether we call them "magical" or dress them up in theological terminology. Whoever believes that ideas as abstract as these preceded the cult phase of deity has to acknowledge *cultus* as a completely new creation and as a break with the past. To do otherwise is to be guilty of applying the concept of evolution in an entirely meaningless way. This rift is barely covered over by a name as futile and yet as pretentious as "Vegetation deity." After all, what we describe by this name is nothing else but a pretext to account for the fact of growth—something just as abstract and lifeless as the concept of growth itself. This pretext we then merely disguise with a veil of reverence in our imagination, which is accustomed to conceive of God in this way.

Consequently, even though they seem to represent totally different principles, both sides share the view that everything which belongs to the living reality of a belief is a chance product of a so-called evolution. As for the primary substance of the belief, nothing remains except anaemic thought patterns.

Undoubtedly this is the reason why recent scholarship, with all its learning and ingenuity, and despite its isolated discoveries of considerable worth to the settlement of specific problems, always ends up with the same old empty statements. The questions of meaning and origin are always answered with vacuous formulations of religious viewpoints or sentiments which are supposed to have validity for all peoples and cultures. Because people have varied ways of life and needs, these formulations became substanceless and endlessly subject to change. Nothing suggests a manifestation of the divine which could be meaningfully characterized as

*Greek*. Nothing bears witness to the spirit which was one day to be imbued with the idea of Greek art and Greek wisdom, and which was to be chosen to become the teacher of a new world. To be sure, the philologists have taken great pains to fathom the religious thought-world of the poets and philosophers. With Wilamowitz,[2] they criticize the "modern historians of religion" for losing their interest with the emergence of the great gods, and regaining it only "when the old religion has started to decay and the repulsive superstition of the magical papyri takes its place." But their individualism is capable of conceiving the creators of all that is significant and profound only in the likeness of the great single personalities. Thus, for the period before these great gods appeared (and that means the epoch when Greek religion began), nothing is left but the unspiritual. So, the "history" of Greek religion begins, not with revelations, but with a nothingness.

It is time to decide to pay more serious attention to the *sources* and to put an end to our suppression, out of prejudice, of half of the awe-inspiring things they contain.

2

Both sides are in unanimous agreement that *cultus* is the only true witness of religious belief, while myth is nothing but poetry. Neither side believes that it has encountered any insurmountable difficulties in deducing from religious rites both the principles out of which these rites arise and the essential nature of the powers for which the rites were intended. Our own emotions, a little thought, the help we can get from primitive cultures which supply us with the analogies we need—these elements, it is believed, will let us arrive rather easily at the primal meaning of ceremonies which must have been practical in their aims, in any case. "The purpose of *cultus* and of all of its practices," so says Wilamowitz,[3] "is union and interaction with deity. This happens on two fronts: winning the good will and grace of the god, or appeasing his anger." Others add that cult practices were originally meant to force the god to do what was wished. In fact, these practices were imputed to have a magical efficacy in and of themselves. It was only at a later stage that the good will of the god was considered necessary for their success. But I shall say no more about this. At any rate, everyone agrees that cult practices, in the beginning, could have had as their purpose only the bringing of *useful* results to man.

In this way the modern mind has been able to make use of an extremely naive premise to adapt to its own method of thinking and its own way of life one of the most awe-inspiring phenomena of man's history. And yet, the religious rites which still impinge upon our being should have served as a warning. For no serious observer can avoid the impression that *cultus* is the most alien of all the elements which seem foreign to modern thought. Consequently, the concepts of utility and self-interest may well be the least suited to explain genuine cult practices.

Oddly enough, the proponents of the utility thesis never notice the contradictions into which they have gotten themselves. "The gods are there!" is the cry of Wilamowitz. He even goes on to speak of "visions" to which man has said, "This is God."[4] But he forgets what he has said at the very moment when its complete meaning should be clear to him. If men ever really spoke in this fashion—men from whom the sound of the name "God" still evoked the electricity which it later lost through usage and dogma—is it self-evident that their first impulse was to solicit the good will of the great one before whom they stood in awe? Why, we ask ourselves, is there such an expenditure of greatness in the economy of the universe if we must believe that men who actually came face to face with the great one remained just as small in this encounter as if they were dealing with patrons who are susceptible to "flattery, promises and gifts"? We must either abandon the assertion that man once consciously believed in a god worthy of the name, or we must confess that the first manifestation, by whose vision man was overcome, must have produced ecstasy, devotion, allegiance, and exaltation. Are the beginnings of *cultus* absolutely without evidence of this? Yet the moment we admit that *cultus* was not only meant for obvious needs, we must, of course, give up our optimistic statements that we can really know it, or that we can easily arrive at the nature of the belief which stands behind it. Can we, therefore, ever actually confine ourselves to an examination of *cultus* and expect to derive no enlightenment at all from myth?

But myth, so we are told, is only poetry.

What have we said when we say that? Do we mean that it rose out of an arbitrary act of the imagination? Nobody seriously believes that. Genuine poetry is never arbitrary. The philologist knows quite well that the poets of antiquity asked the gods to fill them with the spirit of truth. But this truth was supposedly not the truth of religious faith but an artistic truth, as it were, and the great poets (with their own ideas) were the first ones to give it its real meaning. I shall not inquire into the term "artistic." It is strangely obscure, and this obscurity has long stood in the way of an understanding of Greek myth. Whatever we may think about the nature of poetic creativity, and no matter how demonstrable or probable it is that many individual poets wrote and continued to write poetry around myth, it should be quite clear that all of this poetry from individuals has as its basic premise the existence of the world of myth; and that this original myth cannot, in turn, be explained away by that which we call "the poetic process." When Wilamowitz demands, and rightly so, that our first premise must be "The gods are there," then this means, if we examine it more precisely, "The myth is there." For if the gods "are," if they are real, then they cannot fail to have distinctive characteristics. With this, however, we are already in the world of myth. And who will dare to decide beforehand how great a measure of diversity and emotion can be ascribed to the forms of deity in their first manifestation?

But *cultus*, however it may have developed in individual instances in response to the demands made of it, on the whole presupposes myth, even though the myth may be latent. The greatness which *cultus* was called upon to serve must have existed as such: a holy reality, that is to say, a totality filled with true existence. Again we must admit that it is not the business of any general thesis or theory to decide beforehand how complex and interrelated this reality can be thought to be.

Many unquestionably old rituals are obviously connected with mythical happenings. In Eleusis the fortunes of Demeter and her daughter are acted out in public in the form of cult celebrations. The women who serve Dionysus are wholly similar, in their actions and their suffering, to the female attendants who are inseparably bound to him in the myth. Just as these last are hounded mercilessly in the story of Lycurgus, which we know from the *Iliad* (and many other myths tell us of their adversity and their suffering), so there were in the cults of Dionysus a hounding and maltreatment of women. The religion of Dionysus to which this book is dedicated offers many very remarkable examples of this kind of agreement. But in the provinces of the other gods, too, *cultus* and myth are often so similar that one can look like the mirror image of the other.

A naive interpretation, which we encounter even in antiquity, sees cult practices of this type as a reflection, that is to say, as an imitation of myth. More recent scholarship emphatically rejects this thesis and interprets mythology, on the contrary, as a product of the imagination evoked by cult practices. When it comes into existence, moreover, its true meaning has often long since been forgotten. This proposal seems to be supported by a type of legendary story which was obviously invented to explain names and customs which had become unintelligible, and is, therefore, called aetiological. One should think, however, that such inventions can never completely conceal their premeditated purpose, and by this very fact they are different from the old creations in which the unbiased observer is unable to discover anything tendentious. Actually no reasonable man believes that all myths were produced in as rational a manner as this. Rather, they are supposed to be a translation of the ritualistic practices into the form of sacred old events, a poetic metamorphosis of a cult act into a story in which gods and heroes now assumed the roles which, in reality, man in his worship had acted out. Still, one only has to imagine the way in which this so-called transference came about to become certain that no participant in *cultus* ever would have thought of it, if the world of myth into whose theatre its practices were transferred had not already been in existence.

There is no doubt that both sides are both right as well as wrong. *Cultus* was not called to life by myth, nor was myth by *cultus*. Both presuppositions lead of necessity to absurdity, if we try to think them through to their conclusions.

## 3

The somewhat childish explanation of *cultus* which states
that it is an imitation of myth certainly does the significance
of *cultus* no justice. And yet modern theory has misunderstood and disparaged this explanation more than have all previous speculations and reveries. Completely dominated and
blinded by the self-confidence of the rational and technical
civilization of its time, modern theory has never recognized
the astonishing dimensions of *cultus*, grasping merely that
part of its living essence which a mind receptive only to what
is useful would grasp of the living essence of a cathedral.
Were the phenomenon of artistic creation completely lost to
us at some time, we would first have to approach it with
wonder before we would dare to penetrate to its meaning.
So, the phenomenon of *cultus*, which has, as a matter of fact,
been lost to us except for a few ancient remnants, should
awaken in us, above all, a deep sense of awe.

*Cultus* as a totality belongs to the monumental *creations* of
the human spirit. To get a proper perspective of it, we must
rank it with architecture, art, poetry, and music—all of which
once served religion. It is one of the great languages with
which mankind speaks to the Almighty, speaking to Him for
no other reason than that it must. The Almighty or "God"
did not earn these names of Almighty or God only by striking
fear into man and forcing him to win His good will by favors.
The proof of His greatness is the power it engenders. Man
owes the highest of which he is capable to the feeling of His
presence. And this highest is his power to speak, a power
which bears witness to the marvelous encounter through
which it is conceived and brought into being. Every manifestation also unlocks the soul of man, and this immediately

results in creative activity. Man must give utterance to the feeling of awe which has seized him. There was a time when he did this by building temples, a form of expression which the gigantic undertaking of cathedral construction has continued even into the centuries which lie before us. One can call them the habitations of godhead, and yet this term expresses only an insignificant part of their great meaning. They are the mirror, the expression of the Divine, born of a spirit which must express itself in plastic form when the splendor of greatness has touched it.

The most sacred of these great languages is the language of *cultus*. Its age lies far behind us, and it is really not surprising that it is precisely its language which has become more alien to us than all the others. It testifies that the Almighty was so near that man had to offer his own being as the form in which this proximity could be expressed—an expression that the other languages were called upon to create, from a greater distance, through the media of stone, color, tones, and words. For this reason they have become more powerful as the proximity of deity disappeared, while *cultus* slowly lost its vitality. But it continued as the companion of other languages for thousands of years, and many of its forms still had the power, even in later ages, to evoke a deity whose presence they had summoned up in time past.

None of this contradicts the fact that the deity is offered something in *cultus* which will delight it, something which should have value for it. None of it contradicts the fact that this is accompanied by man's natural wish to be blessed by the good will of deity. Wherever men are united by awe and love, the first impulse of reverence and giving is the need to express great emotion. Yet if we suspect self-interest, we consider the giver's sentiments to be base or his piety unwarranted. But must the vulgar intrigues and sentiments of mankind give us the model for man's intercourse with the gods? If so, let us stop using words as awe-inspiring as "faith" and "worship." Let us not speak of "Great Events," and let us not prostitute the name of religion by using it to describe a superstitious delusion and its mercenary exploitation. The man who permits himself to speak of greatness should know that its surest sign is that great emotions must respond to it.

The forms of *cultus* are determined by the proximity of deity. Hence many of them have the characteristics of immediate communion with it. Sacrifice makes its appearance as a gift which deity is to receive, a repast in which it is to participate. Prayer is a salutation, a eulogy, or a request. But the position which the worshipper assumes, his physical acts, are unquestionably older than his words and more primal expressions of his feeling that the god is present. Its force we can no longer conceive of by considering the emotion of which man in our experience is capable. That which he later built out of stones to honor God (and his cathedrals still tell us of this today), that very thing *he, himself*, once was, with his arms stretched out to heaven, standing upright like a column or kneeling. And if, in the course of centuries, the only element which remained generally understood in the infinite meaning of that act was the act of supplication, just a tiny remnant of that meaning, then that is merely an example of the same poverty of understanding from which other forms of *cultus* also suffered in later ages.

The rite of the blood sacrifice is a creation whose greatness we can still experience, even though its significance was, for the most part, already lost in the time when it was still being practiced. Recent theories—regardless of whether they resort to the analogy of the "*do ut des*" thesis or more complex ways of thought—only prove that the entire conception of this rite could not have sprung from motives which stem from our rational being. If we were in a position to feel once more what it means for a god to be in our immediate presence, only an experience of this imminence could open our eyes. Even to hope for such an experience is presumptuous. But this should not make us incapable of recognizing, in the powerful drama of the animal which sheds its life-blood, the expression of a state of mind, the sublimity of which can be found paralleled only in the great works of art. Nothing makes less sense than to confuse the element of expediency, which is never completely lacking in any genuine act of creation, with the spirit which has produced the created whole. To do this is to take the process of fossilization for the process of life. The more the creative spirit is eclipsed, the more prominent interest and utility always become.

If we were to adhere to the utility thesis, we would have absolutely no way of dealing with those acts of *cultus* for which the analogies of our own existence would no longer permit us to divine a purpose. I think of dances, processions, dramatic scenes of highly divergent types. Let us not be confused any longer by the barren ideology with which the members of retrograde cultures presume to explain their customs which still survive but are no longer understood. The serious observer cannot doubt that the dances and evolutions of *cultus* were set into motion and given form by a contact with the Divine. They were so filled with its presence, so transported, that they often no longer expressed the human condition but the reality and activity of the god, himself. Thus later it was said that man was imitating the god and his history. That is still by far the most logical explanation. The idea we like so much today—that man wanted to be transformed into a god—coincides, at best, with a late interpretation. If God were really there, what better thing could man have done than become, in himself, the living monument of His presence?

But God had, as yet, no history which could be related and imitated. His myth lived in cult activity, and the actions of *cultus* expressed in plastic form what He was and what He did. Before the faithful visualized the image of their God, and gave verbal expression to His life and works, He was so close to them that their spirit, touched by His breath, was aroused to holy activity. With their own bodies they created His image. His living reality was mirrored in the solemnity of their actions long before this mute or inarticulate myth was made eloquent and poetic.

The great era of this myth, strictly speaking, dawned only after *cultus* began to lose its original freshness and creative vitality and become fixed. At that time great sculptors drew anew from the same divine abundance out of which practices of *cultus* had arisen. In its emotion-filled richness they found a diversity of Being and Becoming which *cultus* had not made apparent. But the same reality which was expressed in cult institutions was present in the singers, too, who unquestionably created song out of just that element of the existence, effect, and fortunes of this reality which the sponsors of the cult—that is to say, the community—had had to experience in the consummation of the cult.

Living reality is always inexhaustible. Other people may have received in the presence of godhead holy laws and most secret wisdom, but the Greek genius was given the key to a great theatre, whose scenes revealed the wonders of the world of the gods with a clarity which is unparalleled. The sacred Being, which, in the cult of every god, led irresistibly to ritual, became clear, and was revealed in an abundance of forms. The limitless meaning of godhead stepped into the light of living forms—comparable to that which occurred later in a new form in the fine arts.

That is the way of the Greeks. Are we to call it less religious than others because here faith in God does not reveal laws, penance, and the denial of the world, but the sacredness of Him who is and the great circles of Being in which gods, as eternal form, are active? This prejudice, of course, lies at the heart of all research up to now, and for this reason everything which myth created had to be interpreted as a product of the poetic imagination, without the realization that our task is understanding the religion of the *Greek* spirit.

For this religion, myth, as such, is no less of a witness than *cultus*. Actually, it yields more information because the forms of *cultus* are less well known to us and are, unfortunately, all too often obscure. The language of myth, on the other hand, is not only more mobile but also more distinct. To be sure, it reached its point of perfection in those ages in which the singers were no longer the spokesmen for the spirit of the community but had received the revelation of deity as individuals. In the course of the years, moreover, man has used his poetic imagination to subject myth to arbitrary and personal interpretations, meddlesome speculations, and the naive desire he has always had to rationalize everything. Viewed as a whole, however, it still remains the noblest phenomenon of Greek religion.

Myths which concern themselves with heroes are collective revelations of the manifestation of heroism, even though many of these stories were given their form independently by individual poets. Yet the manifestation of heroism cannot be ascribed to poetic creation, as we understand it, but is rather the presupposition behind all poetic creation. Such is the case with myth, which takes its life from the primal forms of deity, which must of necessity reveal their reality to the

Greek spirit in an atmosphere of ever-increasing enlightenment and awareness.

The true purpose of our critical analysis, however, is to
recognize the opinionated—the trivial—for what it is, and to
distinguish it from the great features by which the Divine
made itself visible to the Greek spirit, which was born to
observe.

### 4

Up to this point I have spoken constantly of the reality
of deity, even though it is the custom to speak only of religious concepts or religious belief.

The more recent scholarship in religion is surprisingly in-
different to the ontological content of this belief. As a matter
of fact, all of its methodology tacitly assumes that there
could not be an essence which would justify the cults and the
myths. As a basis for the cult practices of antiquity, it ac-
knowledges nothing objective with which we would not be
intimately acquainted in our everyday lives—nothing we
would not believe we could comprehend far more suitably
with our scientific and practical minds. Wilamowitz still says
too little when he remarks in the introduction of his book,
"The historians of religion too often give the impression that
history leads to the abolishment of religion."[5]

Our new interpretation of cult as a creative act prepares
us best to state and to answer the question of ontology.

If myths and cults did not come into the world as idle
tales and as actions geared to a useful purpose but as creations
of a monumental nature like buildings and sculptures, then
we must criticize the process of their formation in the same
way in which creative processes must be criticized.

The creative ones have always known that the act of creation has to be set into motion by something which man does not have in his power. The greater their creative power was, the surer their belief in an Existence which has reality and the majesty of the One who set all into motion. Even the more modest followers of the great masters could not dispense with the idea of inspiration. Scholarship, unfortunately, has neglected to appreciate the significance of this phenomenon. To be sure, it has been struck by the greatness of the occurrence in which living and life-creating elements were generated, but it believes that it can judge the event itself without regard for the experiences of those who were involved with their whole being in an occurrence of this type. What is known about man—man, as society shows him to be, who has the power to manipulate to his own advantage certain attributes of thought and action, and who allows himself, at times, to be edified by cultural achievements which have long since been created— this well-known fact, given its proper magnification, is all scholarship needs, so it seems, to understand the most powerful thing that has ever been created. Modern man's preoccupation with primitive cultures has supposedly given this narrow point of view a broader focus. But this is an illusion; for it is sheer prejudice that the views and the capabilities which are commonly met in all of these cultures could really explain the structure of their ancient state institutions and cults.

The creative phenomenon must be its own witness. And its testimony has only one meaning: that the human mind cannot become creative by itself, even under the most favorable circumstances, but that it needs to be touched and inspired by a wonderful Otherness; that the efficacy of this Otherness forms the most important part of the total creative process, no matter how gifted men are thought to be. This is what the creative ones have told us in all ages when they appealed to an inspiration which emanated from a higher being. When Homer invokes the Muse and asks her to instruct him; when Hesiod tells us that he has heard the song of the Muses and was ordained poet by them, themselves; then we are accustomed to see in this no more than the necessary result of a belief in the gods, which is no longer meaningful to us. But if we listen to Goethe when he earnestly assures us that great thoughts belong to no man but must be accepted thankfully and reverently as a gift and a blessing, then we learn to see the professions of a Homer, a Hesiod, and many others, in a new light. Whether we believe in Apollo and the Muses or not, we must acknowledge that the living consciousness of the presence of a higher Being necessarily is part of creative acts in the high style, and that our judgment can never do justice to the phenomenon of this type of creation if it ignores this fact. Even the lesser minds who produce new forms of a more polished order in an area which has long since been delineated are probably aware of the mysterious, marvelous thing which is happening to them. But the closer we get to the great, the primal, the epoch-making creations, the clearer and more powerful this awareness becomes.

*Cultus*, more than all other creations, bears witness to an encounter with the supernatural. In the beginning, however, the distinction was not as great as it seems today. The many different creations which we call the arts were formerly much closer to *cultus*, in fact, belonged to its own particular province. Even language was, without a doubt, created in the commerce with the transcendent power which moves the world. Before it could contribute to the mutual understanding of mankind, it emerged with primal force in the form of glorification and prayer. From the arts, we can still observe how they freed themselves from their connection with *cultus* and became secular. They were unquestionably called into life by a more powerful, a more deeply experienced afflatus of the miraculous, whose presence is attested to by the emotions of ecstasy and grace even today when the arts seem to have a completely independent existence.

When we look, therefore, at origins, at fundamental forces, we must characterize all of the creative activities of man, without distinction, as cult practices. But among these there is a more intimate nucleus which could never be secularized because here man himself, as a being having body and mind, is the substance in which the Almighty becomes form. These are the cult forms, in a special sense of the word. They could lose their resilience, they could disappear, but they could not be secularized. The others are somewhat removed from the mystery of the marvelous, and even if they could not exist or continue to exist without receiving the spark of life from the marvelous, still we cannot fail to think of this distance as a part of them.

It is the special characteristic of the creation of *cultus* that it lacks this distance. It is so closely associated with a compelling awareness of the nearness of the supernatural that man is drawn with his whole being into the creative act of form-making. Sculptors and creators of every kind are aware of inspiration and flashes of insight; and the greater they are, the more reverence they show as they refer to the mystery which guides them. *Cultus*, on the other hand, bears witness to the manifestation of godhead. At the center of all religion stands the appearance of God. That He has come, that He is present—this gives meaning and life to all of religion's primal forms. With this we have arrived at a primary occurrence which can no longer be understood as a product of man's thought, his constructs of knowledge, his everyday life, but rather as a prerequisite for them. Hence, it also becomes pointless to ask whether something has taken place in external reality or whether man has been seized by an "idea." The alternative has only surface validity. For even when we say "idea," we must insist that we are dealing with an irreducible something, with an instigator and director of thought processes, not with one of their results.

The derivation of this primary "something" from the well-known laws of thought and sense-perception has become the main concern of scholars in recent years. When these laws do not suffice, other categories of thought analogous to them are assumed (so, for example, Ernst Cassirer). These, supposedly, have made the same contribution to the establishment of a mythic world view as our categories of thought seem to be making to the establishment of our empirical world. The remaining hypotheses, which are quite contrived, at least in part, do not consider the basic phenomenon of the religious element at all. In fact, they are there just to avoid recognizing it, as far as they are able.

But what good does it do to refer to the laws of the intellect if there is no recognition of that which has given rational thought its direction and purpose? What is gained by referring to human needs, human wishes, and human forms of reality when it is just these elements which need explaining most? We really should understand that it is hopeless to derive the main forms of religious belief from an already completed store of ideas, necessities, and ideals. For these, even if they seem to correspond to certain given conditions in the external and internal world, still need something identifying them as a whole before they become what they are. It is only our fragmentized way of looking at things which deceives us in this matter. We focus on individual necessities and needs, thought processes, wishes, goals, and ideals and do not consider the whole. We neglect to see that all of these are actually only single forms of a collective life pattern whose creation is a greater miracle than the accomplishments of the most distinguished creators and inventors. And with that we have returned to the great act of creation. Everything refers back to it, and through it all forms—be they called works, necessities, or convictions—are shown the way.

In the center of everything significant, in the center of every final intention stands the image of man himself—the form in which he wishes to see himself. It is asinine to say that he lent this image to the Almighty, and thus the forms of men's gods came into being. It was in godhead that this image first appeared to him. Before man was in the position to see himself, God manifested Himself to him. His image preceded the human image. What the form and nature of man could and should be, man learned from the appearance of the Divine.

The majestic epiphany, through the contemplation of which man became aware of his own image, also radiated that quickened whole which we called the total life-pattern. *At the beginning stands always the god.* By Him first are created the goal and the road to that goal; by Him, too, the suffering He is supposed to alleviate. It was not because man had wishes that a god appeared to man to grant him fulfillment, but the needs and the wishes, like the granting of the needs and wishes, flowed from the reality of godhead.

Too much time has been spent on the senseless task of deriving the efficacious from the impotent. There is nothing in the world which has shown such productivity as the image of deity. Let us finally be convinced that it is foolish to trace what is most productive back to the unproductive: to wishes, to anxieties, to yearnings; that it is foolish to trace living ideas, which first made rational thought possible, back to rational processes; or the understanding of the essential, which first gives purposeful aspirations their scope and direction, to a concept of utility.

5

Whether we investigate the *cultus* and belief of a particular culture or human life as it is expressed in it, we always arrive at a great act of creation, which cannot be explained by any of the individual configurations of this culture but has endowed them all with their intrinsic nature, and hence, their being.

The total *Gestalt* of what we call culture rests upon a commanding myth which is inseparably bound to the myth of godhead. With the creation of this myth, culture and a national ethos are established. Prior to this they are not there at all. Of course, we do not mean by this that all of the varied perspectives of myth had to enter the world at one moment. The vitality which produced the great event could and had to create constantly something new—constantly new, and yet always the same.

If, thus, the experiencing of an almighty presence, of which cult practices give us overwhelming evidence, is the first link in every chain of vital evolution; if, in short, it cannot be explained by any of the phenomena which succeed it but rather is itself indispensable to the foundation of all future creative activity, then we must label it as the primal phenomenon and must recognize that the manifestation of godhead, from which all religions take their point of departure, is not only not a delusion but the most real of all realities. For its manifestations include everything that we call "real," from the formation of human society and culture to the objects of experience, thought, sensation, and will. The road on which all of them lie has been delineated by the primal phenomenon of the myth—and not by human intentions and circumstances.

I suppose we do not want to base creativity, particularly in those aspects in which it is most significant, totally on an event which originates in godhead, separating it in the process from all of the human powers, capabilities, and inclinations we know from experience. We have the habit of looking at the great spiritual processes with uncreative minds. Consequently, this concept must seem paradoxical to the highest degree. But paradox belongs to the nature of everything that is creative. There is meaning here in the statement that man's most intimate activity is not his own, that an "otherness" allies itself with him in all creation, and that this "otherness" has far more significance than the sum total of everything he instinctively experiences as his own intentions and faculties. Anyone who investigates the cults and myths and does not permit himself to be confused by the concept of theoretical man (who never would have produced anything like this) must see immediately that the paradoxical contradiction which distinguishes all genuine acts of creation, is imperatively evident in cult and myth. In them we acknowledge the greatest creations which give direction to all other creations; for it is they which are supported by such a vital and powerful awareness of a higher presence that man's activity no longer just works together enigmatically with the godlike but has become an out-and-out witness to the higher Being.

All religions bear witness to the experience that every great instance of human efficacy is a revelation of divine efficacy. And at the moment when the first forms of the whole form-making process come into being, that is to say, at the moment when cults and myths appear, this experience becomes an overwhelming event which we can do little else but recognize. And we must admit that the doctrine of the manifestation of deity expresses adequately that which actually occurred and continued to occur as long as *cultus* and myth continued to give living testimony.

6

Rudolf Otto[6] also insists upon the objective nature of the revelation of deity. But his idea of the "holy" is an objectiveness which manifests itself only psychologically and can be comprehended only by the methods of psychology. The soul, we are told, reaches a state where the emotions of terror and nothingness combine with those of rapture and adoration to produce a miraculous experience—the experience of an unquestionable reality. But this reality can be perceived only in emotional seizures of this type. Before it can be related to the objects of empirical knowledge, a special kind of mental activity is needed vis-à-vis these objects, like that which Kant considered necessary for "things in themselves." In itself this reality has no relationship to these objects—in fact, it is not even possible to say anything about it by comparing the two. Rather, it is the "wholly other," something completely different from anything in our world. As such, it is revealed directly only to the experience of the soul, that is to say, to an entirely mystical experience.

There can be no question that this doctrine, too, places at the beginning that which was to come later, even though it does advocate emphatically the reality of revelation. Thus the secret retreat of the soul which has become fearful and confused and has been thrown back upon itself is placed before the original creation of *cultus* and myth—even though this soul could have found nothing without the myth, which had long since been in existence. As for myth and *cultus*, they, too, are supposed to have become alive only through a secondary intellectual activity.

The reality to which our observations have led us is far different.

That which confronts mankind in epiphanies is not a reality which is completely unrecognizable and imperceptible, affecting only the soul which turns its back on the world, but the world itself as a divine form, as a plenitude of divine configurations. These are the primal appearances which stand at the beginning of all of the more profound human activities and endeavors. They transform the horde into the community, the community into the nation, and go on to leave their mark on the creations of all of the basic forms of human existence. Thus none of the institutions and practices which affect the basic existence of a people is to be completely separated from cult. Rather, all of them, in their periods of most vital growth, no matter how practical and useful they may be, are at the same time cult practices, that is to say, expressions or imitations of the glories of being which appeared at the beginning and established the culture through their appearance.

"The greatest creative force is that which succeeds in giving form to human life itself." The truth of this statement is extended here to include the knowledge that the appearance of the highest realities preceded this creation to stir it into action and to make it fruitful. As for these realities, in their totality they were nothing else but the divine vision of the world, seen even as a particular people was called upon to see it and be possessed by it.

7

Current opinion to the contrary, therefore, it is not the application of unusual means to the achievement of a thoroughly natural aim, but the absence of expediency which makes cult practices so alien and strange to the modern mind. The basic character of these acts is not determined by the fact that the men who first participated in them wished to bring about some desirable objective, but the fact that they already possessed the most desirable of objectives—the imminence of deity.

That a faith in future salvation should associate itself with an activity which sprang from such plenitude is natural and inevitable. From time immemorial man has considered it beneficial to assimilate the great occurrences of the earth and the universe. A profound sense taught him to adjust his own actions to their forms and movements: to the course of the sun by turning toward the right; to the three- and four-fold divisions of heaven's and earth's expanse and to the passage of time by ordering his own existence, and so forth. But the assumption that practical considerations impelled him to do all of this, and not the necessity to pour out his heart and surrender himself to the great god, produces a prejudice whose persistence is explained all too easily by modern man's convictions.

To support this assumption, the intellect of ancient man had to be credited with something completely absurd: the notion that certain purely schematic practices affect objects with which they have no contact at all. A circle drawn around an endangered area was supposed to have been credited with the power of protecting everything found within that circle. The pouring of water out of a cask supposedly was expected to call forth the hoped-for rain, and so forth. And, in fact, ancient man is supposed to have thought that these practices had the power to force results even though they had only the most superficial resemblance to that which was wished. Since, however, every sensible man knows today that they really have no power, we have the task of constructing a way of thought or view of life in which such ideas are something natural. This we call the world-view of magic. Its artificially organized system has the virtue of being closely related to modern man's way of thinking. Of course, it is admittedly composed of nothing but gross misconceptions, but here, too, it amounts to a mechanism of isolated causes and isolated re-sults, and here, too, its chief relationship to the world is the will to master it. The modern theoretician would rather credit his ancestors with the crudest blunders in their choice of means than ascribe to them serious actions which did not originate from some concept of utility. Otherwise he would be forced to admit that his own viewpoint could not act as the standard for the conduct of primitive peoples—in fact, it might even be restricting man's intellectual horizon to a serious degree.

The problems which this point of view has forced upon us, leading as they have to some very pretentious theories of evo-lution, are nothing but sham problems. There is, to be sure, a mental attitude which we are completely justified in calling "magical." It draws all of its power from subjectivity and is aware that it can affect men and things in astonishing ways by a mysterious concentration of the total faculties of the heart and soul. Here, external occurrences are considered second-ary and non-essential even though their help is gladly utilized. This is what the true magicians of all ages and all regions tell us—from the miracle workers in primitive tribes to Paracelsus and his followers. It is obvious that this mental attitude presupposes a specific talent. But even though there may have been communities which were dominated by this attitude, this much is certain: those who were destined to live in the world of *cultus* and myth could never have belonged to these communities. Magic is dependent upon the formless world to be found in the inner recesses of the soul—a realm of the infinite, composed of the most mysterious powers. Myth and *cultus*, on the other hand, are meant to serve the true reality of the world of the earth and the stars.

This genuine magic, the significance of which we shall in no way contest, had its name and prestige preempted by that system of absurd practices which is supposedly earlier in origin than myths and cults. If it had not been for this, we would have been more suspicious of certain customs of primitive peoples (and of the northern European peasants). We would have been far more aware of the ways in which the rituals failed to coincide with the ideas out of which they supposedly arose—even though the participants themselves may, on occasion, have accounted for the former in terms of the latter. Anyone who examines the nature of these rituals without prejudice must come away with the impression that they could exist only thanks to a great emotion, a feeling of passionate exaltation. And such exaltation can have been aroused only by a mythic vision which had taken possession of the human spirit. Whatever type of myth this was— whether it revealed the essential form of the animal, or the drama of an awakening procreative force, the story of the course of the sun, the spirit of combat, etc.—it had to enter reality as action. That was the form in which it existed among men, whether it ever was presented as narrative or not. But when the life of this myth is extinguished and the mechanical action is passed on from generation to generation, phantom ideas begin to inhabit the empty shell. Then the declining and impoverished culture might well believe that this artistic structure was erected out of practical needs, the only thing it still understands; and scholarship believes that it must inquire only how that mentality was created which could ascribe an effective force to empty forms.

How this relates at all to the customs of today's primitive man, to the fact that these customs are as non-mythic and as mechanical as theory assumes, will not be investigated here.[7] But there can be no question that the magical way of thinking which is attributed today to the origins of civilization is actually a product of decadence and impoverishment, regardless of where it still appears. It is only after the essential greatness (whose myth had given cult its meaning) has disappeared from man's consciousness that the impoverished followers of static traditions could become the victims of the superstition that a mysterious power inhabited things done *per se*. The essence of superstition, in spite of what Tylor tells us, is not that it clings to something which has already been discarded, even though its presupppositions have long since lost their vitality, but that it adapts behavior which once arose from a great idea to a barren and prosaic train of thought, and makes it serve self-interest.

But the concept of utility, however early it may have attached itself to the cult act, is always secondary and contributes nothing to the understanding of the origins of the act. The more it moves into the foreground, the greater the distance becomes between ritual and the spirit in which it was conceived. Wherever the concept of utility reigns supreme, cult actions have become completely superficial. This natural process has been reversed by scholars who have mistaken the static end product for the beginning of life. The simple ancient traditions, which they ignore with haughty contempt, deserve far greater respect. These traditions trace the cults back partly to direct interventions by exalted Beings who once appeared in the flesh, and partly to occurrences of a higher order whose memory the cult practices were to preserve. They placed, therefore, a great event at the beginning, and to this extent they are entirely consistent with the true nature of the creation of cult. No matter what may have happened to call a cult into life, it must necessarily have been of such a nature that no configuration suited it better than the story which we find in the tradition. Something great must have occurred, a revelation of such miraculous force that the community of men made a living monument for it out of themselves, surrendering themselves completely to the holy ecstasy of being, in themselves, an answer to, and an expression of, the transcendent.

What has been stated here in general terms could and should be illustrated in detail by numerous examples. For the time being, however, it may be enough to advance a few instances which seemed unusually favorable to the modern point of view, and then, finally, to make reference to a few which openly contradict it.

There was a very old ritual of expiation and purification which was widespread in the ancient world. This ritual stipulated that one or two men were to be led through the entire city; they were then to be killed outside the city; and their bodies were to be completely destroyed.[8] The modern interpretation of this terrible act proceeds from the assumption that it must have been engendered by the same practical state of mind which characterizes all the methods by which man, even today, purges his body and his surroundings of the unclean.

In other words, it was supposedly believed that the dangerous and the perilous clung to a man's being as an external defilement and could be removed by a very simple expedient

much like the scrubbings we give our bodies. "The pharmakos was led around throughout the entire city to absorb
every miasma. He was then killed and burned or taken over
the border of the country just as one wipes a dirty table off
with a sponge and then throws the sponge away. . . . That is
quite primitive and understandable."[9] A ceremonial custom
of antiquity is thus "understandable" to the modern scholar
as soon as he thinks he sees in it the characteristics of the same
mode of thought which directs our everyday actions. In the
case we have before us, the disparity between the act itself
and the thought process foisted upon it is so great that the
naive self-assurance of the modern mind must astound us
almost more than the so-called superstition of "primitive"
man.

In spite of the fragmentary nature of the source material,
the grandeur of the original act still reveals itself clearly
enough. The chosen one was beaten with branches, as if he
were being blessed, and he was led around to the music of
the flute. As we are explicitly told once, he was clad in holy
garments and wreathed with sacred plants. Previously he had
also been fed at public expense on especially pure foods. The
entire celebration took place partly because of special circumstances when a pestilence raged in the land, partly at
regular intervals at the time when the fruits of the field were
approaching maturity. It would be foolhardy to wish to
interpret all of the particulars of the rite. They are not what
is significant here, moreover, and the scholars who have
fought over them have lost sight of the main point in the
process. A man is clad and garlanded with great ceremony, he
is led past every home to the accompaniment of music, and he
is finally killed, either by being thrown off a cliff or by
stoning. And all of this is done to purify and protect the
entire community. Filth was wiped off formerly, as it is

today, with cheap cleaning agents. The horrifying pomp of this tragedy, however, demands, as its counterpart, something portentous—a sinister, lofty greatness to whose presence the community responded with such terrible seriousness. There is no name we can give to this dark Being whose giant shadow fell over the habitations of mankind. His myth was the cult practices themselves which created for the destroyer his image in a gruesome drama. But this image would never have been created if he had not been overwhelmingly revealed from a position of immediate imminence. That which appears to our dull, our unimaginative minds as a menace and poison of a material nature endowed the great generations of antiquity with a wealth of forms not because they thought about these matters even more superficially and mechanistically than we ourselves do, but rather because this image reared itself up before them as a colossal form which was not to be avoided, and forced them to express their emotion creatively in an awful monumental act. More exactly expressed—their ceremonial actions and the revelation of this colossal form were one and the same thing. Nor would they have been affected as deeply by the supernatural, as their creativity intimates, had the idea of utility been an integral part of their cult practices. This only came second, as in all creativity, but it made its appearance quite naturally and necessarily. Just as the artist who gives expression and voice to the spirit of a great destiny in an eloquent painting frees himself from that spirit by this act and simultaneously saves everyone who is affected by his work, so the dreadful was abolished after it was given form in cult. The city was purged of its sins, and freedom and health were regained. The nature of the devotion, too, with which the mute chorus approached the sheet lightning of the transcendent, must have been bound up with a trust in grace—a trust, in fact, in the granting of specific prayers. But the greater the focus was on goals and intentions, the more impoverished the essence of the ceremonial activity became, and where they alone ruled, it had become completely static and lifeless. This latter situation the evolutionists, with rare misunderstanding, have taken to be the original one. Their interpretation of the act of expiation proceeded wholly from the concept of utility allied with it, as if it were self-evident that the original meaning of the elements of this act could be divulged only by this concept. That which seemed "primitive" and "understandable" to the evolutionists was that which was secondary in nature: the regard for material well-being, which, it is true, soon had to be valued as the most important element by the unoriginal thinkers of later generations and was suited here, as elsewhere, to make sacred rites into acts of good common sense. In the process, of course, the ancient forms remained behind as highly paradoxical remnants, and it was reserved for our age to be the first to talk of them as evidence for a practical common-sense point of view.

The sacrifice of men or animals on whom the burden of sin of the whole community is loaded is something quite different. We know of such acts from primitive cultures, too (for example, in the detailed descriptions in G.T. Basden's book on the Ibos of Nigeria[10]). They also have nothing to do with the materialistic and mechanistic thinking which seems so natural to us. That which distinguishes them from cult practices *per se* is an idea which must seem just as absurd to the scholarly mind of our day as all cultic matters do. This is the stupendous idea of redemption through a life which has taken upon itself the guilt of all.

Grim customs like these are offset by more cheerful ones which give expression to the idea of divine assistance. It was the custom in Tanagra for the handsomest young man to walk around the city in the Hermes festival with a ram draped over his shoulders. The god himself, as the story goes, once freed the city from a pestilence by making the rounds in this way, and the ritual was established to commemorate this event.[11] Here, too, modern scholarship ignores not only the myth but also the very nature of the cult practice, advancing its own speculations as it confines itself to the apparent purpose of the ritual, and to its self-made hypotheses of what primitive man thinks. The ram was carried around the town "to absorb the miasma." "The meaning of the custom is, therefore, clear. Like all such expiation rites, this one, too, originally was an end in itself. It was associated with Hermes in this instance because the young man who carried the ram was the exact human likeness of the shepherd god who carried the ram."[12] If he was that, however, then the animal which he carried cannot have had the function ascribed to it here. Hermes certainly did not carry the ram on his shoulders to absorb infectious germs. He, like everyone who carries the animal in this way, picked it up to bring it to its destination unharmed. That is what shepherds do. And that Hermes, the shepherd, should walk around the city to protect it is really a more sensible idea than the thesis that the animal, no matter who carried it, had to absorb harmful substances like a sponge. Even if we would seriously credit prehistoric man with this nonsense, we would have to insist that the purpose which the young man supposedly had in mind was expressed by his attitude; that this shepherd, in short, was not that of the solicitous shepherd. And finally, what sense would there have been in choosing the handsomest young man for this ignoble task? The only thing which does justice to this ceremonial act is the cult tradition which associates the rite with the myth of the god who walks around the town. If it had not survived, we would have had to have invented something like it. There is no doubt that once in a time of great adversity it was believed that the god, who lovingly watches over the flocks, was seen walking around the city in this way, and that salvation came, thanks to his protection. To acknowledge this epiphany, there had to be a ritual. It was the living monument of an overwhelming event. How could man who had been touched by the Divine remain inert and motionless when all genuine revelation awakens the power of creativity? The vision which the people of Tanagra saw was far from an hallucination. It was a mythic encounter which demanded that man give it concrete form by using his own body in ceremonial action. And with this the community came into contact with the sphere of the Divine. It was inevitable that man should feel that something salutary was being accomplished, just as the god himself had once brought salvation with his walking. But the primary and actual motive for the act was not usefulness. Even less are we to see in expediency the meaning of the form in which the act was expressed. Without the myth of Hermes, the walk around the city would have been a futile undertaking. Let us not appeal to the cases in which sacrificial animals were led around the community to bless it, as, for example, in the Italic *lustrum* and *amburbium*. We are, after all, still far from understanding the original meaning of these and related acts, and we should finally have done with the process which subordinates the intelligible to artificial hypotheses which the unintelligible seemed to require.

How closely *cultus* is bound to myth, how many cult practices in their original nature are nothing but reflections of a supernatural reality and occurrence—on this the religion of Dionysus is singularly informative. At its center stands the myth of Dionysus himself, with the divine women who reared him and are his constant companions. All of them suffer adversity and persecution and must die, the same as he. And the terrors which afflict them are unmistakably linked to the dreadful action to which their madness incites them. The mother, the nurse, who murderously assault tender living beings, are ever-recurrent forms of the myth whose profound significance will be revealed to us later. A fragment of the mythical story of Dionysus and his female attendants is already present in the *Iliad*.[13] The mighty Lycurgus, the son of Dryas, once hunted the nurses of the frenzied Dionysus over the regions of Nysa. Struck by the terrible weapon of Lycurgus, they threw their holy *thrysi* to the ground. But Dionysus, himself, fled to the depths of the sea, where Thetis took the trembling god into her protection. What this old myth tells us is acted out in cult in the festival of the Agrionia, which will receive our close attention later. In Orchomenus women were pursued by the priest of Dionysus with sword drawn and those who did not escape him were struck down without pity. It was said that they came from the family of Minyas, whose daughters had once torn apart one of their little boys in a fit of Dionysiac madness. The disappearance of the god himself was also the subject of a cult activity. In the festival of the Agrionia at Chaeronea, the women looked for Dionysus until they finally returned with the news that he had made his escape to the Muses.

Every attempt to explain these cult practices independently of myth leads to idle speculation. The women who are cruelly hunted down by the priests are nothing else but duplicates of the frenzied women of the myth who attended Dionysus. In the cult of Dionysus, in general, the main role is played by the women because in the myth they are the inseparable companions of the god. When the Thyiades, on the day of the festival, awaken the child Dionysus in the cradle, they are doing nothing else but what is done by the divine nurses who rear the young god and participate in his revels when he has reached maturity. These cult practices are undoubtedly more awe-inspiring than the mythic story which we learn from literature. But both are born of the same spirit. The women who participate in the cult become, through the primal force of divine revelation, accessories to a holy occurrence which the myth was to express in words. The myth was not created for an ulterior purpose, any more than the cult practices arose from a motive other than the necessity to give form to the miraculous by which the mind had been transfixed. The mediator was man himself, enraptured by the Divine, and on him it had to work its effect. That this cultic realization of the Divine could also be considered a source of blessing is, of course, self-evident. After all, it served the divine presence. But here, too, the natural order of events has been arbitrarily reversed by modern scholarship.

In the course of the discussion which follows, we shall meet still other examples of this significant conjunction of *cultus* and myth.

Finally, let us only mention in passing that religious practices of the so-called primitives, which hitherto have usually been cited as evidence for the rationalistic hypotheses, still permit us to recognize often enough the nature of the genuine mythic process. The solemn ceremony held during a storm, which A. Talbot observed in Nigeria, is particularly impressive and informative.[14] Talbot tells us that each lightning flash, at the moment when it occurred, was answered by a mighty trumpet blast. The effect was tremendous, touching on the sublime. He, himself, had felt as if the flashing lightning were a sword torn out of the scabbard. There the lightning-god of heaven is considered to be the principal deity. Along with him the divine earth mother is worshipped. The cult practice is, as we see, the immediate response of enraptured mankind to his manifestation or revelation. It bears the myth within itself, and in the imminence of deity establishes it as a living form.

The nature of such cult acts, which are one with myth, can

be studied, especially, in the so-called sun dances of the Indians.[15] But all of this is only supposed to be a preliminary reference.

Godhead has appeared to all peoples and has determined the character not only of their cults but, simultaneously, of their own existence and action; and it has left its imprint on the national character. But because of its profundity and its diversity, the godhead to which the belief of the Greeks bears witness will always remain memorable.

## 8

If, then, the cults are not utilitarian in nature but are, instead, mighty creations called into life by the divine afflatus of a god who reveals himself; if the myths are no old wives' tales but witnesses of this same encounter with the Sublime; if then, it is valid to acknowledge primal phenomena and to do justice to great realities; then the study of psychology and logic, of which previously everything has been expected, can benefit us no longer. Knowledge can come to us only from the reality of the world itself; our chosen leaders must no longer be the petty men of limited vision from whom we have previously taken our orientation, but the greatest intellects who have had the most profound views of the world and have been seized most forcefully by that which is.

It is about time, again, to remember the words of Schelling: "It is not a question here of how we must turn, twist, limit, or curtail the phenomenon so that it can still be explained, if need be, by principles which we once agreed not to exceed; but it is a question rather of the direction in which we must expand our ideas to come to terms with the phenomenon."[16]

# II

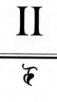

# Dionysus

# 1. *Preface*

ALL of antiquity extolled Dionysus as the god who gave man wine. However, he was known also as the raving god whose presence makes man mad and incites him to savagery and even to lust for blood. He was the confidant and companion of the spirits of the dead. Mysterious dedications called him the Lord of Souls. To his worship belonged the drama which has enriched the world with a miracle of the spirit. The flowers of spring bore witness to him, too. The ivy, the pine, the fig tree were dear to him. Yet far above all of these blessings in the natural world of vegetation stood the gift of the vine, which has been blessed a thousandfold. Dionysus was the god of the most blessed ecstasy and the most enraptured love. But he was also the persecuted god, the suffering and dying god, and all whom he loved, all who attended him, had to share his tragic fate.

The most distinguished poets and thinkers sensed in this diversity a reality of inexpressible depth. But modern scholars are still completely baffled by it. No matter how often they have attempted to trace the diverse back to the simple, the meaning of the collective whole has always escaped them.

Lately they have been astonishingly unanimous in their endorsement of an explanation which can probably be said to be by far the least satisfactory of all such explanations. Dionysus is called "a god of vegetation." Yet, it is obvious that he was known to reveal himself not in the plant world, as such, but in the life of certain specific plants, among which the vine is incomparably the most important. Is it not more likely, rather, that it is the particular nature of precisely these plants which bore witness to the efficacy of the god, and is it not this which can give us an indication of his specific nature? However, such clues are not pursued. Instead, one prefers to believe that Dionysus, for unknown reasons, limited himself, in the course of time, to a special area even though there is no evidence in the sources for a more inclusive area. On the contrary, this can be surmised only through hypotheses, and this is done only because one wishes to derive the remarkable belief, of which the Greek sources speak, from the simplest of concepts. Hence, all of the great attributes which make up the character of Dionysus are supposed to have come together purely by accident, from the outside, and not to have arisen out of an inner necessity because of what he was.

This attempted explanation actually renounces all understanding. It is based on a preconceived idea of nature deities, and disregards everything which is peculiar to the Greek god. In the terrible image of the frenzied god it sees only that which we already know or believe we know from other religions. The obsession of the women, the miracle of the wine, the proximity of death, the tragic drama—these and other essentials of the cult and the myth mean nothing to it. But as long as it is not seen that the manifestation of the divine reality which is called Dionysus is to be discerned in these great forms in which he appears, the inquiry into the religion of Dionysus has not even begun.

An intoxicated god, a mad god! Truly an idea which demands our deepest thought. The ready hypotheses which reduce everything significant to the level of the commonplace have only served to keep us from seeing the tremendous force of this idea. History, however, bears witness to its might and its truth. It revealed to the Greeks such a great and extensive insight into what intoxication meant that thousands of years after the decline of Greek culture a Hölderlin and a Nietzsche could still express their ultimate, their most profound thoughts in the name of Dionysus. So, too, Hegel,[1] who conceived truth in a Dionysiac image, saying it was "the bacchanalian revel in which no member is not intoxicated."

## 2. The Birthplace of the Cult of Dionysus

Nowadays it is believed that research has conclusively proven that Dionysus made his way into Greece as a foreigner, and that he was able to receive recognition only after overcoming powerful opposition. Thrace, and Phrygia, which was inhabited by a related people, are looked upon as his birthplace. It was thought at first that he migrated directly from Thrace to Greece. More recently, however, it is held that compelling reasons have been discovered for the idea that he came, rather, over the sea, out of Phrygia or Lydia. Both views were finally combined by Nilsson.[1] According to him, Dionysus must have made his way into the Greek mainland from Thrace as well as from Phrygia, once in his old-Thracian form, the other time in a form modified by the influence of neighboring religions in Asia Minor. But that is not all. Contrary to the opinion which has prevailed up to now, the mainland of Greece, itself, is designated as the third seat of the Dionysiac movement, because the great excitement which the arrival of Dionysus evoked there is supposed to have been only a re-awakening of an age-old worship. Hence, one is forced to assume that the concepts and rites attached to his name had already belonged to the pre-Greek population.

If we ask for the date when the foreigner supposedly made

his way into the ranks of the Greek gods, Wilamowitz[2] explains that he arrived on the mainland, at the earliest, in the eighth century, and that his victory over the orthodox believers may not be dated prior to the year 700. The Asiatic Greeks supposedly came to know him "proportionately earlier, but," so he concludes, "the society in which and for which Homer wrote his poetry wished to know as little of Dionysus as did Hellas later on, until it had to yield to a movement which came from below."

Whatever judgments one might make about the origin and the birthplace of the religion of Dionysus, it is unthinkable that the Greeks could have become acquainted with it at so late a time. How would it have been possible that absolutely no feeling of strangeness and no remembrance of the violent incursion had been preserved? For the often repeated assertion that certain myths and cults give evidence of such a remembrance rests, as we shall still see, on a confusion of cult migration with epiphany. The Greeks themselves considered their principal cults of Dionysus to be age-old. How right they were in this is shown by the fact that the "old Dionysia," the name given to the Anthesteria by Thucydides,[3] were common to the Ionic tribes, and, as the festival of Dionysus, have to be older than the partition and migration of the Ionians, as Deubner rightly notes.[4] In Delphi the worship of Dionysus could be considered older than that of Apollo.[5] In Smyrna, where the Anthesteria were celebrated by bringing in Dionysus on a ship set on wheels,[6] there is evidence of a festival of Dionysus already for the period when the city was still Aeolic.[7] Homeric epic must be looked upon as the most important witness for the great age of the Greek Dionysus. It is intimately acquainted with his cult and his myths, and it speaks of him in the same manner in which it speaks of the deities who have been worshipped since time immemorial, however the poet himself and his audience may feel about him.

At the center of the cults and myths of Dionysus stand the forms of the frenzied deity and the women, swept along by his wildness, who have taken in the newborn child, have reared him and are, therefore, called his nurses. At certain festivals, rites of pursuit are performed which can have a gory outcome, and the idea of tragic destruction emerges extremely clearly in several of the legends and practices. This essential of the Dionysiac religion is so well-known to the *Iliad* that it can be presented there in all of its details.

In Book 6 of the *Iliad* (130 ff.), Diomedes speaks of the destiny which no man who fights gods can escape. And here he mentions the mighty Lycurgus, who pursued the "nurses" of the raging (μαινόμενος) Dionysus in holy Νυσήιον, so that they struck by his terrible weapon, let their θύσθλα fall to the ground, and Dionysus, himself, fled into the sea, where Thetis received the trembling god fondly. In this passage the women who attend Dionysus are not characterized explicitly as frenzied. But the verse which compares the terrified Andromache, as she rushes off wildly, to a maenad (μαινάδι ἴση: *Iliad* 22, 461) betrays the familiarity the poet and his circle had with the appearance and name of maenad. Did the poet really want to say nothing else with this reference than that Andromache was like an insane person, as Wilamowitz would have us believe?[8] His comparison, after all, like all genuine comparisons, has meaning only if it reminds one of a well-known form. "The frenzied one," however, whose image must have been known to everyone, can be no other but the Bacchante, even though she is characterized, as she is here, with a noun like μαινάς, or, as in the *Iliad* 6. 389, with a verb-form like μαινομένη. *The Hymn to Demeter* gives ample evi-

PLATE 1 Maenads in ecstasy dancing before a robed, masked Dionysus column. Redrawn from the cup painted by Makron (Frickenhaus, *Lenäenvasen*, Pl. 11A and 11B; Beazley, *ARFVP*², p. 462, no. 48 [37]). From the collection of the Staatliche Museen, Berlin. (Acc. No. 2290)

PLATE 2　Maenads ladling out wine before a robed, masked Dionysus column. Redrawn from stamnos painted by the Dinos painter (Frickenhaus, *Lenäenvasen*, Pl. 29A; P.E. Arias, *A History of 1000 Years of Greek Vase Painting*, pp. 372-375, Pl. 206; Beazley, *ARFVP²*, p. 1151, no. 2 [2]). From the collection of the Museo Nazionale Archeologico, Naples. (Acc. No. 2419)

PLATE 3　Maenads dancing at the festival of Dionysus. Another view of stamnos cited above (Frickenhaus, Pl. 29B).

dence of what Homer wants to say here. In line 386 Demeter, as she leaps to her feet, is compared to a maenad "who rushes through the wooded mountains." The relative clause precludes any misunderstanding on our part. Homer's audience, however, would not have misconstrued the word μαινάς even without the clause.

The "frenzied" Dionysus and his "frenzied" women attendants are, therefore, forms with which Homer is intimately acquainted. And the wine-god? Is it really true that Homer knows nothing of him as yet? Aristarchus in referring to the *Odyssey* 9. 198, commented that the poet, who mentions wine so often in both epics, never characterizes Dionysus as the giver of wine. K.O. Müller emphasized this point in his review[9] of J.H. Voss's *Antisymbolik*,[10] and since that time it is taken for granted that wine has nothing to do with the original nature of Dionysus, but that it was only later placed under his protection. No weight should now be given to the story of the golden pitcher, which, according to the *Odyssey* 24. 74, Dionysus gave to Thetis, even though K.O. Müller, himself, was of the opinion that it could be used to object to the validity of his thesis. Let us not appeal either to the fact that the father of the priest of Apollo, Maron, to whom Odysseus is indebted for the wine with which he made the Cyclops drunk,[11] is called Euanthes and has, in other words, a name which we meet in Dionysus, himself, or in one of his sons (Hesiod, for example,[12] makes Maron into a descendant of Dionysus, and Euripides[13] actually calls him the son of Dionysus). But the passage in the *Iliad* (called incongruous, to be sure, by Aristophanes and Aristarchus), in which the son of Zeus and Semele, the woman from Thebes, is called "the delight of mortals" (χάρμα βροτοῖσιν: *Iliad* 14. 325) is unquestionably a reference to the giver of wine. Just as Herakles, in the verse immediately preceding, is called "the strong-

hearted" (κρατερόφρων), so these words are supposed to characterize the son of Semele, and they cannot mean anything
else but what Hesiod is saying when he calls Dionysus, in exactly the same frame of reference, the "joyful" (πολυγηθής).[14]
But this is the title which Hesiod, in another passage, ascribes
to Dionysus as the god of wine.[15] K.O. Müller considered it
conclusive that Homer went out of his way to call grain the
gift of Demeter and yet did not connect Dionysus anywhere
specifically with wine. And yet we cannot overlook the fact
that Demeter's gift is not referred to in the verses which speak
of Demeter herself (*Iliad* 14. 326; *Odyssey* 5. 125) and that
there are remarkably few passages in which the produce of
the fields is linked to her name. The epic poet is fundamentally
no more reserved toward Dionysus than he is toward Demeter. Anyone who knows the gods who rule Homer's world
knows also how significant this reserve is. He is silent about
much which is alien to the spirit of his world and often betrays his knowledge just with a word. What could have been
more alien to him than the frenzied god! The wine-god,
Dionysus, was surely no less known to him than the goddess
of grain, Demeter.

The Homeric epic shows that it has precise knowledge,
too, of the ties Dionysus had with the other gods—those ties
which we know from the history of the cult, or from the
mythic tradition. Of particular importance is his friendship
with Thetis. It is into her arms that he throws himself in his
flight from the fierce Lycurgus,[16] and it is to her that he
presents the golden amphora in which the bones of Achilles
were later laid to rest.[17] What so many cult practices and
legends give evidence of—namely, that Dionysus is at home
in the depths of the sea—is expressed clearly enough in this
Homeric myth. That the golden pitcher which he gave to
Thetis is called a work of Hephaestus may be considered a

reference to his celebrated friendship with Hephaestus. In Nonnus,[18] Aphrodite gives him a crater which had been made by Hephaestus. Finally, it is significant that the Nekyia of the *Odyssey* (11. 325) shows him as associated with Ariadne, the queen of the women of Dionysus. The beautiful daughter of Minos, as we are told there, was snatched from Crete by Theseus. He wished to spirit her off to Athens but Artemis killed her first, at the order of Dionysus. The god must have had a claim on Ariadne, for the story corresponds exactly with the story of the death of Coronis,[19] who was also shot by Artemis, and this at Apollo's instigation because she had betrayed the god with a mortal lover. Artemis is well known as the goddess who brings death to women in labor. Coronis dies even before she gives birth to Asclepius, but Ariadne, according to the legend of her Cyprian cult,[20] is said to have died in childbirth.

After all this, we are willing to believe Pausanias[21] when he says that Panopeus in the *Odyssey* (11. 581) received the designation "place of beautiful dances" ($\kappa\alpha\lambda\lambda\acute{\iota}\chi o\rho o\varsigma$) in consideration of the fact that the Attic Thyiades, on their way to Parnassus, were in the habit of holding their dances there.

Homer, then, not only knows Dionysus, but he alludes to almost everything which is characteristic of the myth and cult of Dionysus. That is even more remarkable because Dionysus had absolutely no importance for the Homeric world. Everything, therefore, which concerns him can be expressed only in incidental references. And, in fact, it is the *Iliad* in which he appears as the "frenzied" one, the one surrounded by "nurses" and "maenads." It is the *Iliad* which knows about the bloody pursuit of the god and his host of women, and his disappearance in the depths of the sea. It is the *Iliad*, also, which can refer to the god of wine, while the *Odyssey* associates him with Hephaestus, Artemis, and, above all, Ariadne.

And nowhere is there the slightest trace that his cult was felt to be something new, something which had forced its way in from abroad.

This familiarity which Homeric epic has with the religion of Dionysus leads us to the same conclusion we could have drawn from the Ionic Anthesteria. Dionysus must have already been indigenous to Greek civilization toward the end of the second millennium at least. Whether he came to the Greeks from the outside in an earlier period of which we have no reliable information is one of those questions which will probably never be answered with complete assurance. This much, however, we can say with certainty. Everything which has been advanced recently and in time past to prove his migration from Thrace or Phrygia is in no way convincing. In its older form this hypothesis was, as we know, represented by Erwin Rohde.[22] He speaks of the "Thracian cult of ecstasy" which invaded Greece with frightening savagery and was adopted only after serious opposition.

It is well known and has been stressed often enough how ardently Dionysus was worshipped in Thrace. A. Rapp has carefully collected what has come down to us from the ancient world.[23] He also stressed that the cult of Dionysus was at its most active in Greece in precisely those areas in which the knowledge of it had been preserved by previous Thracian inhabitants, namely, in Phocis and in Boeotia.[24] Under these circumstances one might well think that the Thracians could have brought this cult to central Greece. But it could just as well have found its way from Greece to Thrace; and the well-known orgiastic cults of Thrace, which are referred to again and again to make it more believable that the god came from there, could, conversely, be used to prove that it was precisely the Thracians who must have been very ready to accept a Greek Dionysus. After all, they became notorious lovers of unmixed wine once the vine became known. It is remarkable that Thrace plays such an extraordinarily small role in the myth of Dionysus. It is for this reason that an expert like K.O. Müller ascribed no significance to the vicinity of Thrace in his deliberations on the origins of the cult of Dionysus; and a scholar as learned as O. Gruppe could come to the conclusion more than a decade after the appearance of Rohde's *Psyche* that Greek colonists "unquestionably" transplanted Dionysus into Thrace.[25] To be sure, almost everyone[26] now believes that the *Iliad*, when it speaks of Nyseion (*Iliad* 6. 133), the place where Lycurgus pursued the rout of Dionysus, must have had in mind a location in Thrace. The reason given is that Lycurgus later[27] is called king of the Edonians, and the site of his destruction is called Mt. Pangaeus,[28] where there was, according to Hesychius, a place called Nysa. And so the *Iliad* scholia also talk about a Nysa in Thrace. K.O. Müller[29] challenged this thesis by saying that "nowhere in the entire geography of Thrace is there any reference to a place actually called Nysa." Moreover, how would Antimachus[30] have been able to have the fight of Lycurgus against Dionysus take place in an Arabic Nysa, if the original myth definitely had a Thracian Nysa in mind?

Recently, as we have mentioned before, there is a general acceptance of the interpretation that Dionysus did not come to the Greeks directly from Thrace, but that he came over the Aegean Sea from Phrygia, from the Thracians who had migrated to Asia Minor. Wilamowitz[31] considers it unlikely that Dionysus took the overland route from Thrace because there are so few traces of the god to be found in Thessaly, through which he first would have had to come. Wilamowitz takes it as proven that the Greeks received their Dionysus from Asia Minor. His arrival in a ship, to which the well-known cult practice of the Anthesteria refers, supports this thesis. But all doubt is removed by the discovery that Semele is the Phrygian name of the Earth Goddess, and that Bakchos is the Lydian equivalent for Dionysus. This verifies perfectly what the Lydian Bacchic chorus of Euripides and Tmolus, as the mountain of Dionysus, had always suggested. What value these observations have will be seen in the course of our investigations. But, even at this stage, some of them can be subjected to a more detailed analysis. In Lydian inscriptions the stem "Baki-" (i.e., Βάκχος) is used to name the god himself. It is further used to designate the month sacred to him and finally—and this is of particular interest—it is used to make up the personal name "Bakiva," which becomes Διονυσικλῆς when it is translated into Greek.[32] The conclusion that, according to this, Bakchos must have been a Lydian word (or a Phrygian word taken into Lydian) is advanced by Littman, himself, who is hesitant, and by Wilamowitz,[33] who, however, is quite positive.[34] But the argument cannot be said to be convincing. At least, it is just as possible to think that the name Bakchos had already made its way in very early times from Greek into Phrygian and Lydian, and that it remained behind solely in Lydian for reasons we do not know. But it is more likely that the name belonged to the pre-Greek inhabitants (of whose language the name Parnassus, the mountain of the Dionysiac orgies, gives evidence), and that it was precisely in Lydian that it was preserved as the principal name of Dionysus. It would, therefore, be rash to look upon the Lydian findings as unquestionable proof of the origin of the cult of Dionysus in Asia Minor. As for the hypothesis that the Phrygian Earth Goddess lies concealed behind Semele—for the present it can only be said that most of our available sources most emphatically contradict it.

Whether we derive the religion of Dionysus from Thrace or from Asia Minor, it is difficult to reconcile either derivation with the ancient observations about Nysa, where the young god was supposedly born and raised.[35] Nysa was, without doubt, the name of a divine mountain country in a distant land of fantasy, similar to the land of the Hyperboreans.[36] In that land Persephone, as she was playing with the daughters of Oceanus and picking flowers, was supposedly snatched away by the god of death, who suddenly erupted from the earth.[37] What was thought about this fairyland is particularly important because its name makes up, without question, the main part of the name Dionysus. P. Kretschmer has made the best comments on this.[38] Its dialectical variants Διόνυσος, Διώνυσος, and Διόννυσος go back to two basic types which combine the word νῦσος, at one time, with the stem Διο-, and the other time with the genitive of Zeus's name. That this νῦσος, as a Thracian word, corresponds to the Greek word νύμφη and means, in other words, "son," as Kretschmer thought, seems to me, in spite of the fact that it is without doubt linguistically possible, not only undemonstrable but also improbable. We can no longer know its original meaning, but we can know the province to which it belongs. The feminine form appears in the name of that Nysa who was, according to Terpander (fr. 8), the nurse of Dionysus. To honor her he supposedly gave the name of Nysa to the city in India. Diodorus (3. 70) calls her a daughter of Aristaius. On a vase of Sophilos[39] three Nysai receive the child Dionysus, and later it becomes commonplace to speak of Nysiai and Nysiades in the plural as the nurses of the god. The fairyland Nysa, therefore, got its name from its female inhabitants, the Nysai, and Dio-nysos, "the divine Nysos" or "the Nysos of Zeus," is characterized as one of them by this name. Living together with women is a part of his nature; and, just as he, as Bakchos, is surrounded by Bakchai, so, as Nysos, he stands in the middle of a zealous host of Nysai. The little boy Dionysus is brought to them in their divine mountain woodland, and from there the god comes to men, as Apollo came from the Hyperboreans.

This Nysa has not only been located in distant lands, but places in the immediate vicinity were also linked with Dionysus through its name. Thus Sophocles[40] mentions a Nysa in Euboea, and this is probably the same place referred to in the *Bacchae* of Euripides.[41] A locality on Helicon was called Nysa, according to Strabo (9. 405), who adds that many saw it as the Nysa of the *Iliad* 2. 508. On Parnassus, too, there was supposedly at one time a Nysa.[42] But neither in Thrace nor in Phrygia, nor in Asia Minor, in general, do there seem to have been any places with this name. All of the accounts of a Thracian Nysa obviously go back to the passage in Homer discussed above, if they did not actually refer to a Thrace near Helicon and Parnassus,[43] as K.O. Müller believed. For Asia Minor there is only one mention of a Lydian Nysa in the alphabetical inventory of Hesychius. The well-known Nysa of Caria first got its name from a wife of Antiochus.[44] This remarkable lack is certainly not favorable to the hypothesis that Dionysus came out of Thrace or Phrygia. The famous choral ode of Sophocles' *Antigone*,[45] in naming the favorite haunts of the god, mentions only Italy in addition to those in the homeland of Greece (Thebes, Eleusis, Delphi, Euboea). The ancient sources tell us that antiquity preferred to look in the far east and the south, that is to say, in the Land of the Sun, for the Nysa in which Dionysus grew up and from which he made his entry into the realms of men. According to Herodotus (2. 146), it was believed that Zeus brought the new-born little boy, who had been sewn in his thigh, to Nysa in Ethiopia (ἐς Νύσην τὴν ὑπὲρ Αἰγύπτου ἐοῦσαν ἐν τῇ Αἰθιοπίῃ).[46] Antimachus[47] transfers the encounter of Dionysus with Lycurgus to an Arabic Nysa, and Diodorus

(3. 66) is of the opinion that the Nysa mentioned in the Homeric hymn 1.8 as the birthplace of the god[48] was precisely the Arabic one. Nonnus, Hesychius, and the scholia of the *Iliad* also have knowledge of this. In addition to Hesychius, Apollonius Rhodius[49] also mentions an Egyptian Nysa. Xenophon already knows of a Nysa situated in Syria.[50] And finally, let us at least mention the Nysa of India, which has been referred to so often since the Hellenistic Age.

Lastly, the ship procession of the Ionic festivals of Dionysus is considered to be an unusually clear piece of evidence in support of the theory that the cult of Dionysus came from Asia Minor to Greece. In Athens, and in all probability on the day of the Choes,[51] the ceremonial entrance of the god in a ship set on wheels occurred. It was thought, therefore, that he came from the sea, as the famous cylix of Exekias pictures him, sailing in a ship which was crowned with vine tendrils.* From this it is concluded that his cult actually must have come at one time to the Greeks of the Greek mainland from over the sea, that is to say, from Asia Minor.[52] It is surprising that Wilamowitz was of the same opinion, too,[53] although he referred to the fact that Dionysus, in Homer's story, plunged into the sea, consequently "could also have come out of the sea." Wilamowitz reminds us, moreover, that, according to the legend of Brasiai on the Laconian east coast,[54] the child Dionysus was supposedly washed up on the shore in a chest together with Semele, and, since his mother was no longer alive, he was reared in a grotto by Ino. It is, then, characteristic of Dionysus that he appears from the sea. His relationship with the element of water will be discussed in detail in a later chapter. Just as he disappeared into the sea in his flight from Lycurgus, so the Argives believed that he was swal-

* See Plate 10.

lowed up by the lake of Lerna; for they regularly called him up from the deep there for the festival of his appearance.[55] If, therefore, he made his entry on the day of the festival on a ship, that signifies nothing else but his epiphany from the sea. In addition, we also know that the ship procession of the general Ionic Anthesteria was held in Smyrna, too—in short, it was held on the other side of the Aegean Sea on the coast of Asia Minor.[56] This was completely without meaning if the rite intended to preserve the memory of an actual arrival of the cult of Dionysus from Phrygia or Lydia. The comments of Wilamowitz[57] cannot detract from the value of this important piece of evidence.

Now that we have completed our prefatory remarks, which were only supposed to show how old was the familiarity of the Greeks with the religion of Dionysus and how unconvincing is the hypothesis that this religion came from Thrace or Phrygia, we turn our attention to the form of the god Dionysus, itself. Once this form has been made clear, let each one ask himself whether it still makes sense to compare the cult of Dionysus with the orgiastic worship of Asia Minor.

# 3. *The Son of Zeus and Semele*

Who is Dionysus?

The god of ecstasy and terror, of wildness and of the most blessed deliverance—the mad god whose appearance sends mankind into madness—gives notice already, in his conception and birth, of his mysterious and paradoxical nature.

He was the child of Zeus and a mortal woman. But even before she bore him, she was consumed in the holocaust of the lightning of her heavenly bridegroom.

> So fell, as poets say, on Semele's hearth
> The bolt of the god she longed to see
> And the god-struck girl gave birth
> To the fruit of the storm, holy Bacchus, to thee.
>
> (HÖLDERLIN)

The father did not let his son perish. Cooling ivy tendrils protected him from the heat by which his mother was consumed. The father himself assumed the role of mother. He took up the fruit of the womb, not yet capable of life, and placed it in his divine body. And when the number of months was accomplished, he brought his son into the light.

Thus, the "twice-born one" has already, before his entry into the world, outgrown everything that is mortal. He has become a god, the god of intoxicated delight. And yet he, the bringer of joy, was predestined for suffering and death— the suffering and death of a god! And to the house of his mother, to which the glory of heaven had descended, he brought not only blessedness but suffering, persecution, and destruction. But his mother, Semele, who had suffered a death in flames in her marriage with the god of the storm, was given leave to ascend from her grave to the gods of Olympus.

She was one of the four daughters of King Cadmus of Thebes. "Peleus and Cadmus," says Pindar,[1] "were the most fortunate of all mankind; for at their weddings the muses sang, the gods banqueted at their tables, they saw the kingly sons of Kronos sitting on chairs of gold and received gifts from them. . . . But there came a time when Cadmus was made joyless by the bitter sufferings of his daughters—three of them; but to the fourth, the beautiful Thyone, came father Zeus, to lie with her on the bed of love." And in another passage: "Great misfortunes the daughters of Cadmus suffered; but the weight of the sorrow sank before the excess of the good. Felled by the lightning, Semele lives in the circle of the Olympians, and Pallas loves her dearly, and father Zeus; and her son loves her, who wears the ivy; and they say that in the sea, too, among the daughters of Nereus, Ino was allotted life imperishable for all time."[2]

Of the four daughters of Cadmus,[3] only these two—Semele and Ino—are of importance as figures for myth. The others—Agave and Autonoe—appear only as the mothers of Pentheus and Actaeon, whose terrible fate—both were torn apart like wild beasts—is associated with the myth of Dionysus. And yet all four, as the *cultus* demonstrates, belong to the genuine ingredients of the ancient myth. Just as in Pindar,[4] Semele, as the beloved of Zeus, is contrasted with the three other daughters of Cadmus, so in the *Lenai* of Theocritus,[5] Ino, Autonoe, and Agave each lead a *thiasos* into the mountains to celebrate the festival of Dionysus, and erect there twelve altars—three for Semele, nine for Dionysus. The same three *thiasoi*, led by Autonoe, Agave, and Ino, appear also in the messenger speech of the *Bacchae* of Euripides.[6] According to the well-known inscription from Magnesia on the Maeander,[7] in former times three maenads from the house of Ino were invited, at the suggestion of Delphi, to come there from Thebes to institute the cult of Dionysus, and each one of them assembled one of the three *thiasoi*. The cult of Semele, who is associated with Dionysus, which the three women's choruses serve, corresponds exactly, therefore, with the myth of Semele, the heavenly bride and her three sisters. On a dedicatory inscription in Cologne,[8] her "divine sisters" are still mentioned along with Semele.*

There are numerous testimonies which prove that Semele was accorded cultic honors. What is true of the mother is also true of Ino, the foster mother of the god. The demolished home of Semele, the ruins of which the Euripidean Dionysus still sees smoking on his return to his native city, Thebes,[9] was still being shown to marveling foreigners in the late centuries of antiquity.[10] It was situated next to the shrine of Dionysos Kadmeios, of whose great significance an inscription of the third century B. C. from the treasury of the Thebans in Delphi first made us properly aware.[11] In this inscription the holy precinct of Semele is called σηκός, precisely as it is in Euripides.[12] Thus there had been a cult of the mother of Dionysus there. But she was worshipped in other places, too. Her principal cult days were the festival of the appearance of Dionysus and the celebration of her resurrection by her divine son, from the realms of the dead. When Dionysus was ceremonially invoked at the Attic Lenaea, he was called "Semele's son" (Σεμελήιος).[13] On the island of Myconos, in

* See Plate 4.

the same festival, Semele received a sacrifice on the eleventh of the month, while sacrifices were made to Dionysus, himself, on the twelfth, the day sacred to him.[14] Her worship in the triennial festivals of Dionysus is explicitly emphasized in an Orphic hymn.[15] The celebrations of her ascent from the underworld appear to have been even more important. Plutarch[16] informs us of a festival, which was celebrated every eight years in Delphi, in which the Dionysiac thyiads participated. The *dromena*, which took place in public, suggested that their subject was the resurrection of Semele. The festival was called Herois. This referred to the central figure, i.e., Semele, who was called ἡρωίς, just as Dionysus, himself, in the famous song of the women of Elis,[17] is called ἥρως. This festival may also have been celebrated elsewhere. In Lerna one said that Dionysus had descended there through the bottomless depths of the Alcyonian Sea to the land of the dead in order to bring Semele back up;[18] and in Troezen, also, one pointed to the place where the god supposedly ascended from Hades with his mother.[19]

Semele's cult and memory are associated throughout with the memory of her great son. Pindar's dithyramb[20] at the Athenian Dionysia says, "Now voices singing songs to the accompaniment of flutes are heard, now the choruses of filleted Semele." The *Lenai* of Theocritus,[21] in which the secret Dionysus celebration of the three daughters of Cadmus and the terrible fate of the inquisitive Pentheus are described, conclude with a salutation not only to Dionysus but also to Semele and her sisters. In Magnesia a marble altar was dedicated "to Dionysus and Semele."[22]

Thus the human mother of the divine son was crowned with immortality and received her share of cultic honors. That is the magnificent finale of the myth of the birth of the son born of lightning from the womb of a mortal woman.

Plate 4   An altar to Semele and her sisters in honor of their sacred motherhood, CIL 13.2.8244. The first four lines read as follows: DEAE SEMELAE ET/ SORORIBUS EIIUS/ DEABUS OB HONOREM/ SACRI MATRATUS. Note the *thyrsus*, castanets, *plakous* (bread), and shepherd's crook. Photograph, courtesy of the Rhineland Photo Archives. From the collection of The Museum of the City of Cologne.

Modern scholarship has dismembered this awe-inspiring myth completely and has reversed its meaning. Semele, so it explains, must have been a goddess from the beginning. She was first made into the daughter of Cadmus by a poet who, according to Wilamowitz, cannot have been active prior to 700 B. C. This poet, then, is supposed to have taken some real event as his starting point and arbitrarily invented from it this myth, whose deep significance any unprejudiced person senses. In the process, however, he supposedly did not anticipate that the human nature of the mother of Dionysus could eventually become significant.

Paul Kretschmer pointed out more than forty years ago in a remarkable piece of research[23] that there was a good probability that the name Semele could be understood linguistically as a Thracian-Phrygian word which was used to characterize the Earth Goddess; that it was related to the Greek words $\chi\theta\acute{\omega}\nu$, $\chi\theta\alpha\mu\alpha\lambda\acute{o}s$, etc.; and that this Thracian-Phrygian Earth Goddess actually appeared as $\Sigma\epsilon\mu\epsilon\lambda\omega$, next to the Heaven God $\Delta\iota\omega s$ (or $\Delta\epsilon o s$), in the formulae of imprecation on Phrygian funerary inscriptions of the Empire. Although Kretschmer's derivation of the name Dionysus from the Thracian, with the meaning "Son of Zeus," appeared to be less convincing because there was no documentary proof for that, his interpretation of the name Semele was accepted enthusiastically; and it has become most recently, in the work of Niisson[24] and Wilamowitz,[25] the basis for the proof that the cult of Dionysus came from Thrace or, rather, Phrygia. Kretschmer, himself, could point to the fact that in antiquity Apollodorus, at least,[26] had equated Semele with Ge. Diodorus[27] also knows of a theory which believed that the Earth Goddess might be recognized in Thyone as well as in Semele. Thus the mother of Dionysus appears in almost all of the new accounts as "the Thracian-Phrygian Earth mother," who was reduced

at only a relatively late period by poetic license to the role
of mortal and the daughter of Cadmus.

But consider the unreasonable demands made of us by this
thesis! The Phrygian inscriptions inform us that this goddess
was still highly regarded there in 200 or 300 A.D. How much
greater her significance must have been a thousand years before! And at that time is someone in Boeotia, which is, after
all, only a short sea voyage away from Phrygia, supposed to
have arbitrarily transformed the great Phrygian Earth Goddess into Cadmus' daughter? And now is there supposedly
no trace, either in the myth or in the *cultus*, of a memory of
her original pre-eminence? This is difficult to imagine, nor
can the supposed analogies of other instances, which themselves first need elucidation, help us past this inconsistency.

But this is not all. The hypothesis does unheard-of violence
to the myth as it comes down to us in all of the sources. The
myth not only presents Semele as a mortal, but it lays the
greatest emphasis on the fact that she was not a goddess and
nevertheless gave birth to a god. Already in the *Iliad* she is
called a woman of Thebes,[28] and Hesiod[29] is not satisfied
with calling her the daughter of Cadmus but adds expressly
that she bore an *immortal* son as a *mortal* woman (ἀθάνατον
θνητή). And this idea of "the offspring of the highest father
and of the Cadmeian woman," as Pindar (*fr. 75*) expresses it,
goes through the entire mythic tradition. The mortality of
the mother, therefore, must have been one of the essentials of
the myth of Dionysus. That the name Semele, which supposedly originally referred to as a goddess, actually was always understood as a human name is proved by the second
name which the mother of Dionysus bears. She is also called
Thyone. The ancient sources do not leave us in the dark
about the real meaning of this honorary title. To be sure,
Pindar already names Semele, in one passage,[30] Thyone, as

the bride of Zeus. Where, however, both names are mentioned, Thyone refers to the new position of the mother freed from the realm of death by her son and crowned with immortality;[31] ("Semele, who is called Thyone" is the reading of the Homeric hymn of the Moscow MS.) Since we also know Thyone as a name for Bacchantes, and Dionysus, himself, is called Thyonidas (Hesychius), there is no doubt that the new name is supposed to give evidence of her admittance to the circle of the divine female attendants of Dionysus. The mother of Dionysus, then, was called Thyone insofar as she had received the position of an immortal. She had to give up the name Semele, or at least had to supplement it with a second name, when she became a goddess. Is it conceivable that a name so decisively felt as human had actually been divine, notwithstanding? In Thebes, Semele was worshipped as one who had died. The area dedicated to her in the holy precinct of Dionysus on the Theban acropolis was a σηκός.[32] Orphic Hymn 44, which speaks of the honors accorded her at the festival of Dionysus, emphasizes that she owes these to Persephone.

The modern hypothesis, therefore, not only disregards the evidence of the ancient myth, but it has no scruples about explaining the very item, which this myth promulgates as its most amazing reality, as an arbitrary correction of the original content of the myth. In so doing, it frivolously destroys the entire myth of the birth of Dionysus, for the strange story of his second birth really loses all of its meaning if his mother was not mortal. When Semele was being consumed, so the myth says, Zeus pulled the six-months-old child from the flames and sewed it into his thigh so that it might mature in his divine body and become a god.[33] It has been maintained that this myth must have resulted from a union of two completely different views. According to the one, Dionysus took his origin from the marriage of Semele with the god of heaven while the other has him born of the father alone, as is told of Athena. But this only exacts new absurdities of the myth. As meaningful as is the image that portrays Athena (the goddess of "Good Counsel" and victorious might, with the mind of a man) springing from the head of the "Counselor," Zeus, without the participation of a woman, so meaningless must have appeared the idea that Dionysus (the womanlike, he who is always surrounded by women, who are his closest confidants) should have been brought forth exclusively by a man. The myth has meaning only as it has actually been told throughout the ages. The tragic failure of the mother is a necessary prerequisite to the birth from the father, and not until they are associated with each other do the two events present a genuine and complete myth. Semele was a child of man, who had conceived a son in the arms of the god of heaven. But the mortal mistress did not have the power to endure the fulminating majesty of the god who loved her. In the blazing storm which killed her she gave birth to a child who was to become a great god. And thus, because as a mortal she was too weak, the father had to take up his son into himself and finish the work of the prostrate mother by means of a second birth.

The idea of an Earth Goddess who is consumed by fire in the arms of the god of heaven would be quite incomprehensible, as O. Gruppe has already said.

Then what gives us the right at all to say that divinity was the original nature of all the higher Beings who, according to the testimony of the myth, were at one time human? Would it not be better to examine first whether such myths could not have had an important meaning, before we attribute their origin to a so-called poet who resorted to cheap devices to combine inconsonants? Ino, too, the foster mother of the

god,[34] many of whose cult shrines, particularly on the Laconian coast,[35] are known to us, is in the myth a mortal who
became a goddess, and as a goddess—and, what is more, as one
of the sea-goddesses[36]—she received the name Leucothea. Just
as Semele's former existence as a mortal is especially emphasized in Hesiod's *Theogony*, so the *Odyssey*[37] speaks of Ino
as "the daughter of Cadmus, Ino, Leucothea, who had once
been a mortal woman but now enjoys divine honors in the
waves of the sea." The association of Ino with Dionysus, to
which the facts of the cult attest,[38] is, without question, age-
old. As a goddess of the element of moisture, she was drawn
into his circle because she was related to him in the essence
of her nature. This will be shown by what we have to say
later. We also meet the other two sisters of Semele—Agave
and Autonoe—again among the Nereids.[39] Thus Ino is in just
the same position as her sister Semele. Both were accorded
cultic honors. Both were once mortal women, according to
the myth. Both have a second name which distinguishes the
goddess from the mortal woman—even if the other name can
very well be used for both designations. We shall not deal,
at this point, with the artificial constructions of Wilamowitz.[40]

To return to Dionysus, himself: the myth of his birth,
which scholars have earnestly tried to reduce to nothing but
historical contingencies, is the most sublime expression of his
Being. Just as the amazing image of Athena's ascent from the
head of her father can be conceived only in the spirit of the
genuine revelation of her Being, so beneath the lightning
flashes of Dionysus grew the certainty that the enigmatic god,
the spirit of a dual nature and of paradox, had a human mother
and, therefore, was already by his birth a native of two
realms.

# 4. *The Myths of His Epiphany*

The myths of his appearance among men, like the myth of the birth of the god, have something unusual and strangely thrilling about them. He entered the world differently from the way in which we are told the other gods did, and he encounters man, too, in a very special way. In both instances his appearance is startling, disquieting, violent. And, like everything violent, it arouses opposition and agitation. Right at his birth gods arise as his enemies. Terrible disturbances are engendered in his vicinity. The destruction of his mother is followed by suffering, bitter distress, and violent death for all who interest themselves in the little boy, beginning with his mother's sister, Ino, who plunges into the sea, out of her mind, with her own child in her arms. And in this way, even the revelation of the god who has become a man creates wild emotion, anger, and opposition among mankind. The daughters of Minyas refuse to follow his call and with good reason, for he rips the ones he has affected out of their wifely decency and morality and mates them with the mysteries and madnesses of the chaos of night. They, however, wish to remain true to their duties as housewives and attend their husbands—until Dionysus incites them with the sharpest goad of his madness. King Pentheus becomes aroused and does not wish to let the women tear their bonds of modesty asunder and dance with the frenzied deity. Perseus in Argos rushes out to meet

Dionysus with armed might. In shifting forms the myth repeats the same image over and over again.

The meaning of such stories, to which we must return later, has been completely misunderstood in recent years. They were considered to be echoes of historical events. They were regularly appealed to when proof was needed that the cult of Dionysus had forced its way into Greece from abroad and had received recognition only after considerable opposition had been overcome. To be sure, Welcker[1] wanted this interpretation to apply only to one part of the legends in question, and Rohde, too, advised caution when he wrote, "These are stories which belong in the category of prefigurative myths through which particular acts of worship are to acquire a prototype and a qualifying explanation from an event in the age of myth which was considered to be historically true."[2] He was, however, of the opinion that "a kernel of historical truth was to be found in these stories," for the idea that this cult met strong resistance in many places (something which is not, after all, said about any other cult) could not possibly be based on "empty fantasies," particularly because its basic assumption that the cult of Dionysus forced its way into Greece "from abroad and as something alien," "obviously" agreed with historical truths.

"Empty fantasies" these myths certainly are not. On the contrary, they contain much more that is real than if they were reporting that which had once occurred. They are not witnesses of that which once was but of that which will always be, as Sallustius[3] says when he is speaking of the myths of Attis: "This never happened but it always is" ($\tau a \hat{\nu} \tau a \ \delta \grave{\epsilon}$ $\dot{\epsilon} \gamma \acute{\epsilon} \nu \epsilon \tau o \ \mu \grave{\epsilon} \nu \ o \dot{\nu} \delta \acute{\epsilon} \pi o \tau \epsilon, \ \ddot{\epsilon} \sigma \tau \iota \ \delta \grave{\epsilon} \ \dot{a} \epsilon \acute{\iota}$). They give a true reflection of the violence, the horror, and the tragedy which are inherently Dionysiac. They do not refer to events which happened in a time when the god was still a stranger, but they refer to that which always occurs when he appears—in fact, to the tremendous efficacy of his being and his epiphany. The more impetuous his nature is, the more unconditional the demands are which he makes on the souls of mankind, the more stubborn the opposition and the resistance must be. The Sibyl, too, struggles long and hard before the spirit of her god overpowers her. This is not to say that the epiphany of Dionysus always had to elicit resistance from man. But the god appeared with such wildness and demanded such unheard-of things, so much that mocked all human order, that he first had to overpower the hearts of men before they could do him homage. Thus the conception of his first arrival—that is to say, the mythic image of a regular coming—became a story of strife and conquest. It was inevitable, moreover, that the character of the savage god and the dangerous wildness of his female chorus found their expression in horrible images picturing the fate of the arrogant and the inquisitive who had hit upon the idea of eavesdropping on the mysterious rites, or breaking in on them with violence. Such a story was told of the appalling destruction of the adversary, Pentheus,[4] who, as an inquisitive young man, meets the fate of dismemberment in the *Lenai* of Theocritus.[5]

But this catches only a smaller part of the meaning of the myths. It is far more important to realize that they deal in the last analysis with the fortunes of the god himself, and of his divine attendants. They are the ones who are excited to madness by him. They are the ones who in such a madness tear their defenseless victims apart, and it is they who are hounded, struck down, and who, like the god himself, perish. That is the content of the awe-inspiring myth of Lycurgus, who pursued and destroyed the "nurses" of the frenzied Dionysus with a terrible weapon and forced the god himself to seek the protection of Thetis in the depths of the sea.[6]

Wherever the location of this skirmish may be sought, it is agreed that it cannot be thought of as being in Greece proper. Rather, it is supposed to have been situated in Thrace,[7] in the country, therefore, which is considered to be the home of the cult of Dionysus. The myth, consequently, can have no memory of oppositions which Dionysus, as a stranger, had to overcome. And yet it speaks of bloody pursuit in which even Dionysus was vanquished and disappeared in the sea—in the watery depths in which he is at home, and from which he is called forth at regular intervals in cult.[8] The story, then, arises from the idea of his Being and his fate, into which his women attendants are inextricably drawn—not from the history of his cult.

And should not this be true, also, of the thoroughly analogous myth of Perseus, who opposed with the force of arms the god and the "sea-women" who came with him,[9] and who, according to one of the sources[10] hurled him into the bottomless lake of Lerna? When, therefore, in the Agrionia the women of Dionysus were pursued and even killed as part of the cult practices, and when the disappearance of the god was also announced during the course of the sacred rites,[11] there can be no doubt that the cult rites were so frighteningly serious because they were concerned with none other than the presentation of the supernatural occurrence which the myth had expressed in words.

In this way both—the myth and the cult—present to view the suffering and dying Dionysus. But this somber form is eclipsed by that of the young victor. Dionysus entered the world as a conqueror. With the strength of a lion he wrestles with and defeats the giants. With the *thyrsi* of his maenads he drives armed bands of men into wild flight. As conqueror he forces his way into the most distant lands and becomes the divine archetype of all triumphant heroes. This Dionysus, who strides along in tumult, is the god whose overpowering nature and epiphany are reported by so many legends which have been interpreted with strange misunderstanding as evidence of actual skirmishes between the entering cult of Dionysus and the guardians of the old religion. Welcker had already made the appropriate remark[12] that "there was no historical probability that in some cities the authorities, in opposition to the people, actually resisted this religion, or that one tribe among the inhabitants opposed another. It was more likely that it was modified or limited."

Like the myth of his birth, therefore, the myths of the appearance of Dionysus also reveal much about his nature.

At his conception the earthly was touched by the splendor of divine heaven. But in this union of the heavenly with the earthly, which is expressed in the myth of the double birth, man's tear-filled lot was not dissolved but preserved, rather, in sharp contrast to superhuman majesty. He who was born in this way is not only the exultant god, the god who brings man joy. He is the suffering and dying god, the god of tragic contrast. And the inner force of this dual reality is so great that he appears among men like a storm, he staggers them, and he tames their opposition with the whip of madness. All tradition, all order must be shattered. Life becomes suddenly an ecstasy—an ecstasy of blessedness, but an ecstasy, no less, of terror.

## 5. *The God Who Comes*

The cult forms give us the clearest evidence of the violence with which he forces his way in—a violence which affects the myth so passionately. These forms present him as the god who comes, the god of epiphany, whose appearance is far more urgent, far more compelling than that of any other god.

He had disappeared, and now he will suddenly be here again.

Other gods, like Apollo, also go off into the distance and return. But only Dionysus disappears in an incomprehensible manner from the circle of his followers or is swallowed up in the deep. As surprising as is his coming, so is his going away. In the Agrionia festival in Chaeronea the women searched for him and returned finally with the tidings that he had fled to the Muses and lay concealed among them.[1] According to the belief of the Argives, he had plunged into the lake of Lerna. That signified, at the same time, his plunge into the underworld; for a sacrifice was thrown down to the "guardian of the door" of the underworld at the festival of Dionysus' return from below. The story is also told that Perseus vanquished the god and hurled him into the lake.[2] An Orphic hymn[3] says that he rested for two years in the sacred house of Persephone after his departure.

And now the one who had disappeared was supposed to reappear suddenly with his tipsy look and his dazed smile, or he was supposed to burst forth out of the darkness in the form of a savage bull.

They were waiting for him—the choruses of women, true images of those higher beings, who followed Dionysus everywhere. In Elis it was the dancing chorus of "the sixteen women,"[4] who invoked the god with the words: "Come, Lord Dionysus, attended by the Graces, into the holy temple of Elis, rushing into the temple with your bull's hoof, venerable bull, venerable bull!" They knew, in short, that the one who would appear would be a wild creature who would bring, through his demonic violence, a breathtaking excitement. In Athens he was invoked at the festival of the Lenaea, which got its name from the Lenai, a chorus of frenzied women worshippers of Dionysus, related to the Bacchae, maenads, and whatever else they are called.[5] It must have been they, above all the others, who called to the god to come, similar to the "sixteen women" of Elis. "Summon the god!" was the cry of the *daduchos* in the night celebration and the assembled peoples cried out, "Semele's son, Iakchos, giver of riches!"[6] This is the way in which he may have been solemnly invoked to appear,[7] by the fourteen Athenian women,[8] who bore the title, *gerarai*, and had, under their care at the Anthesteria, the secret worship in the sanctuary ἐν Λίμναις together with the wife of the Archon Basileus.[9] In Argos trumpets which had been concealed under the leaves of the *thrysi* were sounded when he was called up out of the lake of Lerna, and a sheep was lowered into the mysterious abyss for the warder of the gates (πυλάοχος) who was to release him.[10]

In wintertime on the heights of Parnassus the choruses of the Delphic and Attic thyiads employed an unusual method to call Dionysus to rise up, to appear among them and lead them madly over the mountain top. They awakened him as

Liknites, as a child in the cradle.[11] He had, therefore, just been born and had not yet gained consciousness. That occurred on the site where it was believed Dionysus danced and reveled with the nymphs. "You were seen in the blaze of smouldering torches up high on the two-peaked mountain where the Corycian nymphs, thy Bacchantes, wander"—this is the cry of the chorus in Sophocles' *Antigone*.[12] The priestess in the prologue to the *Eumenides* of Aeschylus also speaks of these nymphs: "I worship the nymphs there in the Corycian grotto, the abode of divine spirits. The place belongs to Dionysus. . . ."[13] It was nymphs, the nymphs of Nysa—and there was, supposedly, a Nysa on Parnassus[14]—who suckled the new-born Dionysus and took loving care of him. Homeric Hymn 26 tells us this. And when it goes on to say that the same goddesses, after they had reared him, made up his riotous train of revelers and roamed through the forests with him who was bedecked with the ivy and the laurel, then we see that the foster mothers and the women who danced with the god are one and the same—just as in Homer the female attendants of the frenzied Dionysus are already called his "nurses"—and it is clear that the choruses of the thyiads, who, like them, concern themselves with the child Dionysus and, like them, dance madly over the mountain tops, take on the role of the divine women and depict in cult their actions, which are partly maternal and partly instinctively ecstatic. This is the way in which they call from his sleep the new-born god, who, as an Orphic hymn says,[15] had rested in the long time between in the house of Persephone. And when he opens his eyes, when he rouses himself, when he grows into glorious maturity, he will fill their hearts with a heavenly terror, their limbs with a maddening desire to dance; and he will go on before them, as the Orphic hymn, which we have mentioned before, says, as it speaks of his revel with the higher beings:

"And when you rouse anew the yearning for the triennial festival, you begin the song in the midst of your female attendants, the beauteously girt ones, who give voice to the shout of joy and excite the choruses to the dance." Just as the Elian women invoked Dionysus with a solemn song, so there is no doubt that the thyiads, too, awakened the divine child with the singing of hymns. We have still another bit of evidence out of the period of the Empire for the part played in a similar ritual. On an inscription from Rhodes,[16] there is a mention of a musician, who "awakens the god with the water organ" (τῷ ὑδραύλῃ τῷ ἐπεγείροντι τὸν θεόν). Here we see, too, how widespread, at least in later eras, the festival of awakening was. "The one in the cradle" (Λικνίτης) is an epithet which Hesychius cites for Dionysus (ἀπὸ τῶν λίκνων ἐν οἷς τὰ παιδία κοιμῶνται). Orphic Hymn 46 invokes the Λικνίτης Διόνυσος.[17]

"Oh, thou leader of the choral dance of the fire-breathing stars, lord of the songs of night, child sprung from Zeus, appear, sovereign, with the women who attend thee, the thyiai, who dance the night through in ecstasy for thee, their king Iakchos!" This is the cry of the chorus of *Antigone*[18] at a moment of appalling tension.

But no matter when and where he may come from, whether he sails over the sea in a wondrous ship, or rises up from the depths of the sea, or as a new-born child suddenly opens his divine eyes—his passion takes possession of the women who awaited him, so that they throw their heads back, toss their hair and rave, just as he himself is the one who raves.

The unique immediacy of his appearance is expressed in the general festivals by a series of special forms. Whereas the other gods, however exciting the experience of their coming may have been (and Callimachus' hymn gives us a famous example for Apollo), are invisible when they enter their temples on their feast days, Dionysus arrives in the flesh, i.e., in a plastic image.[19] In Sicyon one was not permitted to see the images of Dionysus Bakcheios and Lysios the whole year through. Only on one holy night were they brought into the temple from the so-called Kosmeterion, to the accompaniment of hymns and surrounded by torch light.[20] The Ionic Katagogia, the festivals of the return of the god, whose image was ceremoniously escorted by priests and priestesses, are well known through inscriptions.[21] These were the processions which Antony had the audacity to imitate in Ephesus in Alexandreia, where he made his entrance in a cart as a new Dionysus with *thyrsus* and *cothurnus*.[22] In Athens the image of Dionysus was driven to his sanctuary in a ship on wheels, most probably during the Anthesteria (on the day of the Choes).[23] Before the City Dionysia the image of Dionysus Eleuthereus was brought to a little temple in the Academy[24] so that it could be escorted on the eve of the festival in a ceremonial procession of epiphany to the temple of Dionysus.

The strongest proof for the might and triumph of his coming is his marriage at Athens with the wife of the Archon Basileus. This may have occurred on the same day of the Anthesteria on which he appeared as one who had sailed over the sea.[25] Aristotle[26] describes this act with words which convey the meaning of an actual marital union (ἡ σύμμιξις καὶ ὁ γάμος), while the author of the Neaera speech[27] speaks only of a wedding (ἐξεδόθη τῷ Διονύσῳ γυνή); cf. Hesychius, Διονύσου γάμος). We shall never ascertain what actually occurred here. That the divine bridegroom was represented by the Basileus, the rightful husband of the Basilinna,[28] is not only unbelievable in itself, but the wording of our texts eliminates this possibility. There can be no doubt, however, that Dionysus was thought and felt to be present with overwhelming certainty. He whom the women attend, he who always has a

favorite at his side, stepped over the threshold of his earthly
home and took possession of the mistress of that house. The
house in which the holy marriage was consummated, the
Boukolion, was, according to Aristotle, formerly the official
residence of the Archon Basileus. Aristotle knew what he was
saying. Into the house, therefore, of the high official who had
fallen heir to the title of the kings of old, the god set foot to
claim the Archon's wife for his own. That is something quite
different from the sacred nuptials of a god and a goddess
celebrated in cult. There is absolutely no comparison, moreover, between this and that which Herodotus[29] tells us about
the temple of Bel in Babylon, or of the temple of Zeus in
Egyptian Thebes, or of the oracle of Apollo in Lycian Patara
—Wilamowitz[30] notwithstanding. The Babylonian and the
Egyptian god demand the companionship of a woman when
they rest in their temples. Their bedfellows are not allowed
to have any dealings with men. When oracles are given in
Patara, i.e., when Apollo is in his sanctuary, the priestess of
the oracle must spend her nights in the temple. The prophetess unites herself with the god whose higher wisdom she is
called to impart.

The Athenian Basilinna, however, does not belong to Dionysus in this way. She is not a woman whom the god has chosen as his companion, as was the case in Babylon—according to
the express example of the Chaldeans in Herodotus. She is the
wife of the distinguished official who has the name of king.
Nor does she pay her respects to the god in his temple, but, on
the contrary, he presents himself to her in the house of her
husband, to make her his through his embrace. To say that
"to a certain extent the whole community has been placed
under the protection of her divine husband"[31] through this
act is to advance a hypothesis which is as arbitrary as it is
meaningless. It is no better when others are of the opinion

that this act was intended to bring fertility to the land. Dionysus puts himself in the position of the king. He, the confidant of women, he, whose majesty is complete in the intoxicated gaze of the most beautiful of women, claims the queen in Athens, when he comes. This event is of such importance that it had necessarily to be preceded by a great public ceremony of the entry of the god; and if the procession with the ship on wheels took place, as is probable, on the day of the Choes, the next thing, of course, that comes to mind is that the visit to the Boukolion and the marriage took place on this very day.

Just as the appearances of Dionysus, in general, are different from those of the other gods because of their physical immediacy, so there is no precedent in the history of cult for the rite of sexual intercourse with the queen. This visit truly shows that he is the god who appears. In no other act of his epiphany is his nearness revealed with such impetuousness in taking possession.

# 6. *The Symbol of the Mask*

The galvanic entrance of the god and his inescapable presence have found their expression in a symbol which is even more expressive than the cult forms we have previously discussed. It is an image out of which the perplexing riddle of his two-fold nature stares—and with it, madness. This is the mask.

Dionysus was present in person in the form of a mask at the ceremony of the mixing of the wine, which was performed by the women attendants, probably on the day of the Choes.[1] We have rather exact knowledge of this sacred practice from a series of vase paintings which Frickenhaus has assembled* and discussed.[2] The large mask of the god hung on a wooden column, and the wine was not just mixed and ladled up in front of it, but it was also presented with the first draught.[3] A long robe (or a double robe) extends down from beneath the bearded head, and this gives one the impression of a full-figured idol. Ivy sprigs are bushed up over the mask much like the crown of a tree; and ivy twines around the unobstructed parts of the wooden column or grows up from its base, at times even growing out, like tree branches, from the robes of the god himself.

Frickenhaus was wrong in believing that this copied the ivy-clad column in the sanctuary of the Theban Cadmeia.[4] This was the column whose leaves once supposedly protected

* See Plates 1–3 and 5.

the new-born infant Dionysus from the fire. But our sources tell us nothing about a mask on the Theban column. And here the mask is the all-important object. At times it is pictured to be of such a size that it covers most of the column.[5] In fact, most black-figured paintings show only the mask—or even two masks—without the robe.[6] Nor is it at all correct to maintain, with references to May-poles and the like, that the column was supposed to represent a tree because of the tendrils which grow out of or entwine themselves around the unobstructed areas of the column, or because of the bushiness at the top of the mask. It is true we know of a "tree-Dionysus" (Ἔνδενδρος, Δενδρίτης), of whom Plutarch[7] says that he was worshipped almost everywhere in Greece.[8] In this instance, however, the column has been intentionally and distinctly identified as such by its base and capital, and the ivy tendrils which appear on it and form a sort of crown by being heaped above the mask do not make the column into a tree but accompany the epiphany of the god present in the mask—a god whose favorite is the ivy.

It was Dionysus, himself, then, who appeared in the mask. There was no column made of stone, no primitively crude carved image to bear witness to his sacred presence, but just the external flat surface of a face, apparently suited for nothing else except to be worn by a living face as a disguise. And yet this—and this alone—is to represent the god. What is this supposed to mean?

It is true we encounter the mask in other Greek cults. A large number of masks, quite grotesque in part, have come down to us from the sanctuary of Artemis Orthia in Sparta. In Arcadian Pheneos a mask of Demeter Kidaria was stored in a niche above the holy Petroma. On the so-called greater festival of consecration the priest put the mask over his face and beat "the infernal ones," as they were called, with staves.[9] The masks of Gorgo, Silene, and Achelous are well enough known.[10] Dionysus, however, is the genuine mask god. In Methymna on Lesbos an olivewood mask of Dionysus Phallen was worshipped, the mask supposedly having been pulled out of the sea by fishermen.[11] On Naxos there were masks of Dionysus Bakcheus and Meilichios made out of the wood of grape vines and fig trees.[12] There is mention that a mask was known in Athens, too.[13]

Only in the case of the masks of Dionysus do we know that they had to represent the god at his epiphany, all by themselves. They were large scale reproductions made out of lasting materials, and a number of these masks are still extant.[14] One of them, out of marble, more than life size, with an ivy wreath, comes out of the second half of the sixth century B.C. and belonged to the sanctuary of Dionysus of Attic Icaria, which is still called Dionyso today. This mask was obviously used in the cult practices which we have come to know from the vase paintings.[15] Because of their size, which at times is colossal, these masks or those from which they may have been copied, which were made out of lighter materials, could never have been worn by humans in front of their faces. They were thought of as representations of the god—however strange that may seem to us. But it is just this strangeness which can show us the way to the mysteries of the Dionysiac.

It is not every superhuman being who presents himself in the mask, but only those who are elemental, the ones who belong to the earth. In their honor, too, masked men danced their many and varied dances. The mask remained especially popular for the appearance of spirits and apparitions from the depths, and as such it has come down to us through the Middle Ages to modern times in Mardi Gras customs.[16] But how does the mask make its way into the sphere of earthly

PLATE 5 Detail from vase showing maenad dancing in a grotto before a large, bearded Dionysus mask. Oinochoe (Frickenhaus, *Lenäenvasen*, Pl. 1; Beazley, *ABFVP*, p. 573, no. 2). From the collection of the Staatliche Museen, Berlin, Hauptverwaltung. (Acc. No. 1930)

spirits and deities? Moderns are quick to turn to magic for their ultimate explanations, but anyone who has thought this over seriously will see that magic does not help us much here. What good is it, anyway, to say that in prehistoric times the masks of earth spirits were put on to ward off evil or to promote vegetation, and that this was done so that man could change himself into these spirits or gain control of their powers? It is doubtful that this would have ever occurred had not the mask, in itself, been thought to have within it the mysterious might of such beings—even without a man wearing it. The proof of this is to be found in the awe which masks as such always inspired, and in the fact that masks were kept in holy places.

It is characteristic of the age-old gods and spirits who appear in the masks that they appear with exciting immediacy before the faithful. In contrast to the Olympians, they are always close at hand, and, as a consequence, they appear now and then among men and live with them for longer or shorter periods of time. It is for this reason—and only for this reason—that men can appear in their role. And it is this miracle of their breath-taking, unavoidable presence which must have given the mask its meaning.

The modern, who has removed himself so far from these origins, can see the importance of the mask only in the fact that someone wears it. And when certain supernatural beings are themselves impersonated in mask form, he sees himself forced into the curious assumption that the artificial make-up of the human imitator has been transferred to the original image itself. Thus even the Gorgon is first supposed to have received her well-known masklike image because people once were in the habit of wearing her mask in apotropaic rituals.[17] Yet when we look at the mask, even we can still be so moved by it that we understand in a flash why it—and it alone—conveys the most compelling immediacy more than any complete image and thus had to serve as the representation of those spirits who appear in man's immediate proximity, with Dionysus, in particular, the most powerful of them all.

We have long since noticed that, in the procession of the gods on the François vase, Dionysus assumes a different pose from the other gods. While the latter are shown in profile, he is the only one who turns his terrible face with its large eyes directly at the viewer. This remarkable peculiarity, however, is usually explained by the fact that primitive man and his successors preferred to present Dionysus in the mask. It would be much closer to the truth to say, *vice versa*, that Dionysus was presented in the mask because he was known as the god of confrontation. It is the god of the most immediate presence who looks at us so penetratingly from the vase painting. Because it is his nature to appear suddenly and with overwhelming might before mankind, the mask serves as his symbol and his incarnation in cult.

From earliest times man has experienced in the face with the penetrating eyes the truest manifestation of anthropomorphic or theriomorphic beings. This manifestation is sustained by the mask, which is that much more effective because it is nothing but surface. Because of this, it acts as the strongest symbol of presence. Its eyes, which stare straight ahead, cannot be avoided; its face, with its inexorable immobility, is quite different from other images which seem ready to move, to turn around, to step aside. Here there is nothing but encounter, from which there is no withdrawal—an immovable, spell-binding antipode. This must be our point of departure for understanding that the mask, which was always a sacred object, could also be put on over a human face to depict the god or spirit who appears.

And yet this explains the significance of only half of the

phenomenon of the mask. The mask is pure confrontation—an antipode, and nothing else. It has no reverse side—"Spirits have no back," the people say. It has nothing which might transcend this mighty moment of confrontation. It has, in other words, no complete existence either. It is the symbol and the manifestation of that which is simultaneously there and not there: that which is excruciatingly near, that which is completely absent—both in one reality.

Thus the mask tells us that the theophany of Dionysus, which is different from that of the other gods because of its stunning assault on the senses and its urgency, is linked with the eternal enigmas of duality and paradox. This theophany thrusts Dionysus violently and unavoidably into the here and now—and sweeps him away at the same time into the inexpressible distance. It excites with a nearness which is at the same time a remoteness. The final secrets of existence and non-existence transfix mankind with monstrous eyes.

This spirit of duality which already distinguishes Dionysus and his realm, in his epiphany, from everything which is Olympian, returns over and over again in all the forms of his activity, as we shall see. It is the source of the fascination and the confusion which everything that is Dionysiac evokes, for it is the spirit of a wild being. His coming brings madness.

# 7. *Pandemonium and Silence*

"Oh deathly quiet pandemonium!"
(NIETZSCHE,
*Dionysosdithyramben*)

The wild spirit of the dreadful, which mocks all laws and institutions, reveals itself in the initial phenomena which accompany the approaching and imminent god. These are the phenomena of pandemonium and its related counterpart: deathly silence.

The pandemonium in which Dionysus, himself, and his divine entourage* make their entry—that pandemonium which the human horde, struck by his spirit, unleashes—is a genuine symbol of religious ecstasy. With the horror which is at the same time bewitchment, with the ecstasy which is like paralysis, overpowering all natural and habitual sense perceptions, The Dreadful suddenly springs into being. And, at its greatest intensity, it is as if the insane din were in reality the profoundest of silences.

There are other deities, too, who appear in the midst of pandemonium. They are the ones who are by nature close to Dionysus and are also associated with him in *cultus* and myth. Above all, there is Artemis, who, of course, is called by Homer the Lady of Clamours (Κελαδεινή), Demeter, the Great Mother. But none of them takes such joy in a stupefying din as does Dionysus.

* See Plates 1–3.

His titles already mark him as the god of pandemonic wildness. He is called "the roarer," Bromios, a surname which appeared early, all by itself, as the name of the god.[1] In a Homeric hymn he introduces himself as Dionysus (ἐρίβρομος).[2] "A din (βρόμος) filled the forest," as the god who had just come of age passed through with his female attendants.[3] He is the "loud shouter."[4] He, himself, is called Εὔιος from the echoing shouts of joy (εὐοῖ), and the women of his rout are called Εὐάδες. Bellowing, shrill-sounding instruments accompany him; we often see them pictured in sculpture. A series of mythic stories and descriptions make us keenly aware of the overpowering spirit of the Dionysiac din which makes its violent entry as it captivates and inspires dread at one and the same time. The daughters of Minyas, who reject Dionysus and remain true to their household duties, are startled suddenly by invisible drums, flutes, and cymbals, and see the ivy of the god hanging down miraculously from their looms.[5] As a prisoner of the Tyrrhenian pirates, Dionysus suddenly transforms the mast and the oars into snakes. Flute music fills the ship, and everything is overgrown with ivy.[6] As Philostratus[7] describes it, Dionysus' own ship is rocked by waves of bacchantic sound. On its exterior hang resounding bronze cymbals so that the god is not forced to continue his voyage in silence even when his satyrs are deep in a drunken sleep. To the astonishment of the inhabitants of India the troops of the militant Dionysus also advance to the sound of flutes, drums, pipes, and crashing cymbals.[8]

However, there is nothing which reveals the supernatural meaning of the incredible noise-making, which announces the god and accompanies him, so well as its counterpart of deathlike silence into which it suddenly changes. A wild uproar and a numbed silence—these are only different forms of the Nameless, of that which shatters all composure. The maenad, whose shrill exultation we think we have just heard, frightens us with her rigid stare, in which we can see the reflection of the horror which drives her mad. We see her this way on the earlier vase paintings (the most impressive example is that on the famous cylix from Munich [No. 2645]): her eyes stare wildly, a snake coils itself around her windswept hair and lunges up with vibrating tongue over her forehead.* In this picture and others like it the silent maenad is in frenzied motion with her head slumped to one side. And yet she holds herself bolt upright, sunk in a speechless trance, like an image made of stone. Horace sees her in this way[9] "when at night on the mountain tops she looks down in wonder at the Hebrus river and the land of Thrace, glistening with snow."

The picture of the Bacchante who stands motionless and stares into space must have been well known. Catullus is thinking of her when he tells of the abandoned Ariadne,[10] who follows her faithless lover with sorrowing eyes as she stands on the reedy shore "like the picture of a maenad."[11] Indeed, melancholy silence becomes the sign of women who are possessed by Dionysus. Silent melancholy characters were said to behave like Bakchai because silence was a characteristic of theirs.[12]

Aeschylus, in the *Edonians*, has given us a picture of the wild tumult of the Thracian orgy. According to him, the sound of the flute excited madness.[13] The presence of the frenzied god, himself, was both felt and heard. This is quite clear from the verses which we shall consider below. Madness dwells in the surge of clanging, shrieking, and pealing sounds; it dwells also in silence. The women who follow Dionysus get their name, *maenades*, from this madness. Possessed by it, they rush off, whirl madly in circles, or stand still, as if turned into stone.

* See Plate 6.

PLATE 6  Maenad carrying the *thyrsus* and brandishing a leopard cub. Detail from inside of a cup painted (ca. 490 B.C.) by the Brygos painter (Arias, *A History of 1000 Years of Greek Vase Painting*, pp. 337-338, Pl. xxxiv; Beazley, *ARFVP*², p. 371, no. 15). From the collection of Staatliche Antikensammlungen, Munich. (Acc. No. 2645)

# 8. *The World Bewitched*

What is the reason for this tremendous excitement, this deep trance? What did this bewildering clamor proclaim?

The world man knows, the world in which he has settled himself so securely and snugly—that world is no more. The turbulence which accompanied the arrival of Dionysus has swept it away. Everything has been transformed. But it has not been transformed into a charming fairy story or into an ingenuous child's paradise. The primeval world has stepped into the foreground, the depths of reality have been opened, the elemental forms of everything that is creative, everything that is destructive, have arisen, bringing with them infinite rapture and infinite terror. The innocent picture of a well-ordered routine world has been shattered by their coming, and they bring with them no illusions or fantasies but truth—a truth that brings on madness.

Greeted with wild shouts of joy, the form in which the truth appears is the frenzied, all-engulfing torrent of life which wells up from the depths that gave it birth. In the myth and in the experience of those who have been affected by this event, the appearance of Dionysus brings with it nourishing intoxicating waters that bubble up from the earth. Rocks split open, and streams of water gush forth. Everything that has been locked up is released. The alien and the hostile unite in miraculous harmony. Age-old laws have suddenly lost their power, and even the dimensions of time and space are no longer valid.

The ecstasy begins—in the mythical sphere—at the moment when the god enters the world. The hymn which Philodamus of Skarpheia composed for Delphi in the middle of the fourth century tells us that all of the immortals danced at the birth of Dionysus. Semele, herself, during her pregnancy, was supposedly seized by an irrepressible desire to dance,[1] and whenever she heard the sound of a flute, she had to dance; and the child in her womb danced, too.

"The earth flows with milk, flows with wine, flows with the nectar of bees. And there is a vapor in the air as of Syrian frankincense."[2] The *Bacchae* of Euripides gives us the most vital picture of the wonderful circumstance in which, as Plato says in the *Ion*,[3] the god-intoxicated celebrants draw milk and honey from the streams. They strike rocks with the *thyrsus*, and water gushes forth. They lower the *thyrsus* to the earth, and a spring of wine bubbles up. If they want milk, they scratch up the ground with their fingers and draw up the milky fluid. Honey trickles down from the *thyrsus* made of the wood of the ivy.[4] They gird themselves with snakes and give suck to fawns and wolf cubs as if they were infants at the breast.[5] Fire does not burn them. No weapon of iron can wound them, and the snakes harmlessly lick up the sweat from their heated cheeks.[6] Fierce bulls fall to the ground, victims to numberless, tearing female hands,[7] and sturdy trees are torn up by the roots with their combined efforts.[8] Wine suddenly streams forth on the ship of the pirates who take Dionysus along with them. Vines with swelling grapes wind themselves around the sails, ivy grows around the mast, and wreaths hang down from the tholepins.[9] Miracles of this type also announce the imminence of the god to the daughters of Minyas. The loom on which they are working is suddenly overgrown with ivy and grape vines, and wine and milk trickle down from the ceiling of their chamber.[10]

The same miracle which calls forth nourishing streams from the hard and the rigid also bursts chains asunder, causes walls to fall in ruins, and lifts the age-old barriers which keep the future and the remote concealed from the human mind. Dionysus is, after all, given the highly significant name of the "liberator" (Λύσιος, Λυαῖος). In the *Bacchae* of Euripides, the maenads who have been thrown into prison at the king's command are suddenly free again. The chains dropped from their feet of their own accord, and the locked doors swung open untouched by any hand.[11] The maenads who had been seized and imprisoned by Lycurgus were said to have been freed suddenly in the same manner.[12] Still much more miraculous than the freeing of the women is the arrogance with which Dionysus, himself, derides the deluded fool who dared to throw him into chains only to see his captive suddenly before him again without his bonds.[13]

To open that which has been locked away is also to reveal the invisible and the future. Dionysus, himself, "is a prophet, and the bacchic revel is filled with the spirit of prophecy."[14] We shall say more about the holy places of his oracles later. Plutarch makes the general assertion that the ancients credited Dionysus with an important role in divination.[15] According to the myth, Semele, as she carried Dionysus in her womb, was already filled with a divine spirit, and so, too, were the women who touched her blessed body.[16]

The public cult festivals were also witnesses of the marvels of this transformed world. In many places the epiphany of Dionysus was accompanied by wondrous streams of wine. Grape vines bloomed and ripened on one and the same day. The inhabitants of the island of Teos cited as proof of Dionysus' having been born there the astonishing fact that a spring of wine with a lovely fragrance gushed from the earth regularly at his festival.[17] In Elis the miracle was confirmed by eyewitness accounts: in the festival, which bore the name Thyia and was celebrated in an area which was eight stades away from the city, three empty basins were put into a room in the presence of citizens and any foreigners who happened to be present. The room was then locked and sealed, and anyone who wanted to could bring his own seal to add to the seal on the door. On the next day the seals remained unbroken, but those entering the room found that the three basins had been filled with wine. Pausanias, who was himself unable to be present at the time of the festival, assures us that the citizens and the foreigners had vouched under oath for the reliability of this report.[18] A similar miracle was reported on the island of Andros, and here we also are told when the festival usually took place. On the fifth of January, so Mucianus tells us in Pliny,[19] a stream of wine flowed in the temple of Dionysus there, and for seven days, at that. Samples of it, whenever they were taken out of the sanctuary, immediately turned to water. Pausanias, who tells us of the same phenomenon,[20] adds that the festival was celebrated only every second year and hence belonged to the "trieteric" class. Undoubtedly we are to see, in this, one of the winter epiphany festivals of Dionysus. And from it we learn what sort of miracles accompanied the coming god.

On Naxos wine gushed forth from a spring.[21] This miracle, which is mentioned by Propertius in his hymn to the god,[22] supposedly took place for the first time at the marriage of Dionysus and Ariadne.[23]

The most amazing miracle, however, was that of the so-called "one-day vines" (ἐφήμεροι ἄμπελοι). These flowered and bore fruit in the course of a few hours during the festivals of the epiphany of the god. Particularly famous was the miraculous vine of Parnassus, the holy site where the women danced their wild dances for Dionysus in the wintertime and awakened the divine little boy in his cradle. A choral song in Euripides' *Phoenissae*[24] reveals what this vine meant to Delphi. It sings of the twin peaks lit up by the fire of the Bacchic festival and of the vine which "daily bears its yield of juicy thick grape clusters."[25] As Sophocles tells us in his *Thyestes*,[26] on Euboea one could watch the holy vine grow green in the early morning. By noon the grapes were already forming, they grew heavy and dark in color, and by evening the ripe fruit could be cut down, and the drink could be mixed. We discover from the scholia of the *Iliad*[27] that this occurred in Aigai at the annual rite in honor of Dionysus, as the women dedicated to the god performed the holy rites (ὀργιαζουσῶν τῶν μυστίδων γυναικῶν). And finally, Euphorion knew of a festival of Dionysus in Achaean Aigai in which the sacred vines bloomed and ripened during the cult dances of the chorus so that already by evening considerable quantities of wine could be pressed.[28]

This was a miracle which commanded serious belief, a miracle which Sophocles and Euripides considered worthy of their praise. We do not intend to dismiss it with the flippant remark that it was nothing but a hoax perpetrated by the priests. For the faithful, it was a genuine sign of the presence of the god, who appeared in person at his festival. At Eleusis at the supreme moment of revelation was not a freshly reaped ear of grain exhibited to the initiates (ἐν σιωπῇ τεθερισμένον στάχυν)?[29] The conjectures which have been recently advanced to explain this act[30] are quite unsatisfactory. Foucart,[31] who, like most scholars today, construes the words ἐν σιωπῇ in Hippolytus not with τεθερισμένον στάχυν, which would be natural, but with that which went before, is quite right when he says we would have to understand otherwise that the ear was cut off silently in the presence of the initiates and was then shown to them. And yet that is undoubtedly what happened. The ear of grain which grows miraculously suits the mysteries of Demeter as well as the miraculous vine suits those of Dionysus. It is not without interest to learn that the so-called sun dance of the American Navajos has in it, among other occurrences, the miracle of a plant which becomes green, blooms, and bears fruit between midnight and dawn.[32]

However, wine itself—even if it does not appear as suddenly and in as astonishing a manner as this—enters the world as a miracle. This is the way in which it is received and enjoyed at the Anthesteria when Dionysus makes his ceremonial entrance into the city. The vase paintings still show us clearly the mood in which the god was honored, and his miraculous gift received.[33] Before the citizens drank it, the wine was mixed for Dionysus, who was there in person in the mask.[34] Apparently a priestess, perhaps the wife of the Archon Basileus himself, took over the mixing of the wine, and the fourteen *gerarai*, whom she had to swear in,[35] were probably her assistants in this rite.[36] The celebrants lined up and had their pitchers filled by these priestesses. Then, to the accompaniment of trumpet blasts, began the famous drinking bout in which the crowd joined together to honor the drunken god.[37] Finally, each celebrant placed his wreath around the wine jar, handed the wreath—in the sanctuary of Dionysus—to the priestess who had mixed the wine for him, and then poured out the wine remaining in the jar as a libation to the god.[38]

The vase paintings, which Frickenhaus has assembled, show the mixing and the initial tasting of the wine in front of the mask of Dionysus.* Again, it is women who pay homage to the

---

* See Plates 2, 3, and 5.

newly manifested god, no matter what we may wish to call them. Those who are not immediately engaged in administering to Dionysus, himself, or to the holy wine ritual, are in a visible state of ecstasy, which, in some of the pictures, has reached the well-known form of maenadic frenzy. Of these actions we can no longer determine which ones corresponded exactly to the actual practice of the ritual. The forms of Dionysiac frenzy which belong by nature to mountain forests would hardly have been manifested in this way at the Anthesteria festival in the precinct of Dionysus. There is no question that the artists have inserted mythic elements into their work. But none of that was in any sense foreign to the subject. The women who served the god represented, after all, the divine entourage spoken about in the myth, and the painters did something quite significant when, in depicting the women's actions, they took up the reality into the myth. It is out of such pictures that the emotions with which the god was received address themselves vividly to us. He, the god who appeared among men with his ripe intoxicating drink, was the same as the frenzied one whose spirit drove the women to madness in the loneliness of the mountains.

Wine has in it something of the spirit of infinity which brings the primeval world to life again. It is doubly significant, then, when in the transformed world not only milk and honey but streams of wine spurt forth from the earth before the eyes of the dancers, who are bewitched by the presence of Dionysus and sport with the elements.

But they are so bewitched that their maternal instinct knows no limits anymore, and they suckle even the young of wild beasts. They are, after all, mothers and nurses—like the nurses of Dionysus in the myth, who swarm around the matured god in the forests and accompany him on his journeys.[39] We see these divine "nurses" ($\Delta\iota\omega\nu\acute{\upsilon}\sigma\omicron\iota\omicron$ $\tau\iota\theta\tilde{\eta}\nu\alpha\iota$)[40] in many sculptures[41] receiving the divine child from the hands of Zeus or of his messenger, Hermes.* But there are other little boys whom they rear, as mothers or as foster mothers; for "many a nymph with whom Dionysus so loves to play upon the mountain peaks delights him unexpectedly with a child."[42] In the *Bacchae* of Euripides[43] the maenads steal little children from their homes. In Nonnus,[44] who elaborates on the Euripidean scene, the maenad who stole the little boy offers him her breast. And now in the forests where they live a life in the wild with the beasts, they suckle the animal young as if they were their own children. "The young mothers, who had left a child behind in their homes, held fawns or young wolves in their arms and suckled them with their white milk," so the messenger in the *Bacchae* of Euripides reports.[45] Nonnus' poem even speaks of young lions,[46] and the picture of the maenad who gives suck to a beast of prey appears often in works of art.

* For a vase painting of this scene, see Plate 7.

PLATE 7 Hermes bringing the new-born Dionysus to the nymphs and Papposilenus at Nysa. White-ground calyx-krater painted by the Phiale painter (Arias, *A History of 1000 Years of Greek Vase Painting*, p. 367, Pl. XLIV; Beazley, *ARFVP²*, p. 1017, no. 54). From the collection of the Museo Gregoriano Etrusco, Vatican Museum. (Acc. No. 559)

# 9. The Somber Madness

But the splendor of the god, to whom all of the treasure rooms of the world have been opened, is overcast suddenly by a profound darkness. Behind the enraptured truth there looms another truth which brings on horror and catches up the dancers in a madness which is no longer sweet but somber.

This is represented in the myth, first of all, by the motif of severe persecution. The first account which Greek poetry gives us of the plight of the women of Dionysus speaks of their horror-stricken flight from Lycurgus, who beats them unmercifully.[1] In their fear they drop the holy objects and think only of saving themselves. They have reason for their despair. Dionysus, himself, is beaten and in his fright has to take refuge in the depths of the sea. What this myth relates was cult practice at the festival of the Agrionia. There the priest of Dionysus in Orchomenus pursued a band of women with the sword and struck down all whom he could reach.[2]

Thus death encroaches upon the realm of the god, who is extolled as "the joyful one" ($\pi o \lambda v \gamma \eta \theta \acute{\eta} s$), and the "giver of riches" ($\pi \lambda o v \tau o \delta \acute{o} \tau \eta s$). In fact, his realm actually becomes the realm of death, for the Agrionia festival, like the Anthesteria, the spring festival of Dionysus, was a festival of the dead (see p.118). Dionysus, himself, is a suffering, dying god who must succumb to the violence of terrible enemies in the midst of the glory of his youthful greatness. His grave was in Delphi, in the Holy of Holies. Like him, the women who had raised him and had played his ecstatic games with him all met violent deaths as well. It was said that the "women of the sea" ("Αλιαι γυναῖκες), whom he had brought along with him from the islands, lay buried in Argos, where Perseus had confronted him.³ And there, too, it was believed, were found the graves of the three Theban maenads who were supposed to have established the cult of Dionysus in Magnesia on the Maeander.⁴ Ariadne, the symbol of womanhood which gave itself up to Dionysus in love, is at the same time the symbol of the suffering and death of all those who are associated with him. Her grave was exhibited in several places. She, too, was supposed to have hanged herself like the daughter of Icarius, the murdered friend of Dionysus, Erigone, who was commemorated on the day of the dead of the Feast of the Pots.⁵ In her cult not only days of joy were celebrated but also days of sorrow, and it is highly significant that the corpse of the murdered Hesiod was said to have been washed up on the shore by the waves of the sea on the day of an Ariadne festival in Locris.⁶

We have a report out of Arcadian Alea whose grimness brings to mind the ritual of the Agrionia. At the biennial festival of Dionysus celebrated there, called the Skiereia, women were flogged.⁷ It is futile to attempt to strip the rite of its sinister nature by referring to fertility rites which are apparently similar.⁸ Pausanias, himself, to whom we owe our knowledge of the ritual, compares it to the flogging of the Spartan youths at the festival of Artemis Orthia, and the well-known barbarity of this custom makes a mockery of all innocent interpretations. Artemis Orthia is associated with Dionysus through her epithets.

But the tragic destiny of which the myth is aware and to which the ritual gives expression did not occur without warning. It was generated with inexorable necessity out of a mad act of violence. Only because Dionysus, himself, is not merely the enraptured one but also the terrible one, has the terrible demanded him as its victim. That sinister truth which creates madness shows its horrible face in his actions no less than in his sufferings. The most celebrated myth of his destruction has him suffer as Zagreus, the "great hunter," the same fate inherent in his appalling actions. The "hunter" is himself hunted; the "render of men" (ἀνθρωπορραίστης) is himself rent. But the dark shadow of terrible deeds lies behind the persecution, suffering, and death of his female companions, also. In the merciless assault on a band of women at the festival of the Agrionia, the daughters of Minyas were commemorated—they who once had consummated that mad, bloody act toward which the sinister manifestation of the Dionysiac nature is irresistibly pressing.

According to the myth,[9] they were the only ones who did not wish to listen to the summons of Dionysus but remained at home, modest and diligent women, awaiting the return of their husbands. There suddenly the spirit of Dionysus came upon them with marvels and terrors, and in the madness which seized them they cast lots for their little boys. The story goes that they had developed a violent lust for human flesh. The lot fell on Leucippe's little son, who was then torn into pieces by the three. The gruesome savagery of these women, who had been previously so virtuous and motherly, appears here as a punishment inflicted upon them by a scorned and neglected god. But this, as Welcker has already observed correctly,[10] does not explain the real significance of their actions. It was the wildest eruption of the destructive madness which belongs to the reality of Dionysus as much as do the ecstasy and abandon which accompany him. This same savagery also re-occurs where there can no longer be a question of an affront to the god. It finds its expression also in the cult sacrifices made to Dionysus. And as the counterpart of the maternal instinct, it repeats itself even among the beasts of the wilderness, whose young the maenads not only suckle at their breasts but tear apart and devour—a representation of those mothers who pounce upon their own infants with hideous desire.

When Dionysus came to Argos, and the inhabitants there did not wish to worship him, he drove the women mad so that they stormed off to the mountains and devoured the flesh of their own little children.[11] Here, too, the implication seems to be that the women were affected in this way because they were being punished. But the god punishes by revealing the absolute terror of his reality. And this terror attacks innocent victims, too—in fact, it constantly threatens to make a victim of the god himself. According to Nonnus,[12] Aura, too, the beloved of Dionysus, killed one of her new-born children and devoured it. Like the mothers, so the foster-mothers. It is already said of the daughters of Lamos, the first foster-mothers of the new-born Dionysus, that they would have torn the child into pieces in their madness had he not been snatched away in time by Hermes and given over to Ino.[13] Ino, herself, Dionysus' mother's sister, who had reared the divine child, is said to have killed her own infant son, Melikertes, in a fit of madness.[14] This son of Ino's was worshipped on the island of Tenedos as Palaimon, and since children were sacrificed to him, he was called the "child-killer" (βρεφοκτονός).[15]

Thus the same brutality speaks to us out of the cult as out of the myth. We feel its presence clearly; the infinity which the ecstasy of life inhabits threatens with the ecstasy of destruction everyone who approaches it. Happy that soul whose madness is tempered by Dionysus as the "deliverer" (Λύσιος)! The appalling side of his own nature stands out clearly enough in several of the acts of worship offered him by man. On the island of Chios, where the women, as we hear, were seized by a Bacchic madness,[16] a man was torn into pieces to honor Dionysus Omadios, the bestial deity who feeds on raw flesh.[17] The same is said of Tenedos.[18] From this island we hear also that there the "render of men" ('Ανθρωπορραίστης), Dionysus, received an unusual sacrifice.[19] Buskins were put on a new-born calf whose mother was given the treatment of a woman who had just given birth to a child, and then it was slaughtered with an axe. But the slaughterer who had struck the fatal blow with the axe had to flee under a shower of stones to the sea. The buskins make it plain who the victim was really meant to be: Dionysus, himself, who, the myth tells us, as a regal child was torn to pieces by the Titans. This ritual, to which we must return later (pp.131-32 and 192), is generally interpreted today as a so-called sacramental sacrifice, which was supposed to bestow upon its participants the power of the god who had been killed and eaten.[20]

Yet, in everything which has come down to us about Dionysus and his cults, we find nowhere the intimation that his flesh might have been eaten by a society which wanted to appropriate his divine power. Rather than give such a baseless hypothesis credence, let us ask the cult itself for evidence. And the cult tells us that it was the Dionysus who was the "render of men" who was slaughtered here. What the myth tells us of the god, namely, that the Titans overpowered him as Zagreus, as the "great hunter," was a cult act in Tenedos. And just as the myth tells us that he was overpowered as a regal child in the form of a bull, so a calf dressed in buskins was slaughtered there. The meaning of the myth is this: the god himself suffers the horror which he commits. That which the myth tells in words, the *cultus* repeats in regular sacrificial actions.

We recognize, then, in the suffering, persecutions, and

destruction of the attendants of Dionysus and the god himself, the destiny which their own horror breeds. The memory
of their actions is still preserved in many other legends. Take,
for example, the story of Procne and Philomela.[21] Procne,
together with her sister, kills her own little son and serves
him up to her father, whereupon the two are hunted down
with a sword or an axe.[22] It is worth noting that this occurs on the day when an orgiastic festival of Dionysus takes
place.[23]

Consider also the myth of the destruction of Pentheus in
which it is his own mother who tears her son to pieces. The
*Lenai* of Theocritus[24] tells us that the three sisters, one of
them his mother, dismembered the unfortunate one who had
driven them mad with his prying curiosity.

Still, it is not just human children with which the women
of Dionysus concern themselves in good and in evil. The vital
spirit of the primeval world which has affected all of creation through Dionysus drives the young of the forest to their
embrace. We have seen how the women mothered fawns and
young wolves and gave them the milk from their breasts. But
here, too, the sweet madness of overflowing tenderness does
not continue long but suddenly reverses itself and becomes a
destructive frenzy.

Wherever poets or artists represent the madness of the
maenads at its height, there the dancers appear with young
animals in their hands, tear them into pieces, and swing the
bloody members through the air. In the *Bacchae* of Euripides[25] they pounce on a herd of cattle, fell the most powerful animals among them, and tear them limb from limb. The
same picture appears again in later authors.[26] The true victims
of their gruesome hunt, however, are the animals of the forest,
the very ones they have mothered. In Euripides,[27] Orestes
and Pylades, who have seized Hermione, are compared to
Bacchants who have in their hands a young animal. The verb

νεβρίζειν (from νεβρός "fawn") is used to describe the tearing
to pieces of a young deer by a maenad. Since, however, the
women also suckled the young of other animals, wolves and
bears are also mentioned as the victims of their murdering
lust.[28]

Thus the madness of these bloodthirsty huntresses has
evolved from the magic of a motherliness which has no
bounds. The revel rout, however, is only following the example of its divine leader. Dionysus, himself, is a hunter.
"Like a hare" (Aeschylus, *Eumenides* [26]), he hunted down
Pentheus, a victim who is torn to pieces in a horrible manner. Agave in Euripides[29] calls him "an experienced hunter"
(κυναγέτας σοφός), and the chorus answers, "Yes, our king is
a hunter!" (ὁ γὰρ ἄναξ ἀγρεύς). He hunts the blood of young
male goats.[30] The maenads are compared to hunting dogs.[31]
But they, too, are considered hunters,[32] and so one of them
is given the eloquent name Θηρώ.[33]

But what a hunt that is! Killing is dismemberment, and
with it, at the height of the frenzy, comes the devouring of
the raw flesh. "Dressed in the holy deer-skin, he hunts the
blood of dying goats with a ravenous lust for raw flesh
(ὠμοφάγον χάριν)." This is the song of the Euripidean chorus
of Dionysus.[34] Like their master, the maenads, too, pounce on
their victims to devour their flesh raw.[35] That no longer describes the hunter. That describes the beast of prey. And this
is just what the epithet ὠμηστής means to say, for it was to
the god as the "eater of raw flesh," that is to say, as a beast
of prey that three Persian youths were sacrificed before the
battle of Salamis.[36] Elsewhere this word ὠμηστής usually describes lions.[37] But other beasts of prey (wolves, eagles, vul-
tures, and dogs) are characterized by it. When Hecuba in the
*Iliad*[38] calls Achilles this, she is comparing him to a merciless
beast of prey.[39] The same is true of ὠμοφάγος, an adjective
used with the maenads, and of ὠμόσιτος. That the murderous

and bloodthirsty actions of the maddened women were actually looked upon as those of beasts of prey is substantiated by Oppian's tale[40] (which surely goes back to ancient accounts) that Dionysus changed into panthers the women who were to rend Pentheus. Dilthey has compared these passages with a vase painting in which Pentheus, who is being seized by a maenad, is at the same time pounced upon by a panther.[41]

With this the god of magical grace has entered a state of the most terrible contrasts.

His ability to transform himself into something else is often stressed. He is the "god of two forms" ($\delta i\mu o\rho\phi os$),[42] the "god of many forms" ($\pi o\lambda\nu\epsilon\iota\delta\grave{\eta}s$ $\kappa a\grave{\iota}$ $\pi o\lambda\acute{\nu}\mu o\rho\phi os$),[43] "Appear as a bull, or as a many-headed dragon, or as a lion breathing fire!" This is the invocation of the chorus to Dionysus in Euripides' *Bacchae*.[44] In the battle against the giants he was a lion.[45] To the daughters of Minyas he appeared in the form of a young girl and suddenly changed himself into a bull, a lion, a panther.[46] In Nonnus (who also tells of the many transformations of Zagreus in his battle with the Titans[47]), the Indian Deriades complains of the impossibility of conquering him— Dionysus—because the $\pi o\lambda\nu\epsilon\iota\delta\grave{\eta}s$ (the many-formed one) was now a lion, a bull, a boar, a bear, a panther, a snake, and now a tree, fire, water.[48]

More frightening and serious than the multiplicity, however, are the duality and contrast in Dionysus' nature. Plutarch, in his life of Antony, reminds us of this when he speaks of Antony's entrance into Ephesus as the new Dionysus who is acclaimed by many as if he were Dionysus "the friendly god who lavishes blessings" ($\chi a\rho\iota\delta\acute{o}\tau\eta s$ $\kappa a\grave{\iota}$ $\mu\epsilon\iota\lambda\acute{\iota}\chi\iota os$), even though he was for most "the bestial and wild one" ($\grave{\omega}\mu\eta\sigma\tau\grave{\eta}s$ $\kappa a\grave{\iota}$ $\grave{a}\gamma\rho\iota\acute{\omega}\nu\iota os$). Similar distinctions are not uncommon in our sources.[49] Even the animals who accompany him and in whose forms he himself appears from time to time stand in sharp contrast to one another, with the one group (the bull, the goat, the ass) symbolizing fertility and sexual desire, and the other (the lion, the panther, the lynx) representing the most bloodthirsty desire to kill.

The panther, as is well known, appears in descriptions of a later period as the favorite animal of Dionysus and is found with him in countless works of art.* As Philostratus tells us,[50] the panther leaps as gracefully and lightly as a Bacchant, and this is the reason the god loves him so. It was even maintained that he had a passionate love for wine.[51] At the same time, however, it was because of his intractable savagery that he was compared with Dionysus.[52] As the Gigantomachy can illustrate, the lion was already associated with Dionysus very early in history.[53] In *Homeric Hymn* 7, Dionysus frightens the pirates who had captured him by having a lion appear. In Euripides, he himself is invoked to appear as a lion (see above), and it is as such that he appears to the daughters of Minyas, to their horror (see above). There are other references which could be made here: there is, for example, Dionysus Κεχηνώς on Samos, who is said to have received his shrine there because of the gratitude and loyalty of a lion. Euphorion wrote a poem on the incident.[54]

Usually it is said that the lion and the panther were not originally associated with Dionysus but entered his retinue by way of Asia Minor through contact with the cult of the Great Mother.[55] But there were lions on the Balkan peninsula itself even in later eras,[56] and even if the panther was not indigenous there, it need not have become a member of the god's retinue because of external borrowings. It is very doubtful whether gods and cults were as ready to accommodate themselves to one another as moderns—to whom they have no serious import—like to imagine. As long as a god was still thought to exist, what he actually was had to determine

* See Plate 8.

whether he attracted or repelled this or that to his orbit. Whenever or however the worshippers of Dionysus got to know the panther, which was as beautiful as it was dangerous, its nature told them immediately that it was akin to Dionysus and had to belong to his realm. That is confirmed by the other beasts of prey, similar to the panther, who were associated with Dionysus earlier or later.

Ever since the Augustan Age, Roman writers, following, of course, the Greek tradition, like to name the lynx as a beast of Dionysus.[57] This animal had been native to Greece from a very early time and is still found there today.[58] The panther or leopard, and the lynx (the tiger, too, is added in the references out of Roman literature) have that very thing in common which justifies comparing them in more than one respect with the nature and actions of the maenads. This makes itself felt most in the panther, which was, after all, the most loyal attendant of the god. Of all the cats devoted to Dionysus, it was not only the most graceful and fascinating but also the most savage and bloodthirsty. The lightning-fast agility and perfect elegance of its movements, whose purpose is murder, exhibit the same union of beauty and fatal danger found in the mad women who accompany Dionysus. Their savagery, too, fascinates those who watch them, and yet it is the eruption of the dreadful impulse to pounce on the prey, tear it into pieces, and devour its flesh raw. We are told that the leopard and the lynx are the most murderous of all the larger beasts of prey. Many more victims must bleed to death under their teeth than would be needed for their sustenance. And when one hears that a female leopard which is suckling her young is the bloodthirstiest of all the carnivores, one cannot help thinking of the maenads who were also nursing mothers.

It is true that the worlds of the other gods are not without paradox. But none of these worlds is as disrupted by it as is the

PLATE 8    The panther of Dionysus. Detail from the Roman (ca. A.D. 200) Dionysus-mosaic in the Rheinisches Museum, Cologne (A-2200). Photograph, courtesy of the German Tourist Information Office, Chicago.

world of Dionysus. He, the nurturer and the god of rapture; he, the god who is forever praised as the giver of wine which removes all sorrow and care; he, the deliverer and healer (λύσιος, λυαῖος, σωτήρ, ἰατρός, etc.), "the delight of mortals" (χάρμα βροτοῖσιν),[59] "the god of many joys" (πολυγηθής),[60] the dancer and ecstatic lover, the bestower of riches" (πλουτοδότης),[61] the "benefactor" (εὐεργέτης)[62]—this god who is the most delightful of all the gods is at the same time the most frightful. No single Greek god even approaches Dionysus in the horror of his epithets, which bear witness to a savagery that is absolutely without mercy. In fact, one must evoke the memory of the monstrous horror of eternal darkness to find anything at all comparable. He is called the "render of men" (ἀνθρωπορραίστης),[63] "the eater of raw flesh" (ὠμηστής),[64] "who delights in the sword and bloodshed."[65] Correspondingly we hear not only of human sacrifice in his cult[65a] but also of the ghastly ritual in which a man is torn to pieces.[66]

Where does this put us? Surely there can be no further doubt that this puts us into death's sphere. The terrors of destruction, which make all of life tremble, belong also, as horrible desire, to the kingdom of Dionysus. The monster whose supernatural duality speaks to us from the mask has one side of his nature turned toward eternal night.

It is only among the monsters of the world of the dead that we find the epithet of the beast of prey who "eats flesh raw" ὠμηστής, etc.) repeated. Hesiod[67] uses it to describe Cerberus and also[68] Echidna. The latter had mated with Typhon and had spawned, according to Hesiod, not only Cerberus, the Lernean Hydra, and the Chimaera, but also Orthus, Geryon's hound. By her own son, Orthus, she gave birth to the Nemaean lion and the Theban Sphinx. The hound, Orthus, bears a name which is unquestionably connected with the well-known epithet of Artemis: Orthia. Significantly

enough, this name turns up again in the case of Dionysus
('Ορθός).[69] There is also a tradition that it was Dionysus who
sent the Sphinx to the Thebans.[70] There is no reason why we
should reject this evidence. Euripides, himself, says[71] that the
Sphinx was sent from Hades to Thebes (ὁ κατὰ χθονὸς "Αιδας).
This man-eating lion-woman reminds us vividly of Dionysus,
and not just of him but also of his maenads. According to one
tradition (see above, p.110), the bloodthirsty panthers are
supposed to be transformed maenads. As for the Sphinx,
among the references which tell of her origin[72] there is also
the one which says that she was once a maenad, that is to say,
one of the Theban women whom Dionysus drove mad

However, the mad Dionysus and his women attendants are
also close enough to other spirits of the underworld. Take
the Erinyes, in particular, who also like him have a dual nature. Dionysus is worshipped as Melanaigis;[73] the Erinys is
similarly called μελάναιγις.[74] The Erinyes are represented as
mad, as are those under the spell of Dionysus. In Aeschylus[75]
they call themselves μαινάδες,[76] and in the vicinity of Mega-
lopolis they were worshipped as Maniai.[77] Lyssa ("canine
madness") also belongs to the realm of Hades, and it is her
"dogs" which are to arouse the women in Euripides' *Bacchae*[78] so that they pounce upon Pentheus and tear him into
pieces. In Euripides' *Hercules Furens*[79] she is compared to a
Bacchant (βακχεύσει). The women who kill and dismember
the children of Polymestor are called "Bacchants of Hades"
in the *Hecuba*.[80] Dilthey, in a very learned article,[81] has called
our attention to numerous analogies which exist between the
participants in the revel rout of Dionysus and the spirits of
the underworld, even though the examples are not all equally
convincing. Certainly we cannot accept his conclusion that
"the god-intoxicated frenzy of Greek women at the festival
of Dionysus" is to be interpreted as "a mimetic presentation
of the riotous procession of the dead." This is too one-sided.

Still, it cannot be denied that the god and his maenads, in their bloodthirsty ecstasy of madness, approximate the forms of the world of the dead. The frozen silence which is characteristic of the maenads makes this relationship particularly clear. After all, the spirits of the dead are "the dumb ones," and it is well known that the Romans called the goddess of death *dea Tacita*, and the spirits of the dead, in general, *di silentes.*

Tradition has much to say about Dionysus the god who visits or even lives in the world of the dead. The well-known Horatian hymn (*Car.* 2. 19) closes with the picture of Cerberus, who quietly watches the god with the golden horn enter, and licks his feet as he leaves. The god went below to bring his mother, Semele, back.[82] According to *Orphic Hymn* 46, he himself grew up in Persephone's home, and *Hymn* 53 says that he sleeps in the house of Persephone in the intervals before his reappearances—in fact, he is even called Χθόνιος Διόνυσος. His death and his grave have already been mentioned, and more will be said about them in a later chapter. The cry of the *Lenai*, "giver of riches,"[83] points in the same direction. The dead of the Golden Age, who wander over the earth as invisible guardian spirits, are called this by Hesiod.[84] One might also think of the "night festivals" of the god (Νυκτέλια),[85] and that he himself was called "the nocturnal one" (Νυκτέλιος).[86] He leads his nocturnal dances by torchlight. How correct E. Rohde was when he declared that the world of the dead, too, belonged to the kingdom of Dionysus![87]

But let us conclude our arguments with the evidence that best supports our case. The similarity and relationship which Dionysus has with the prince of the underworld (and this is revealed by a large number of comparisons) is not only confirmed by an authority of the first rank, but he says the two deities are actually the same.

Heraclitus says,[88] "For if it were not Dionysus for whom
they held their processions and sang their songs, it would be a
completely shameful act to the reverent; Hades and Dionysus,
for whom they go mad and rage, are one and the same."
(εἰ μὴ γὰρ Διονύσῳ πουπὴν ἐποιοῦντο καὶ ὕμνεον ᾆσμα αἰδοίοισιν
ἀναιδέστατα εἴργασται [εἴργαστ᾽ ἄν Schleiermacher] . . . ὡυτὸς
δὲ Ἀίδης καὶ Διόνυσος, ὅτεῳ μαίνονται καὶ ληναΐζουσι).

These words have never been forgotten, to be sure, but
curiously enough they have had no great influence on the
critical evaluation of the religion of Dionysus. Scholars obviously hesitated to use the evidence of a philosopher, especially
when the context in which the words appeared had been lost.
It is unfortunate, moreover, that the first part of Heraclitus'
statement is unclear—in fact, one part of the text is undoubtedly corrupt although no one has as yet succeeded in restor-
ing a meaningful text. Heraclitus could not have written what
Diels has him say above, following Schleiermacher's conjectures.[89] But the second part is intact and impossible to mis-
understand. And here Heraclitus says explicitly: "Hades and
Dionysus, for whom they go mad and rage, are one and the
same." For Heraclitus, Dionysus is the god of insane wildness,
the god of what the Μαινάδες and their affiliates, the Λῆναι,
do.[90] This god, he says, is the same god as Hades. What can
keep us from believing him? Is it his practice to indulge in
arbitrary interpretations? His aphorisms, however paradoxical they may sound, bear witness to the nature of things.
Should what he saw in Dionysus mean nothing to us? Consider, too, how much he must have known about the Dionysus of the sixth century which is lost to us today. Consequently his comments must stand as one of the most important
bits of evidence that have come down to us.

We can now understand why the dead were honored at
several of the chief festivals of Dionysus.

The festival of the Anthesteria was the most important festival of the dead in Athens and among the Ionians. To it belonged in all probability the entrance of Dionysus in a ship followed by the mixing of the sacred wine and the subsequent drinking contest and, perhaps too, the marriage of the god with the Basilinna. It was believed that on these days the dead came to visit the living and remained with them until a ceremonial pronouncement was made which signified to them that their time was up, and they had to take their leave. For a distinguished account of this belief, which is found to reoccur in the All Souls' celebrations of other peoples, let us turn to Erwin Rohde. Rohde called Dionysus, in whose retinue the dead seem to come to the upper world, the "Lord of the Souls"—in fact, Rohde believed that the meaning of the Dionysiac religion, in general, was to be understood from this vantage point. Today, on the contrary, one only asks how Dionysus, who was originally, after all, nothing but a fertility god, could have made his way into a festival of the dead. The answers which, for example, Nilsson[91] and Deubner[92] attempted to give to this question could just as well have been used to support the thesis that Dionysus must have been the god of the Anthesteria from the very beginning. Folklore has given us much evidence for believing that the pleasure man takes in the fruits and flowers of the earth, the enjoyment he has in her intoxicating liquids—in fact, that gaiety, in general, can be linked with those moments when man salutes his dead. The words of Thucydides[93] (as Deubner, himself, noted) can lead to the conclusion that Dionysus was already honored at the Anthesteria when the Ionians were still together in their homeland. Whoever considers this association (in spite of its great antiquity) as more or less fictitious can be speaking only from preconceived notions of the nature and origin of Dionysus. The modern hypothesis that he entered Greece as a foreigner relatively late has become more than doubtful. Let us adhere, rather, to the facts of the cult. They have that much more right to be considered original and genuine since the Anthesteria is not the only festival of the dead in which Dionysus took part.

The Agrionia (or Agriania, Agrania) were also clearly days of the dead. Much has already been said about them. Their great antiquity and wide diffusion are assured by the name of the month Agrianos,[94] which is attested to in so many places. Unfortunately we have detailed reports only of the type of celebration held in Boeotia. In Orchomenus the women were hounded ruthlessly by the priest of Dionysus. They were supposedly descended from the house of the daughters of Minyas, who were said to have cast lots for their children in a fit of Dionysiac madness and to have dismembered the child upon whom the lot fell.[95] In Chaeronea it was the custom for the women in this festival to make a search for Dionysus, who had fled. Finally they returned with the explanation that he had fled to the Muses and had concealed himself there.[96]

We hear of the Agrionia in Argos, however, that they were a festival of the dead.[97] E. Rohde was right when he thought the same was true of the Boeotian Agrionia. Consequently we are again confronted by the fact of a festival which combines the elements of both Dionysus and the dead. To be sure, it is supposed here, too, that Dionysus came later and forced himself on a festival which had previously existed as a festival of the dead.[98] But there is nothing to recommend this supposition. Quite the contrary. The sources show quite clearly that the two cults—that of Dionysus and that of the dead—were inherently related and amounted basically to one cult. The Argive festival, which is characterized as a festival of the dead by the above-mentioned gloss of

Hesychius, was held in honor of a daughter of Proetus, according to a second gloss of Hesychius. Thus women are given a dominant position here, too, just as in the festivals of Boeotia, and in both festivals it was the women belonging to Dionysus' circle who were in the foreground. But there is more to it than this. When it is said that the Argive Agrionia were celebrated in honor of a daughter of Proetus, we must associate with this the myth in which the daughters of Proetus, who were driven mad by Dionysus for the same reasons as the daughters of Minyas, were hunted down, and the oldest of them, Iphinoe, died as a result of this persecution.[99] Women were hunted down in this way in the ritual of the Boeotian Agrionia, as we know, and this was not without its element of tragedy either, for the women were threatened with the sword, and when one of them could not save herself, she was killed. What happened here in the cult, the myth of Lycurgus tells us. He fell upon the "nurses" of Dionysus with a deadly weapon and forced the god himself to seek refuge by leaping into the sea. Is not this feature repeated in the ritual of the Agrionia when in Chaeronea the women searched long for the god, who had escaped, and finally brought back the news that he had fled to the Muses and had concealed himself there?

Thus the Argive festival which the sources call a festival of the dead was clearly the same as the Boeotian festival which was intended for Dionysus. On the face of it, it is obvious that a festival which called such tragic experiences to mind and acted them out could very well be a festival of the dead, too. Perhaps, too, the Agrionia were held also at approximately the same time of year as the Anthesteria— if, as is likely, they actually took place in Elaphebolion, that is, one month after the Anthesteria.[100]

# 10. *Modern Theories*

It is in the nature of Greek myth to seize upon the basic forms of that which has being. These forms appear in a clear and distinct light with all of the freshness of the elemental. All modifications which come from a soul that has been moved, all of the excesses which come from a spirit that breathes defiance remain at a distance. The primitive world looks out from and breathes from the living form. Goethe, as he examined the horse's head on the pediment of the Parthenon, was overcome by the impression that here the artist had created a primeval horse. This says something of unusual importance about the perspective of the Greeks and their forms. The primeval is that which is most alive—in fact, it alone is truly alive. It is not the subjective talent of the artist which gives the creations of Greek myth their incomparable vitality, quickening man's pulse as they have through the ages; but it is the appearance of the primeval world, which these creations have been able to evoke.

It is for this reason that the polarities of that which has being appear here, too, in all their colossal proportions, in mutual confrontation. No arbitrary concept, no desire for salvation reconciles them. It is only in the opposite of all agreement, in supreme tension, when the antitheses become wild and infinite, that the great mystery of oneness is proclaimed from the very depths of being. Nor is it just proclaimed. Oneness itself is revealed to Greek myth and cult as the deity who is mad—as Dionysus.

His duality has manifested itself to us in the antitheses of ecstasy and horror, infinite vitality and savage destruction; in the pandemonium in which deathly silence is inherent; in the immediate presence which is at the same time absolute remoteness. All of his gifts and attendant phenomena give evidence of the sheer madness of his dual essence: prophecy, music, and finally wine, the flamelike herald of the god, which has in it both bliss and brutality. At the height of ecstasy all of these paradoxes suddenly unmask themselves and reveal their names to be Life and Death.

Dionysus, who holds them together, must be the divine spirit of a gigantic reality, an elemental first principle of being in whose essence lies the reason why he, himself, is called a madman, and why his appearance brings madness with it. But before we follow this line of thought, we must test the hypotheses which have been advanced recently to explain Dionysiac madness.

A generation ago it still sounded quite convincing to say that the madness of the maenads took its origins from a romantic empathy with the fate which befell the year's vegetation. "It was," said L. Preller, "the excruciating grief of earth and nature, the wildest despair of a soul alarmed by the agonies of winter, illuminated, to be sure, by the ray of hope that spring must surely return again, and with it the god of youth, of joy, of the power of nature which wells forth eternally in endless creation." Recently, however, a valid objection has been raised against this thesis. Nature in the winters of the south does not evoke an image of dying, nor does it give the human spirit any reason to take part in sympathetic laments or even storms of despair. Besides, the cult of Dionysus does not know of any alternation of outbursts of lamentation and joy which could have corresponded to the growth and death cycle of vegetation.

Several decades before Preller's *Mythologie* appeared, K.O. Müller had already recognized that there was something quite mysterious about Dionysiac μανία.[1] He expressed his viewpoint in sharp opposition to the opinion held by, among others, J.H. Voss with his thesis of Antisymbolism. Dionysiac μανία could not, he said, have been provoked by outside forces, particularly not by the drinking of wine, since it was principally women who were seized by the madness of the god. We must recognize in this madness the conduct which was peculiar to those who believed in Dionysus, and the explanation for it could be found only in the worship itself. These words pointed the way for the research which followed. K.O. Müller did not venture to give the required explanation itself—even though he believed that he had found definite parallels in Oriental priests. A few years later he expressed himself somewhat differently in his *Archäologie der Kunst*.[2] But his earlier thoughts bore fruit in Erwin Rohde, who referred specifically to Müller's precedent in the beginning of his justly famous presentation of the religion of Dionysus.[3]

Even though Rohde's artistry and perspicacity deserve great praise, today we must no longer be deceived by the fact that his conclusions were arrived at under the influence of the psychological presuppositions of his day. Every interpretation he made of religious phenomena had to start with human subjectivity. Nietzsche, in his *Birth of Tragedy*, had traced the Dionysiac orgies back to the "influences of the narcotic potion of which all primitive men and peoples speak in hymns" or to the emotions which awaken with "the powerful imminence of spring which permeates all of nature with its joy. As the emotions are intensified, the subjective element disappears completely into self-forgetfulness." In this Rohde could no longer follow him. But now Rohde had lost the re-lationship with the realities of the world in general. The only thing left was the world of the mind within us with its own characteristic experiences, and thus the explanation he gave had to be completely psychological in nature. The most amazing element about it, however, was the dialectic he em-ployed. He believed he was proceeding with all necessary vigor and, in his own words, "was keeping clear of all theories which derived from patterns of thought alien to the subject in hand," when, to help him understand the phenomenon in question, he permitted himself one assumption: "that the re-sult evidenced in the participants in the celebration—namely, the state of ecstasy—was to be regarded as willed and de-liberately induced; and that it was to be looked upon as the purpose, or at least one of the purposes, of these amazing observances."

It is odd that Rohde could have thought this to have been such a natural and unbiased assumption. With the one little word "willed" he had imposed a theory on the facts to be explained—and a very audacious theory at that. Indeed, one could say that with this assumption everything he wanted to make plausible in the rest of the work was already pre-sumed. According to Rohde, then, the mad ecstasy was in-tentionally induced. The wild dancing, the shaking of the head, the shrieks which pierce the darkness of the night were not involuntary outbursts of unleashed wildness but devices to arouse fanatical emotions which sought union with the deity and bliss by losing themselves in ecstasy. It was no true madness. Nothing supernatural, which sends the mind reeling when it has been perceived, had confronted them in their rapture. They only wished "to break loose from the narrow prison of the body, to embrace the god, and become one with him." If, however, we go on to ask how the god exer-

cised this power of attraction, or what the nature of his essence was that one wished to rush to him to become one
with him, we fail to get an answer. Obviously he is being
thought of as a god who follows the Oriental pattern, as the
Divine or the Infinite, in general, in whom the individual
soul would gladly like to lose itself. This is why it seems so
obvious to Rohde to compare the various methods which are
supposed to strengthen this desire. According to him, the
smoking of hashish and other similar methods used in the
Orient to bring on a state of bliss are "absolutely identical"
with the Dionysiac.

How far these ideas are from what Dionysus actually is!
The "Thracian ecstasy cult" is for Rohde the manifestation
of a religious impulse which is found throughout the world,
an impulse "which must well stem from a profound need in
man's nature, a condition of his psychological and physical
makeup." He says, "In his moments of greatest exaltation
man does not wish to face the more than human vital power
he feels surging around and over him by locking himself up
in his own private existence and following his normal practices of worshipping it timidly. Rather, he wishes at these
moments to throw all restraint to the winds and with passionate exuberance" achieve complete "oneness" with the god
—that "oneness" which we have just discussed above in
Rohde's own words.

Rohde was very conscious of the fact that a self-hypnosis
which leads to complete illusion is not to everyone's taste. It
presupposes, so he says, a morbid predisposition. Certainly
the hereditary morbidity of the Asiatic shamans and those
like them, whom Rohde likes to cite for comparison's sake,
is well known. Nor does Rohde hesitate to remind his readers
of how religious epidemics, in more recent eras, have inun-
dated whole countries at times. A "religious epidemic," simi-

lar to the dancing epidemic after the Black Death in Europe, "must have made people's minds receptive to the Thracian Dionysus and his festivals of ecstasy." He is even quite serious in believing that there was a "severe disturbance in psychic balance" as a result of the Doric migrations. But the most surprising of all: "A morbid state of mind remained with the Greek temperament as an after effect of the profound Bacchic excitement which once had raged through Greece as an epidemic and still broke out again periodically at the nocturnal celebrations of Dionysus."

One can see from this how far-fetched the comparisons and how forced the interpretation of historical phenomena had to be to make Rohde's psychological theory seem even vaguely plausible. We would be hard put to understand the cogency of his statements if we did not know how established and widespread the idea was and still is that religious ecstasy and passions can be explained only with the help of psychology and, if need be, psychiatry. If, however, we adhere to the Greek phenomenon itself, as it is presented to us in the sources, then Rohde's theory immediately loses all of its plausibility. The well-known forms of the maenads do not at all create the impression of a pathological state of mind and are as far removed as possible from the image of the ecstatic shaman. It is true that Nietzsche, also, cites the comparison with the dancing epidemic of the waning Middle Ages, and Rohde's characterization of Dionysiac frenzy as an epidemic disease had a decisive effect even on Wilamowitz's presentation in *Glaube der Hellenen*. But shall we really be permitted to believe that the Greeks in the centuries during which they were at their prime could be seized by an ecstatic frenzy as easily as the people of the Middle Ages who had been unhinged by a frightful disease and palsied by their fear of hell? The shamans, the Angekoks, the medicine men, the dervishes, and whatever else they are called, to whom Rohde constantly refers, are priestly individuals or religious societies that have learned how to induce a self-imposed sort of madness by artificial means. Among the Greeks, however, the priest remained completely in the background, and the orgies are an affair of the community—above all, of the women, even though they may be represented by sodalities.

Now the fact that the women play a dominant role in the cult of Dionysus is precisely what Rohde and his followers have seized upon as best authenticating their opinions. Everyone knows how excitable women are, how easily frightened their imagination is, and how inclined they are to follow without question. These frailities in the character of women supposedly explain the unexplainable: that a people like the Greeks could fall victim to a religious frenzy. "It is to them, above all," i.e., the women, Rohde explains, "that it [the cult of Dionysus] may well owe its introduction." Wilamowitz even says "that the women forced recognition of the alien god." In other words, of all of the characteristics of women, who are the principal supporters of the Dionysiac religion, only their credulity and their fanaticism are taken into account. And just as there is no desire to understand that the enthusiasm came from the unique nature of the god himself, there being the view instead that it came only from the human longing for redemption, so the role of the female element in the religion of Dionysus serves only to explain its adoption and diffusion. If, however, we stop dealing in generalities and focus our attention on the women of Dionysus and their clearly defined role, then the possibility of comparing Dionysiac practices with the ecstatic pageantry of alien religions becomes more and more remote. Even the well-known orgiastic rites of Asia Minor, which are so often said to be related to the rites of Dionysus, present in actuality a completely different picture. Dionysus is surrounded by raving women. These women are—and are called—foster mothers. They nurse and take care of new-born male infants and suckle the young animals of the wilderness. But they also hunt down these animals, tear them into pieces, and devour the bleeding flesh. The analogies drawn by Rohde do not apply in the slightest to this whole existence and these actions which are peculiar to the maenads, and his interpretations of them misses the mark completely. How can this create the impression that man wished in this way to transcend himself and throw himself into the arms of the god!

Still, there is no need to pursue this line of analysis any further. The rug has already been pulled out from under Rohde's theory by an extremely important bit of evidence which, surprisingly enough, has remained entirely ineffective until now. The god, in whose honor the wild dance rages, is himself mad! Whatever explanation is advanced must then be applicable to him, first of all. The oldest reference to him, that of *Iliad* 6. 132, calls him μαινόμενος, and a series of important titles, descriptions, and presentations leaves no doubt that almost everything which is said of the maenads also applies to him—in fact, to him most of all. He, himself, is the mad one; he, himself, is the brandisher of the *thyrsus,* the render, the eater of raw flesh. The ease with which this unambiguous evidence has previously been ignored is simply amazing. K.O. Müller[4] was already of the opinion that "the epithet of 'The Mad One' " must have come "to the god through his worship since in ancient religions the manner in which the god was honored quite often gave the god his character." And Rohde[5] says, in referring to a grammatical reference in the scholia of Homer, "Actually there is probably a mythological or a sacral hypallage to be found here. The nature of the atmosphere, which the god has produced, recoils upon the god himself." He adds, "This would not be without example." But then he contradicts himself with the example he cites:

"Dionysus, who causes intoxication, is himself presented as intoxicated." It is as natural that a god himself partake of the blessings which he imparts, as it would be absurd to conceive of a god himself in the posture which god-inspired man assumes toward him. If madness, as Rohde insists, is really supposed to be a condition into which the believers deliberately transfer themselves so that they can thereby be lifted up to godhead, then it is overdoing it a bit to want to convince us that the same madness was transmitted to the god himself, and that there is not even anything odd about this procedure.

Rohde, therefore, has not succeeded in throwing any real light on the phenomenon of madness, the understanding of which is a prerequisite for any really deep insight into the nature of the religion of Dionysus.

However, even today, in spite of its mistakes, his presentation deserves the respect it has received. For Rohde considered it essential to explore the most sacred areas of human existence for the rationale for a movement which was as momentous and great as the Dionysiac was. To a pupil of Schopenhauer and a friend of Nietzsche it could not yet be self-evident that primal religious ideas and procedures had to be derived from a sphere of the crudest kind of practice and an extremely materialistic or "common sense" way of looking at things.

This manner of thinking became increasingly more common in the last decades of the past century and finally dominated the scene. The interpretation now given to the Dionysiac movement took its point of departure from Wilhelm Mannhardt's research, which basically has much to commend it. From it came, however, a principle which emerged victorious: that, insofar as they had anything to do with vegetative nature, the cults of ancient peoples could in the last analysis have meant nothing more than or nothing different from what even today's roughly corresponding practices of northern European peasants mean or seem to mean.

Dionysiac madness, in which Rohde had found such a deep and noble meaning, now is supposed to have been staged for a very materialistic purpose, tailored completely to the needs and way of thinking of simple peasants. With it one aimed to instigate and encourage growth in the fields. "Vegetation magic," to use Mannhardt's term for the rioting and capering of the peasants, is the ultimate secret behind the enraptured frenzy. Warding off evil from the fields, wresting a fruitful year from the spirits on whose activity all that grows is believed to depend—this and nothing else was what the simple country people of antiquity had in mind when they held their riotous processions on specific days of the year. In these celebrations the shouts, the dancing, the running, and the brandishing of torches seemed to be excellently suited to awaken the spirits of the field and goad them into action. Thus the riddle of the raging of the Θυιάδες and the frenzy of the Μαινάδες is solved. Voigt,[6] who adhered closely to Mannhardt, spelled this theory out in detail a considerable period before Rohde's *Psyche* appeared. Rapp[7] continued it. Later it was combined with Rohde's thesis of redemptive ecstasy in a very strange mixture,[8] and today it can be said to be the generally accepted theory—in spite of a few modifications here and there.

There is no reason why we have to waste time in criticizing the basic viewpoint of this thesis. It clearly contradicts the most important facts of the cult which it is supposed to explain. We do not know that the orgiastic elements in Dionysus and his rout were in any way related by the ancients to the fertility of the fields. Dionysus' theatre was also as far away from the fields as it could possibly be. The followers of Dionysus, as we know, left the areas where men worked and lived, to revel with the god in the loneliness of the mountain forests and on the peaks of the highest mountains. And is there the slightest parallel to draw between the maternal association with wild animals, the tearing to pieces of fawns, and the devouring of their raw flesh and that which we hear about the northern European peasants? Do actions like this make us think of vegetation magic? And dare we forget that the maenads were, first of all, mythical and divine beings and that the mortal women, when they rave as Bacchants, were only imitating them? Dare we forget that Dionysus, himself, was mad? Folklorists, however, dispose of this evidence, too. They demand, namely, nothing less than that we believe that all the actions and practices performed by humans, which supposedly forced the spirits to help them by means of a vegetation magic, were transferred to these spirits themselves together with all of the regalia which went along with them. We can ignore the conjectures which Rapp[9] advanced in order to make such an unnatural hypothesis plausible. We can ignore, too, related viewpoints[10] which vary in their particulars from the one we have mentioned above but, on the whole, give rise to the same reservations.

One further interpretation which has become unusually popular still needs to be discussed briefly. This concerns one individual practice. No satisfactory explanation could be found in the framework of Rohde's view for tearing animals into pieces and devouring them. Voigt,[11] on the contrary, noted that this occurred generally to just those animals which could be considered to be personifications of vegetation spirits because of their vitality and sexual potency, inasmuch as Dionysus, himself, often appeared in their forms—that is to say, in the forms of the bull and the goat. This led to the thought that raw meat dripping with blood must have been devoured so that "the actual sap of life" could be absorbed into the self, and thus the conclusion followed that the raging women wanted to appropriate "the power and blessings of creative nature" to themselves and "at the same time dedicate this power to the earth, to nature which conceives and gives birth." But if Dionysus, himself, was a spirit or god of fertility, the worshippers who devoured the flesh and blood of animals they had torn into bits must have believed they were devouring him and incorporating his power of fertility into themselves. The myth of Zagreus does say, after all, that he was torn apart by the Titans, and in the guise of a bull, at that. And Orpheus, who was intimately connected with him, suffered precisely this fate at the hands of the maenads. Therefore, one must see in the wild actions of the maenads a form of what people, following a theory which has enjoyed such great popularity for some time, call "sacramental sacrifice."

Thus the solemn moments when the god who appears with such overpowering force is invoked and welcomed are endowed with a basic meaning which leaves little to be desired as far as brutality goes. The women of Elis, who called upon him in a song[12] we have already discussed, saw him appearing as a bull, but he came only "to be killed and butchered by the mad Thyiads so that they could appropriate the power of the god to themselves."[13]

This is not the place to test the theory of the "sacramental sacrifice." Whatever one may think of it, it cannot be applied to the rites of Dionysus unless one uses the most artificial hypotheses and the most daring jumps of logic. In the myth in which Orpheus is torn apart by the maenads, nothing is said about any eating of flesh. The same is true of the rending of Pentheus. In both cases this terrible vengeance fell upon men who despised the god and were his enemies. Dionysus, however, or Zagreus, is not cut into pieces by his own people, but by his bitterest enemies. And even though it is true that they consumed his flesh, the mythic tradition is in complete agreement that this flesh was not eaten raw but cooked.[14] We have already referred in a previous chapter to the meaning which the portrayal of the violent death of Dionysus had. There is no question that it served as a basis for certain cult practices, and we shall have more to say about it later. At the same time it will also become self-evident what is meant by the statement that the rending of the fawns reproduces the sufferings of Dionysus.[15] It takes a good deal of courage to think of "transference" in the case of the rites at Tenedos, where a calf dressed in the cothurnus is sacrificed for the "render of men," Dionysus. To do this (and Voigt[16] does it) suggests that the act of violence perpetrated on the god had been charged to him. Nowhere in all the sources does the idea appear that the devout partook of the flesh of the god for their own benefit. To be sure, we do hear of initiates who, in mentioning the rites of consecration through which they became Βάκχοι, also name the "meal of raw flesh."[17] There is nothing, however, in the sources which suggests that the body of the god is meant here. Consequently Wilamowitz, too, with his respect for the Greek sources, ridicules this presumptuous hypothesis: "That they [the frenzied women] thought they were eating the god or divine food is only a modern assumption. They also suckle fawns."[18]

But the first premise of this bizarre doctrine is already in error. In the famous account which Euripides gives us in the *Bacchae*, it is true that the band of raging women pounces upon a herd of cattle and tears even bulls into pieces. Yet in the scenes, both literary and artistic, in which this motif re-occurs at regular intervals, the victims of this savagery are, as we know, specifically not those animals which conjure up thoughts of the abundance of fertility in nature and which have served as the forms in which Dionysus made his appearances. Instead, they are the inhabitants of the wilderness— above all, young does and stags, but bears and wolves, too.

# 11. *The Mad God*

Thus previous attempts to explain the madness of the Dionysiac orgies in terms of human needs, whether spiritual or material, have ended in complete failure. Their conclusions are not only unbelievable in themselves, but they are intolerably contradictory of the most important and the most explicit sources.

We must return again to K.O. Müller's point of view. Madness is a cult form which belongs to the religion of Dionysus. The god who sends the mind reeling, the god who appears to mankind in the most urgent immediacy is welcomed and feted by the women in an absolute ecstasy and excess of rapture. They respond to his coming with the behavior of the insane. The myth tells again and again how his fury ripped them loose from their peaceful domesticity, from the humdrum orderly activities of their daily lives for the purpose of making them into dancers in the wilderness and the loneliness of the mountains, where they find him and rage through the night as members of his revel rout.

"Soon the whole world will dance when Bromios leads his throngs into the mountains. Into the mountains where the women flock, driven from the shuttle and the loom by the goad of Dionysus."[1] Thus the daughters of Minyas, who wished to remain faithful to their household duties and attend their husbands,[2] were driven out by Dionysus with miracles and portents of horror. The Argive women, too, are said to have been seized with Dionysiac madness and to have left their homes.[3] In Nonnus we find again and again[4] the picture of the woman who runs away from domestic life and the handiwork of Athena to rush with hair dishevelled to the choral dances of Dionysus.

But the wild actions of mortal women had their proto-type[5] in the actions of a higher being. Dionysus was pictured as being surrounded by goddesses,[6] by nymphs who had reared him as a child and raged through the woods with him when he had become a man.[7] Whatever their name, these were the true maenads, and the art works—when they depict the revel rout of Dionysus—are thinking of them far more often than they are of human scenes. But, for all of that, there is no question that the human choruses of maenads, thyiads, and whatever else they are called, rushed about with a similar wildness. Among other things, a story, such as the one in Plutarch,[8] can give us some idea of this (even Rohde, incidentally, used this episode to combat Rapp's excessive scepticism). If, however, the human followers of the god, copied the behavior of the divine followers, the god, in turn, is reflected in the behavior of the latter. We hear of the Λαψύστιαι, a type of Βάκχαι, that they wore horns in imitation of Dionysus.[9]. Dionysus, himself, is a wild and boisterous spirit. He is invoked by the women of Elis as a raging bull.[10] The Rhodians knew him as Θυωνίδας,[11] and his mother as Θυώνη. In his pictures and in the description of him, he has the same bearing and the same attributes as the maenads. The prologue of Euripides' *Hypsipyle* talks of "Dionysus, who bounds through the pine forests of Parnassus with *thyrsus* and deerskin."[12] The chorus of the *Bacchae*[13] sings, "With the smouldering torch on his fennel wand Bacchus frolics as he runs, as

PLATE 9 A maenad dancing. Skyphos (ca. 490-480 B.C.) attributed to the Brygos painter (Beazley, *ARFVP*², no. 176 [132]). From the collection of The Metropolitan Museum of Art, Fletcher Fund, 1929. (Acc. No. 29.131.4)

he dances, inciting the stragglers as he stirs them with shouts. His hair streams in the wind."[14]

The bloodthirstiness of the maenads is the bloodthirstiness of the god himself. In the same tragedy, in a passage immediately preceding the one cited above,[15] it is said that the god "storms down from the raging choral dance, dressed in the holy deerskin, hunting down the blood of goats he has killed, greedily lusting for raw flesh to devour." According to Oppian,[16] he already delighted, as a child, in tearing kids into pieces and bringing them back to life again. In a red-figured vase painting,[17] like a maenad he has torn a fawn into pieces, and dances in wild excitement, swinging the two halves in the air. He is explicitly characterized as "the raging one," "the mad one"; the nature of the maenads, from which they get their name, is, therefore, his nature. The *Iliad* knows him as μαινόμενος Διόνυσος.[18] According to Clemens Alexandrinus,[19] it is the μαινόλης Διόνυσος whom the Bacchae worship in the orgies in which raw flesh is eaten.[20] He dances with the nymphs.[21] It was supposedly the goddess Hera who had driven him mad.[22] This characterization cannot be pushed aside by skillful interpretation, however embarrassing it may have proven to have been to scholars in the past. They have overlooked the most important element, the central concept from which all research must, by rights, proceed.

Dionysus is the god who is mad. For his sake the maenads are mad. We must not inquire into the reasons why they are distraught and wild, but we must ask, rather, what *divine madness* means.

It is the nature of the finite to have within its essence the seeds of extinction; the hour of its birth is the hour of its death. (HEGEL, *Logic*)

> Dionysus: sensuality and cruelty. Transitoriness could be
> interpreted as the enjoyment of the power to generate and
> the power to destroy, as continual creation.
>
> (NIETZSCHE, *The Will to Power*)

A god who is mad! A god, part of whose nature it is to be
insane! What did they experience or see—these men on whom
the horror of this concept must have forced itself?

The visage of every true god is the visage of a world. There
can be a god who is mad only if there is a mad world which
reveals itself through him. Where is this world? Can we still
find it? Can we appreciate its nature? For this no one can
help us but the god himself.

We know him as the wild spirit of antithesis and paradox,
of immediate presence and complete remoteness, of bliss and
horror, of infinite vitality and the cruelest destruction. The
element of bliss in his nature, the creative, enraptured, and
blessed elements all share, too, in his wildness and his madness.
Are they not, then, mad just because they, too, already carry
within themselves a duality, because they stand on the threshold where one step beyond leads to dismemberment and
darkness? Here we have hit upon a cosmic enigma—the mystery of life which is self-generating, self-creating. The love
which races toward the miracle of procreation is touched by
madness. So is the mind when it is staggered by the impulse
to create. Plato recognizes the madness of the philosopher
(μανία καὶ βακχεία).[23] But Schelling says, "Ever since Aristotle
it has become a commonplace to say that no one ever creates
anything great without a dash of madness. We would rather
say: without a constant solicitation to madness" (*Die Weltalter*).

He who begets something which is alive must dive down
into the primeval depths in which the forces of life dwell.
And when he rises to the surface, there is a gleam of madness

in his eyes because in those depths death lives cheek by jowl
with life. The primal mystery is itself mad—the matrix of the
duality and the unity of disunity. We do not have to appeal
to the philosophers for this, although much could be quoted
from Schelling here. All peoples and ages testify to it through
their life experiences and their cult practices.

Man's experience tells him that wherever there are signs of
life, death is in the offing. The more alive this life becomes,
the nearer death draws, until the supreme moment—the en-
chanted moment when something new is created—when death
and life meet in an embrace of mad ecstasy. The rapture and
terror of life are so profound because they are intoxicated
with death. As often as life engenders itself anew, the wall
which separates it from death is momentarily destroyed.
Death comes to the old and the sick from the outside, bringing fear or comfort. They think of it because they feel that
life is waning. But for the young the intimation of death rises
up out of the full maturity of each individual life and intoxicates them so that their ecstasy becomes infinite. Life which
has become sterile totters to meet its end, but love and death
have welcomed and clung to one another passionately from
the beginning.

This eternal bond of existence is the reason for the note-
worthy fact that peoples from time immemorial have been
aware that the dead and the powers of the underworld are
present at life's central moments and festivities—that is to say,
at birth and puberty. Recent research, which rarely has the
courage to penetrate deeply, prefers to look for the meaning
of the significant cults and myths in the idea world of a popular belief which has become petty and timid, rather than in
the seriousness of existence itself. As a result, it has traced
these customs and attitudes back to man's fear of harmful
spirits and ghosts. But there is no progress to be made if we
constantly assume an attitude of superiority and think only

of convincing the founders of venerable institutions of their mistakes and their superstitions. They knew more about life than we do. At its great moments of change they looked death in the eye—because it was really there. At every type of birth, life is shaken to its foundations, not by sickness nor by some external menace but by its most important function. It is just in this circumstance that its association with death becomes clearest. The peoples who celebrate festivals like this are not just thinking of dangers. They firmly believe that the presence of the nether world is absolutely indispensable to the great miracle which takes place at birth. Is that an empty illusion? Does not each one of us have the face of one who has died? Does not each one live the death of those who came before him? Does he not reproduce their features, their movements, their thoughts and emotions—yes, the expression of the entire world of the past? In the new-born child the ancestor rises up out of the darkness of death. This is the reason why the divinities of birth and fertility are so close to the divinities of death. Indeed, this is the reason why they often merge completely.

The puberty rites still celebrated today among primitive peoples bear witness to the same thing. Here where preparations are made and celebrations are held for the thrilling life's miracle of newly emerging virility, the symbols and the spirits of death are always present with their anguish—yes, even with their most terrible dangers. Interpretations, some of them rational, some of them mystical, have been proposed for these customs, too. They could even refer to eyewitness accounts, at least in part. But the future will undoubtedly show that in this case, too, it was the stirring up of life's depths which summoned Death's dancing choruses and called his spirits and his horror to attend the primordial process of a change in life's rhythm.

The festivals of the dead which coincide with the beginning of spring show us how forcibly life at the height of its vitality has always spoken this language. Recent interpretations of this phenomenon look like child's play beside the high seriousness of the primal concept that the spirits of the realm of the dead are present at the awakening of nature. Like all primal concepts, this, too, is eternal. Generation after generation must constantly rediscover that the most uninhibited growth and fertility are shrouded in the exhalations of death. This is not to be taken as a warning or an admonition, but it symbolizes the most profound never-ending nature of desire.

Philosophy, the heir of myth, when it first emerged, already expressed the realization that death was based on and enclosed within the nature of being, itself. In the oldest statements which have come down to us the mortality of existing things is characterized as a penance which they must pay one another.[24] The same idea reappears often later. Schelling says,[25] "Nothing which is and becomes can be or become without the simultaneous being and becoming of something else; and even the death of one product of nature is nothing but penance for an obligation which it has assumed towards all the rest of nature. Consequently, within nature there is nothing primal, nothing absolute, nothing which exists by itself." And a poet with the eminence of Calderon dared to say:

> For man's greatest sin
> Is that he was born.
> (*Life Is a Dream*)

Here the inextricable association of life with death—not in spite of, but precisely because it is alive—is invested with an unusual meaning. However, an idea remains which is held in common with the primitive beliefs of mankind testified to by the myths and cults. This is that death is not to be sought first at the end of life but at its beginning, and that it attends all of life's creations.

All intoxication arises from the depths of life which have become fathomless because of death. From these depths comes music—Dionysiac music—which transforms the world in which life had become a habit and a certainty, and death a threatening evil. This world it obliterates with the melody of the uncommon which mocks all attempts at reassurance. "Richard Wagner says of civilization that it is neutralized by music as lamp light is neutralized by the light of day."[26] From this abyss come also ecstasy and inspired prophecy. These are no baseless "risings outside of one's self" nor clairvoyance. How could ecstasy be creative if it arose from an insufficiency, from a not-having coupled with a desire to have? The elemental depths gape open and out of them a monstrous creature raises its head before which all the limits that the normal day has set must disappear. There man stands on the threshold of madness—in fact, he is already part of it even if his wildness which wishes to pass on into destructiveness still remains mercifully hidden. He has already been thrust out of everything secure, everything settled, out of every haven of thought and feeling, and has been flung into the primeval cosmic turmoil in which life, surrounded and intoxicated with death, undergoes eternal change and renewal.

But the god himself is not merely touched and seized by the ghostly spirit of the abyss. He, himself, is the monstrous creature which lives in the depths. From its mask it looks out at man and sends him reeling with the ambiguity of nearness and remoteness, of life and death in one. Its divine intelligence holds the contradictions together. For it is the spirit of excitation and wildness; and everything alive, which seethes and glows, resolves the schism between itself and its opposite and has already absorbed this spirit in its desire. Thus all earthly powers are united in the god: the generating, nourishing, intoxicating rapture; the life-giving inexhaustibility; and the tearing pain, the deathly pallor, the speechless night of having been. He is the mad ecstasy which hovers over every conception and birth and whose wildness is always ready to move on to destruction and death. He is life which, when it overflows, grows mad and in its profoundest passion is intimately associated with death. This unfathomable world of Dionysus is called mad with good reason. It is the world of which Schelling was thinking when he spoke of the "self-destroying madness" which "still remains the heart of all things. Controlled only by the light of a higher intelligence and calmed by it, as it were, it is the true power of nature and everything she produces" (*Die Weltalter*).

The fullness of life and the violence of death both are equally terrible in Dionysus. Nothing has been mitigated, but neither has anything been distorted and changed into something fantastic, as would be the case in the Orient. Everything follows the Greek way of looking at things and is seen as clear and structured. The Greek endured this reality in its total dimensions and worshipped it as divine. Other peoples were touched by the same entity, so that they had to respond to it with a variety of representations and practices. This is made clear by their birth celebrations, puberty initiations, and many other customs. But to the Greeks this entity appeared as a god in the form of a god. And the mad god who appeared with a host of raving female attendants summoned mortal women to share his madness with him. He brought the primeval world along with him. This is the reason why his onslaught stripped mortals of all of their conventions, of everything that made them "civilized," and hurled them into life which is intoxicated by death at those moments when it glows with its greatest vitality, when it loves, procreates, gives birth, and celebrates the rites of spring. There the most remote is near, the past is present, all ages are mirrored in the moment of the now. All that is lies locked in a close embrace. Man and animal breathe in the same maternal warmth. Cries of joy fill the air everywhere at the miracle of the springs which flow forth from an earth unlocked—until madness becomes a lowering storm and lets the frenzy of horror and destruction burst forth from the frenzy of ecstasy.

We should never forget that the Dionysiac world is, above all, a world of women. Women awaken Dionysus and bring him up. Women accompany him wherever he is. Women await him and are the first ones to be overcome by his madness. And this explains why the genuinely erotic is found only on the periphery of the passion and wantonness which make their appearance with such boldness on the well-known sculptures. Much more important than the sexual act are the act of birth and the feeding of the child. But more will be said about this later. The terrible trauma of childbirth, the wildness which belongs to motherliness in its primal form, a wildness which can break loose in an alarming way not only in animals—all these reveal the innermost nature of the Dionysiac madness: the churning up of the essence of life surrounded by the storms of death. Since such tumult lies waiting in the bottom-most depths and makes itself known, all of life's ecstasy is stirred up by Dionysiac madness and is ready to go beyond the bounds of rapture into a dangerous wildness. The Dionysiac condition is a primal phenomenon of life in which even man must participate in all of the moments of birth in his creative existence.

This feminine world is confronted by the radically different masculine world of Apollo. In his world not the life mystery of blood and of the powers of earth but the clarity and the breadth of the mind hold sway. However, the Apollonic world cannot exist without the other. This is why it has never denied it recognition. This is a point to which we will return at the conclusion of this book.

## 12. *The Vine*

The divine essence of Dionysus, the basic characteristic of
his nature, has now been discovered. It is madness. But this
word has infinitely more meaning here than the temporary or
lasting disturbance which can affect a mortal and is depicted
in Greek thought as a demonic force called Lyssa or Erinys.
The madness which is called Dionysus is no sickness, no de-
bility in life, but a companion of life at its healthiest. It is the
tumult which erupts from its innermost recesses when they
mature and force their way to the surface. It is the madness
inherent in the womb of the mother. This attends all moments of creation, constantly changes ordered existence into
chaos, and ushers in primal salvation and primal pain—and in
both, the primal wildness of being. For this reason Dionysus,
in spite of his association with the spirits of the underworld,
with the Erinyes, Sphinx, and Hades, is a great god, a true
god; that is, the unity and totality of an infinitely varied
world which encompasses everything that lives.

The deep emotion with which this madness announces
itself finds its expression in music and dance.[1] What these
mean to the followers of Dionysus can be seen in innumerable
works of art. Dionysus, himself, is called Μελπόμενος[2] and
Χορεῖος. In Argos the grave of a maenad with the name of
Χορεία was exhibited.[3] We come across maenads making music
on vase paintings and in the poetry of Nonnus.[4] Bacchus

teaches the nymphs songs.[5] He is said to have danced already
as a child in his mother's womb. There are numerous references to his connection with the Muses. In the legend of Lycurgus when he sought refuge in the depths of the sea, he
escaped to the Muses, according to the belief of the women
who celebrate the Agrionia in Chaeronea.[6] On the island of
Naxos he is called Μουσαγέτης.[7] In the hymn of Philodamus of
Skarpheia,[8] it says that he went from Thebes to Pieria, where
the Muses received him, decked with ivy, with festive songs.[9]
There were altars to Dionysus and the Charites at the Pelo-
pion in Olympia and between them were altars to the Muses
and the nymphs.[10]

In the art of prophecy, madness is represented as secret
knowledge. Plutarch[11] explicitly says that in the opinion of
"the ancients" Dionysus played a large part in prophecy.[12]
In the process he also recalls the passage in Euripides' *Bacchae*
where the god is called μάντις, and this is followed by the
added explanation that the madness and the nature of the
Bacchants are filled with prophecy.[13] As for the Bacchanalia
which were transferred to Rome, we hear still that men
prophesied there when they were in a state of ecstasy.[14] According to Herodotus,[15] there was an oracle of Dionysus in
Thrace with a prophetess, as in Delphi.[16] Euripides calls
Dionysus point-blank the "prophet of the Thracians."[17] He
supposedly gave oracles in Delphi even previous to Apollo.[18]
In Greece itself, of course, we know of only one Dionysiac
oracle, that in Phocean Amphicleia.[19]

We have, unfortunately, too little information about the
nature of Dionysiac prophecy. In one of the works ascribed
to Aristotle there was an interesting statement that the proph-
ets belonging to a Thracian oracle of Dionysus prophesied
after they had imbibed a good deal of wine, while the Apol-

Ionian seers in Claros gained their inspiration by drinking holy water.[20]

Like the glories which arise from a primal world renewed, music, dance, and prophecy—these three paragons—emerge like blessed miracles from Dionysiac madness. But there is a sacred plant in which this madness itself rises out of the earth in the form of an elixir which intoxicates. This is the vine.

Strangely enough, scholars have maintained that Dionysus could not have been the god of wine from the beginning. K.O. Müller was convinced of this by the fact that Homer never mentioned wine as the gift of Dionysus. But Müller, at least, added that it was "consistent with the character of the cult" when the consecration of the wine was later associated with it.[21] Scholars of more recent times think that wine was part of the cult of Dionysus even at an early age, but it was used only as a means to produce ecstasy.[22] "Only?" Did the age in which the cults and myths came into existence look at things in the same way we do? For us things have this or that use and mean very little in themselves. But is it conceivable that the ancients could have assigned to wine the miraculous power to lead man to the divine, without, at the same time, worshipping the spirit of the divine within it? The significance which one believed had to be ascribed to wine in the earlier cult of Dionysus is proof enough in itself of the antiquity of the belief in the wine god, Dionysus. Admittedly, the element which distinguishes the grape from all other plants is precisely that which has always assured it its place in the cult of Dionysus. This is its intrinsic power to enchant, to inspire, to raise up the spirit. And this is the power whose effect brings even us in contact with the ancient belief that a god reveals himself in wine.

However, we do not have to confine ourselves to general

considerations. The facts in the sources themselves make it certain that wine was always looked upon as the gift of Dionysus. Homer, in whose world this god means little, still is aware of all of the basic characteristics of his cult and myth and knows him quite well as the wine god. This we have already shown on p.55 above. But still more significant is the evidence which comes from the festivals of his epiphany in which a miracle caused the wine to flow or vines to bloom and bear fruit in a few hours (see above, p.98). A belief which expresses itself in forms like these is unquestionably age-old. The tremendous significance which the vine has had in historical times as a plant of Dionysus should also have made scholars wary of the thesis that this was an accidental innovation, relatively speaking. For only that which is part of the basic structure can spread with such force. The next chapter will show how incorrect it is to see in Dionysus a general vegetation deity who becomes a god specifically concerned with wine only in the course of time.

Wine, which, as Aeschylus[23] says, "the wild mother" brought into existence, "the fiery drink of the black mother," as Euripides calls it,[24] is a metaphor for the god himself. Like him, it, too, is complete only through the miracle of a second birth. Dionysus, who was ripped out of the burning womb of his mother, had flames of lightning for his nurses (as Nonnus so often says). He is called "the one who is born of fire" ($\pi\nu\rho\iota\gamma\epsilon\nu\eta$ς),[25] the "fiery one" ($\pi\nu\rho\delta\epsilon\iota$ς).[26] Wine, too, has a fiery nature. Some thought they might explain the myth of the fiery birth of the god from this fact.[27] Archilochus begins his hymn to Dionysus with the words "struck by wine's lightning bolt."[28] Posidonius ascertained that the fire-containing soil in volcanic areas produced the best wine.[29] Some[30] tried to use this as a basis for the idea found in the words $\pi\nu\rho\iota\gamma\epsilon\nu\eta$ς $\Delta\iota\delta\nu\nu\sigma\sigma$ς. Plato[31] wishes to deny adolescents wine so that fire is not poured into their fire. The ethics of Posidonius make allowances for wine's fiery content.[32]

The mysterious process of the fermentation and ripening of wine still has the power today of evoking a way of thinking in vintners and connoisseurs which reminds us vaguely of mythopoeic thought. They regard wine as a living being which evolves step by step from the chaotic boisterousness of youth to a lucid clarity and strength. In the process, when the ripening is over and the highest degree of excellence seems to have been achieved, the chaotic movement starts again, like a person who might relapse into puberty in order to pass through this stage of development once again to rise to an even nobler refinement. Some even believe that a mysterious sympathy exists among wines approaching maturity, and consider it rash to bring them into contact with one another indiscriminately, because the development of each wine can be furthered or deterred by the company it keeps. Through its transformation wine seems to bring out again the heat of the sun which the grape received outside in nature, and an old folk belief is of the opinion that it remains associated with the life of nature. This supposedly explains the renewed action of the ripening wine in spring when the vines bloom.

> When the vines bloom anew,
> The wine moves in the keg;
> When the roses glow anew,
> I don't know what is the matter with me.
> (GOETHE)

This miraculous plant, which has been the inspiration for thousands of profound thoughts, has been considered in all ages the loveliest gift of Dionysus and his epiphany in nature. Even if we did not know it, we would be forced to see that wine carries within it the wonders and secrets, the boundless wild nature of the god. The moment the belief in Dionysus became alive, the devout could learn from wine and could get an ever deeper awareness of who he really was. After all, pleasure and pain and all the antitheses of Dionysus are locked up in the deep excitation with which he seizes the soul. "Whether you bear in yourself complaints or laughter, or whether you contain strife and mad love or friendly sleep, O faithful cask."[33] This is the way in which the touching hymn of Horace addresses the forty-year-old wine born in his own birth year. All the world praises wine because it brings joy; but its pleasure is unspeakably deep because there is something which flows in it that is related to tears. According to the beautiful story which we read in Nonnus, it is supposed to have sprung from the body of Ampelos, the dead favorite for whom Dionysus shed hot tears. So the joy of men flows forth from the tears of a god.

"Bacchus, the lord, wept to still the tears of mortals."[34] And when the sorrowing god himself drank in, in the fruit of the vine, all of the splendor and grace of the dead youth, his heart was glad within him.

Even though this myth appears late in the literature of Dionysus, it can direct us to the dark mystery out of which rises the sacred madness which transfigures existence with such suddenness. Semele bore Dionysus as a "joy to mankind" ($\chi\acute{\alpha}\rho\mu\alpha\ \beta\rho\sigma\tau\sigma\tilde{\iota}\sigma\iota\nu$), to use the phrase in the *Iliad* 14. 325. In Nonnus,[35] Zeus says to his love after he has embraced her, "Blessed are you who will give birth to intense joy for gods and men, for you have conceived a son who brings forgetfulness to the sorrows of mortals." This is Dionysus, who is "filled with joy" ($\pi\sigma\lambda\upsilon\gamma\eta\theta\acute{\eta}\varsigma$), to use Hesiod's epithet for him.[36] No plant should be planted in preference to the vine, says Alcaeus[37] and following him Horace,[38] who calls the vine "sacred," as does Ennius.[39] A drink from the divine spring suddenly transcends grief and misery, the poor man feels himself rich, the slave free, the weak strong and power-ful—to quote numerous passages of poetry full of reverent praise.[40] But there is no more beautiful nor profound a passage than that which appears in the hymn of Horace (3. 21): "You move with soft compulsion the mind that is often so dull; you restore hope to hearts distressed, give strength and horns to the poor man. Filled with you he trembles not at the trucu-lence of kings or the soldiers' weapons."

In this way all violent bonds and orders are cancelled as if the freedom of the primal world had been restored with one blow. Man, too, is made open and true by this freedom. Wine, as Plutarch says so nicely,[41] frees the soul of subservience, fear, and insincerity; it teaches men how to be truthful and candid with one another. It reveals that which was hidden.[42] Wine and truth have long been associated in proverbs.[43] It is a good thing, so it is said, to search for the truth in earnest conversation while one drinks wine, and agreements arrived at over a wine glass were at one time considered to be the most sacred and inviolable agreements.[44]

Indeed, it must have been a god who was familiar with suf-fering who endowed man with such a comforter and de-liverer. It is said that wine was given to mankind after the great flood as divine assistance. As Nonnus[45] tells the story, Aion complained to Zeus about the laborious care-ridden life of the new men and begged him to grant them the divine nec-tar as a solace. But Zeus declared that he would beget a son who was to bring to the human race another dispeller of cares and messenger of joy, the vine. The ancient Israelites had similar thoughts when they told how a Noah appeared among the wicked, and at his birth his father cried, "He shall com-fort us in our work and in the toil of our hands with the very ground which Jehovah hath cursed."[46] After the flood, it was this Noah who planted the first vineyard.[47] Thus, out of the

same soil which let man earn his bread only after much toil
and trouble grew the miracle of solace, deliverance, and joy—
the drink which was offered, in accordance with an Israelite
custom of mourning, to those burdened with sorrow.[48] *Proverbs* 31.6 says of it, "Give strong drink unto him that is perish-
ing, and wine unto the distressed in soul: Let him drink and
forget his misery and remember his sorrow no more!"[49]

But wine is also a conqueror. It reveals to the strongest and
to the most headstrong the greatness of the tender-eyed,
dancing, and exultant god who is at the same time the most
powerful conqueror and the hero with the greatest triumphs.
Countless myths tell of these wonders. Dionysus alone has
the power, with wine's magic, to bend the will of the im-
placable Hephaestus, against whom even Ares cannot prevail.
Wine even has the ability to dispel the restlessness of Fate's
goddesses when Apollo, out of love for Admetus, used it to
dupe them.[50] Wine overcame "even the centaurs," to quote a
famous line in the *Odyssey*.[51] With its help Midas masters
Silenus, who then has to reveal hidden knowledge to him. As
many myths known to us from the poetry of later eras report, Dionysus, himself, overcame the opposition of his
strongest enemies and his coyest lovers with the help of this
confederate. Odysseus takes it along as his companion for this
reason when he makes up his mind to confront the gigantic
Cyclops, who will have nothing of law and custom.[52]

And finally, in the same drink which has within it the
power to free, to comfort, and to bring bliss, there slumbers
also the madness of the god of horror. Wine so disturbed the
mind of the centaur, Eurytion, that he commited crimes in
his madness ($\mu\alpha\iota\nu\acute{o}\mu\epsilon\nu\sigma$) which plunged him into ruin.[53] Not
many references are needed to substantiate the terrible pro-
gression of immoderate drinking. Frequently, the growing
intensity of the effects of wine is described in successive

steps:[54] from well-being, love, desire, and sleep, to wantonness, cries, deeds of violence, and finally madness (μανία). Plutarch says that in Egypt the terrible effect of the drunkenness which transports men into madness is explained by the fact that wine is the blood of enemies of the gods from whose bodies the earth, which covers them, brought forth the vine.[55]

Thus, of all that earth produces, the vine mirrors best the god's two faces and reveals most clearly his miraculous nature—both his endearing and his terrible wildness. It was doubtless always recognized as such, ever since one knew of him and of wine. We, on the other hand, are accustomed to use the gifts of nature to suit ourselves without being amazed by its secrets, and whenever there is talk of wine, we think of geniality, high spirits, and, perhaps, also of the dangers to health and morals. But the Greek of antiquity was caught up by the total seriousness of the truth that here pleasure and pain, enlightenment and destruction, the lovable and the horrible lived in close intimacy. It is this unity of the paradoxical which appeared in Dionysiac ecstasy with staggering force.

# 13. *Dionysus Revealed in Vegetative Nature*

The madness of Dionysus is engendered in the vine and is shared by everyone who imbibes its miraculous elixir. This is why it is the principal symbol of the god and the best guaranty of his presence.

But he does not live in it alone. As a genuine god, he must pervade a great realm of natural phenomena with his spirit. He must be actively manifest in them in a thousand ways, and yet always remain the same. This realm must be a whole, and not just a part or a section of the world, but, instead, one of the eternal forms of its totality.

There is no way to express the essence which holds this Dionysiac realm together. We recognize it, however, by its spirit of madness which is so tangibly present in wine. All of the many other creatures of nature in which the god principally reveals himself are, therefore, related to the vine in their way; and the nature of the vine can teach us that it enjoys a special function in relation to those who belong with Dionysus. His theatre of operation is not vegetation in general, as is said currently, but a mysteriously aroused element of life which appears in an unusually clear focus in certain plants but also can be perceived in numerous aspects of the human and animal world.

Along with the vine, the ivy is the favorite plant of Dionysus.[1] As the laurel adorns Apollo and distinguishes him, so the ivy, Dionysus. This is the reason why he is called "the ivy-crowned" (κισσοκόμης).[2] The more than life-size mask of the god in Icaria is wreathed with ivy.[3] In the Acharnian deme he was specifically invoked as Κισσός, and the first ivy supposedly grew there.[4] Allegedly in the past there had been none in all of Asia, and it was to be found only in Nysa in India and on Mt. Meros as a token that the god had been there.[5] Thus the ivy wreath was worn in the cult of Dionysus;[6] ivy vines twined themselves around the *thyrsus*, and from the Hellenistic period we even hear that initiates had themselves tattooed with the mark of the ivy leaf.[7] The myth says that the ivy appeared simultaneously with the birth of Dionysus in order to protect the little boy from the flames of lightning which consumed his mother.[8] In the house of Cadmus it is supposed to have wrapped itself around everything and to have checked the shocks of the earthquakes which accompanied the lightning bolts.[9] This is why the Thebans considered an ivy-twined column sacred to the god[10] and, in fact, called Dionysus, himself, the "one who is entwined around pillars" (Διόνυσος Περικιόνιος).[11] The spring at Thebes in which the nymphs supposedly bathed the child Dionysus after his birth was called Kissusa after the ivy.[12]

It was not hard to understand why the grapevine belongs to Dionysus. But the ivy, too, has peculiar properties which suggest the god, and this relationship becomes particularly illuminating when we compare and contrast it with the grapevine.

The vine and the ivy are like siblings who have developed in opposite directions and yet cannot deny their relationship. Both undergo an amazing metamorphosis. In the cool season of the year the vine lies as though dead and in its dryness resembles a useless stump until the moment when it feels the renewed heat of the sun and blossoms forth in a riot of green and with a fiery elixir without compare.

What happens to the ivy is no less remarkable. Its cycle of growth gives evidence of a duality which is quite capable of suggesting the two-fold nature of Dionysus. First it puts out the so-called shade-seeking shoots, the scandent tendrils with the well-known lobed leaves. Later, however, a second kind of shoot appears which grows upright and turns toward the light. The leaves are formed completely differently, and now the plant produces flowers and berries. Like Dionysus, it could well be called the "twice-born." But the way in which it produces its flowers and fruit is both strikingly similar to and yet startlingly different from that found in the vine. It blooms, namely, in the autumn, when the grapes of the vine are harvested. And it produces its fruit in spring. Between its blooming and its fruiting lies the time of Dionysus' epiphany in the winter months. Thus, after its shoots have opened out and up, it shows its reverence, as it were, to the god of the ecstatic winter festivals as a plant transformed with a new spring growth. But even without this metamorphosis it is an adornment of winter.

While the vine of Dionysus needs as much light and heat from the sun as it can get, the ivy of Dionysus has surprisingly little need for light and warmth, and grows green and fresh in the shade and in the cold, too. In the middle of winter when the riotous festivals are celebrated, it spreads its jagged leaves out boldly over the forest floor or climbs up the tree trunks precisely as if it wished to welcome the god and dance around him as the maenads do. It has been compared to the snake, and the cold nature ascribed both to it and to the snake has been advanced as a reason for their belonging to Dionysus.[18] The way in which it creeps over the ground or winds itself around trees can really suggest the snakes which the wild women accompanying Dionysus wind around their hair or hold in their hands. There is an episode in Nonnus[14] which tells of snakes, hurled by maenads against tree trunks, twining themselves around the trunks and becoming ivy plants. In fact, the ivy, whose slender vines glide so easily over the ground and climb into the air, seems also to reveal a mysterious relationship with the lither animals like the panther, the kid, and even the dolphin, the favorite animals of Dionysus,* which, because of their agility, were compared with the maenads.

Thus these two plants sacred to Dionysus face each other in an expressive counterplay. The vine intoxicated with light is a child of warmth and gives birth to the fiery stream which sets body and soul aglow when it is drunk. The ivy, on the other hand, seemed to be cool in nature—in fact, the sterility and uselessness of its shade-seeking stems suggested night and death, and it had to be kept at a distance from many sanctuaries.[15] After all, it was used to decorate graves. Its nature was contrasted with that of fire, to which wine seemed to be related. This is the reason why it supposedly protected the new-born Dionysus from the flames. Its coolness had the power, so one said, of extinguishing the heat of the wine, and for this reason Dionysus was said to have told his fellow celebrants to wreath themselves with it.[16] Nor did it seem without significance that the ivy, in contrast to the enlivening and invigorating grape, produces a poison which, it was believed, caused sterility or worked as a medicine which cooled and purified.[17] The story is told of the companions of Alexander the Great[18] that when, on the Indian mountain of Meros, they wreathed themselves with the ivy which, to their astonishment, they found growing there, they were imme-

* See Plates 6 and 10.

diately seized by the spirit of the god and were transported into a wild state of joyous ecstasy. According to Plutarch,[19] the women who were possessed by Dionysus pounced on the ivy to tear it to pieces and devour it. One might well believe, he says, that it possesses the power to excite madness and can produce a state of intoxication, much like wine. Some of these ideas are confirmed by more recent observations.[20]

The vine and the ivy, the two plants closest to Dionysus, which we see as interrelated because of the amazing manner in which they agree and differ, are also classified by modern botany as near relatives. In their botanical family tree, the ivy is close to the vine. For the worshipper of Dionysus the relationship of the two is based on the dual-formed god whose nature is born out of the earth through them. Light and dark, warmth and cold, the ecstasy of life and the sobering exhalation of death, the contrasting and yet related plurality of the Dionysiac state, are revealed here as plant life; they enter into conflict with one another, and are transformed, to our amazement, from one into the other. But if we ask what the material element is which acts as the carrier of the Dionysiac power and thus permeates plant life, then Plutarch gives us the answer that Dionysus, according to Greek belief, was the lord and bearer of all moist nature.[21] Proclus, in his account of the teachings of Philolaus, follows the same frame of reference when he establishes that Dionysus held sway over moist and warm creation (τὴν ὑγρὰν καὶ θερμὴν γένεσιν), whose symbol also was wine, it being a moist and warm element.[22] The warmth has been intensified in wine to a white heat, to the fiery drink which inflames body and soul and subdues all. Moist warmth, however, is the opposite of moist cold, which Proclus, in the passage above, following Philolaus, assigns to Cronus (τὴν ὑγρὰν καὶ ψυχρὰν οὐσίαν). As a Dionysiac element this is revealed in the ivy, the snake-like plant, which grows

PLATE 10 Dionysus as seafarer. Inside of a cup painted by
Exekias (Arias, *A History of 1000 Years of Greek Vase Painting*,
pp. 301-302, Pl. xvi; Beazley, *ABFVP*, p. 146, no. 21). From the
collection of the Staatliche Antikensammlungen, Munich. (Acc.
No. 2044)

green even in winter and recalls the mysteries of darkness and death in spite of its exuberantly growing tendrils.

It is conceivable that Dionysus must exercise the same power in nature over the growth of trees that is so miraculously manifest in the vine. This should be true especially of trees which produce succulent fruit. To corroborate his interpretation of the Dionysiac nature, Plutarch, in the previously mentioned passage, acquaints us with a fragment out of Pindar[23] in which the following wish is expressed: "May Dionysus, rich in joys, make the trees to prosper with the holy splendor of ripe fruit." Thus Dionysus, to quote another passage of Plutarch,[24] is worshipped "almost everywhere in Greece" as " the tree god" (Δενδρίτης). In Boeotia he is called "he who lives and works in the tree."[25] According to Diodorus, the care of fruit, in general, is ascribed to him.[26] In the cult legend from Magnesia on the Maeander it is said that the likeness of Dionysus was once found in a plane tree which had been split asunder,[27] and the myth of Icarius, to whom Dionysus gave the vine, ends, as we know, with Icarius' daughter, Erigone, hanging herself from the tree under which her murdered father was buried.

But actually among trees, as among creeping and climbing plants, there are unusual ways in which the spirit of the god is revealed. And it is immediately clear that in them, too, the element of moisture plays a prominent role.

First of all, let us mention the pine tree, which, like the ivy, also grows green in the winter. In the cult and the myth it is considered a tree sacred to Dionysus. In the wild night celebrations of the god its wood flames as a torch.[28] Its cones crown the *thyrsus*. The unfortunate Pentheus supposedly sat on a pine, and the Corinthians received an oracular order from Delphi to worship the tree "as the god," whereupon they had a statue of Dionysus carved out of its wood.[29] A mysterious relationship seemed to connect the pine with the vine. It grows, so it was said, in warm earth, in those places where the vine prospered best also.[30] Its resin was much used to conserve wine and refine it.[31]

The rich sap which oozed from its trunk seemed to point to a mysterious abundance within it which could be compared with the contents of the vine. As Plutarch said, it was just because Dionysus was the lord of the moist and the pro-creative that the pine belonged to him (and also to Poseidon).

The elements of moisture and procreation were revealed with unusual clarity in the fig tree, which was also sacred to Dionysus. After all, Priapus claimed it likewise. It is well known and certainly understandable enough that it should stand as the symbol for sexual intercourse.[32] Phalli were carved out of fig wood, and an epithet of Dionysus, Θυωνίδαι, was used to describe them.[33] Dionysus, himself, was called Συκίτης, Συκεάτης.[34] The swollen fruits with their juicy blood-red pulp must always have conjured up thoughts of secret significance, and it is, therefore, unnecessary to cite further Greek sources.

The scholium to line 330 of Aristophanes' *Frogs* lists the myrtle, in addition to the ivy and the vine, as the third favorite plant of Dionysus. In it, again, the other dark side of the two-fold god seems to reveal itself. Dionysus supposedly turned it over to Hades, at Hades' wish, as a surrogate for Semele, whom he carried away from the dead. This is the basis for the belief that the myrtle belonged both to Dionysus and to the dead.[35]

Even though it sounds at times as if the promotion of plant life were quite generally connected with Dionysus, we must learn from his cult and myth that his efficacy in the plant world is of an unusual nature, and this makes plants with very specific qualities symbols of his nature. Such general names as Καλλίκαρπος or Αὐξίτης, etc. cannot change this in any way. The epithets which characterize him as the god of flowers, Ἄνθιος,[36] Ἀνθεύς,[37] Εὐανθής,[38] probably do not refer to flowers or blossoms in general but to those of the Dionysiac plants— above all, the vine blossoms. And when the "Festival of Blossoms" of the Anthesteria is held in his honor, when Pindar, in his dithyramb written for the City Dionysia at Athens (*fr.* 75), alludes to roses and violets with special affection, when it is said quite specifically, in fact, that "Bacchus loves flowers,"[39] there is nothing more in all of this than that he happens to make his marvelous appearance in the beginning of spring, and the lovely progeny of earth's floor announce his coming and adorn his path.

It is the life-giving element of moisture, therefore, to which the plants sacred to Dionysus bear witness. The next chapter will give us a closer understanding of the deep and wide, indeed, the infinite significance of this bearer of the Dionysiac mysteries.

# 14. *Dionysus and the Element of Moisture*

HOMUNCULUS:  This holy moisture damp,
                 Which gleams here 'neath my lamp,
                 Is all so passing fair.

PROTEUS:  Within this vital damp
               Now light shines from your lamp
               In tones without compare.

This is how Goethe, in the classical *Walpurgisnacht*, has that flickering creature which is just on the threshold of becoming speak with the old master of transmutation. It is the moment when Galatea, glory of the waters, rides over the the sea in a conch chariot. Thales calls out in rapture:

Hail again, all Hail!
What joys I feel prevail
Within my soul, with truth and grace possessed. . . .
All things have water as their source confirmed!
It nurtures all, each living thing!
Forever, Ocean, be thou our king!

With this, Homunculus is disintegrated and is incinerated at Galatea's feet in order to enter Becoming through the element of the waves and of love.

These words and these images, which transmit the most amazing knowledge, have their origins in the same vital depths out of which myth appeared thousands of years ago. But this is genuine myth, which has nothing to do with little stories and even less with allegorical or symbolic word camouflage for all sorts of cheap knowledge. Rather, this is the myth which deals with living images of reality as it presented itself to mortals who had not yet wilfully severed their connections with the world and set themselves up in opposition to it. Our modern way of thinking has made this alienation complete. But the poet is a diver who constantly re-enters the eternal depths. And Goethe, who even as scholar and scientist could remain true to these depths, received from them such mighty visions that the gigantic chasm dug by the passage of time seems to be closed just for an instant.

To the mythopoeic mind, water is the element in which the primal mysteries of all life dwell. Birth and death, past, present, and future intertwine their dances here. Where the sources of Becoming are, there too is prophecy. This is why the water spirits have the power of prophecy. And beauty omnipotent, the enchantment for whom all the treasure-houses of Becoming fling wide their gates—Aphrodite—rose out of the sea, begotten in the middle of the waves from the seed of Uranus. With water come vitality, re-invigoration, and nourishment to flood through all creation. The daughters of moisture, the nymphs of myth, nourish and care for the newly-born. Oceanus in the *Iliad* is called the father of the gods, yes, the universal father.[1] These fundamental concepts of the myth are continued in philosophical doctrines. Thales declares that water is the origin of all things and of all beings, and Aristotle conjectures[2] that he was persuaded by obser-vation to believe that everything nourishing is moist, that warmth arises out of moisture, and that the seeds of all living things have a moist nature. Aristotle also suggests that some people believe that the more profound meaning of that fa-mous Homeric passage[3] was precisely this.

Water is, then, the element in which Dionysus is at home. Like him, it betrays a dual nature: a bright, joyous, and vital side; and one that is dark, mysterious, dangerous, deathly. The spirits which rise up and out of it are, like the Dionysiac spirit, not only bearers of prophecy but also bearers of madness. An insane person is called "one who has been seized by the nymphs" (νυμψόληπτος, *lymphatus*). Myths tell us that Dionysus had the ability to change his form, and this, too, makes him like the forms to be found in moving water: Proteus, Thetis, and the others.

The cults and myths are as explicit as they can be about the fact that Dionysus comes out of the water and returns to it, and that he has his place of refuge and home in the watery depths. At the festival of his epiphany, the Argives called Dionysus βουγενής out of the lake of Lerna with trumpet blasts and plunged a lamb into the bottomless depths as a sacrifice to the "guardian of the gates."[4] Once Perseus is supposed to have thrown Dionysus into the lake after he had vanquished the god and the "sea women" who had accompanied him.[5] The same idea lies behind the myth in the sixth book of the *Iliad* (130 ff.): the god makes his escape into the depths of the sea, where Thetis receives him as he runs from Lycurgus, who gives the women of Dionysus a savage and bloody beating. In Nonnus, who tells the story of Lycurgus in detail,[6] Dionysus remains on the bottom of the sea for a considerable period and does not reveal himself to his devotees until later.

According to a legend which comes from Brasiai in Laconia, the child Dionysus was washed ashore in a chest. Cadmus, so the story goes, was enraged by his daughter's love affair and had had her and the boy thrown into the sea.[7] Dionysus' mother's sister, Ino, who took care of the child after Semele's death, is also supposed to have thrown herself into the sea. The next chapter will show how important water is in the legends which concern the women associated with Dionysus. In Methymna on Lesbos people thought they owned a statue of the god which had been fished out of the sea.[8]

In spring, then, he comes riding over the sea to celebrate his epiphany in the Ionian city states.[9] Hermippus[10] speaks of the many good things he brings with him in his black ship ever since he has been sailing the wine-dark sea. The famous cylix of Exekias shows him on the high seas in a ship equipped with sails and overgrown with a mighty vine. The ship-car in which he makes his entrance at the Anthesteria still carries memories of his journey over the sea. In this representation of Dionysus as seafarer, there is surely something more than just the idea that he came from a great distance—that is to say, from across the sea. The evidence already cited clearly indicates how close his association with the sea and with water, in general, was thought to be. There is other evidence, too. In Pagasae he was worshipped as the "god of the sea" (Πελάγιος); in Chios, as the "god of the seacoast" ('Ακταῖος). In Athens his oldest sanctuary was situated ἐν Λίμναις. So, too, in Sparta[11] and possibly also in Sicyon.[12] He, himself, is called Λιμναῖος[13] or Λιμναγενής.[14] Wrede[15] has already given us a fine description of the damp forest valley in Attic Icaria where his old cult site lay. The grotto, too (ἄντρον), which shows up so often in his cults and myths, points to his predilection for the element of moisture. On Euboea there was a "grotto of Dionysus" (Διονύσου σπήλαιον).[16] In Laconian Brasiai the grotto was exhibited in which Ino was said to have brought up the child Dionysus after he was washed ashore in a chest.[17] Homeric Hymn 26 also has the god grow up in a grotto as a protegé of the nymphs. And a Berlin vase painting[18] shows the huge mask of the god mounted in a grotto.*

Dionysus, himself, dispenses the water which enlivens and invigorates. In Cyparission in Messenia there was exhibited near the sea a spring which his *thyrsus* supposedly struck out of the earth. The name given to it was, therefore, Διονυσιάς.[19] On the Phineus bowl in Würzburg we see him riding with Áriadne in a fantastic chariot on his way to a wine fountain while three nymphs wash their naked bodies in a bubbling spring. The Charites from Orchomenus who bathe in the Acidalian spring are called his (and Aphrodite's) daughters.[20]

Inherent in the Dionysiac element of moisture is not only the power which maintains life but also the power which creates it. Thus it flows through the entire human and animal world as a fertilizing, generative substance. The learned Varro was very well informed when he declared that the sovereignty of Dionysus was not only to be recognized in the juice of fruits whose crowning glory was wine but also in the sperms of living creatures.[21] From this sphere of the god's activity he traced the origin of the custom in which a phallus was crowned with wreaths and carried around in the god's cult. We certainly know how great a role this symbol of procreative power played in his festivals. "A wine jar, a vine, a goat, a basket of figs, and then the phallus"—this is the description Plutarch gives us of the original simplicity of the Dionysiac celebration.[22] A song was sung to the phallus.[23] We have inscriptional evidence for the use of a large wooden phallus in the processions of the Dionysia in Delos.[24] Each colony sent a phallus regularly to the Athenian Dionysia.[25]

There is no need to pile up more evidence. We see that the

* See Plate 5.

phallus enjoyed a high position as the attendant and announcer of the god. The phallus out of fig wood was called by the Rhodians Θυωνίδας,[26] as was Dionysus, himself, and in Methymna the god, whose statue was reputed to have been fished out of the sea, carried the epithet of Φαλλήν.[27] Dionysus could even be identified with Priapus,[28] who was otherwise considered to be his and Aphrodite's (or one of the nymphs') son.[29] However, the phallus is, after all, only an attendant of Dionysus, a potency which looms absurdly large in his circle but betrays in the process how far it is separated from the majestic reality of the god. The animal-like power and drive of sex is certainly not the least of the life miracles of his realm, and it bursts forth wildly and impetuously from the element in which he reveals himself. But his divine nature stands aloof from this in the dignified and majestic manner in which the god appears on the vase paintings whenever he is depicted in the company of his lustful satyrs.[30] In Aristophanes' *Acharnians*, the phallus celebrated in the rural Dionysia festival is expressly addressed as the "friend" of the god (Φαλῆς ἑταῖρε Βακχίου),[31] and the other references are of the same type.

There was, however, a mighty beast, in whose bodily form the river gods generally appeared when they emerged from their element, who was so close to Dionysus that he revealed himself to the devout in its form above all others. This is the bull.

It is well known that the bull was looked upon by ancient peoples as a symbol of fertility and prolific generation, and it was just for this reason that the spirits of nurturing and fertilizing streams had to be depicted in its image. In the *Iliad* it is said of the wildly boiling Scamandrus that it roared "like a bull."[32] This comparison would hardly have appeared if the poet had not been familiar with the viewpoint that the river god was a bull.[33] Thus the bull form of Dionysus again suggests the element of water, which we have perceived to be the carrier and agent of his divine power in nature. Like Dionysus, Achelous is also represented by the mask.[34] Moreover, this association of bull and water is explicitly established by the cult, for in Argos the Bull Dionysus (Βουγενής Διόνυσος) was summoned out of the deep with trumpet blasts.[35]

But it is not only the vitality and generative powers of the bull which make it one of the forms in which Dionysus reveals himself, but there are also its frenzy and its dangerousness. Like all the genuine revelations of the god, it, too, exhibits the duality of the giver of life and the destroyer. In it the life element boils up into a truly Dionysiac wildness and horror which are discharged in a storm far more violent than the fury of the panther and the lynx, the bloodthirsty favorites of Dionysus. According to a passage in Athenaeus,[36] Dionysus was compared to the bull because of the wildness which intoxication by wine evokes.

It is precisely the wild and raging bull whose image the devout have before their eyes when they summon Dionysus. The women of Elis[37] cry for "Lord Dionysus," "Noble Bull" (ἄξιε ταῦρε), "raging with the bull's hoof" (τῷ βοέῳ ποδὶ θύων) to come. This is certainly also what was meant when Aeschylus said in the *Edoni*[38] of the Thracian orgies that "frightening apparitions roared from somewhere out of the darkness with the voice of the bull" (ταυρόφθογγοι δ' ὑπομυκῶνταί ποθεν ἐξ ἀφανοῦς φοβεροὶ μῖμοι). In the *Bacchae* of Euripides the chorus calls to the god to appear in bull form.[39] Pentheus sees him as a bull when he is on his way to the destruction which the god is preparing for him.[40] Dionysus is called the "bull-horned one."[41] Bull statues were not rare in Greece, according to Plutarch,[42] and Athenaeus[43] bears witness to the fact that Dionysus was depicted with horns[44] and was called "bull" by many poets. In Cyzicus his statue was set up in bull form.

Zagreus is overpowered and torn to pieces by the Titans after he has undergone numerous transformations and has appeared in the form of a bull.[45] The ritualistic rending of a living bull on the island of Crete supposedly recalls this incident.[46] The Laphystian maenads wore horns to be like their god.[47] It would be easy to cite many other sources for the bull form. The bull is also the prey of Dionysus, and his sacrificial animal. Sophocles[48] calls Dionysus the "devourer of the bull" (ταυροφάγος). In Arcadian Cynaitha, at the winter festival of Dionysus, a number of men, after they had been filled with the spirit of the god, seized a bull out of the herd and carried it in their arms to the sanctuary.[49] And, in conclusion, reference should be made to the fact that Dirce (according to Euripides' *Antiope*) came to a Dionysiac festival on Cithaeron and was dragged to her death by a wild bull.

In the case of the other domestic animals sacred to Dionysus, the most productive sexual desire and fertility are also combined with a characteristic trait which was felt to be sinister.

The he-goat is one of the most loyal associates of the god. In the simple celebrations to Dionysus held in earlier times, as Plutarch describes them,[50] the wine jar came first, then a vine stock, a he-goat, a basket of figs, and finally the phallus. Its highly touted lecherousness is what reputedly made the goat into one of the members of the Dionysiac circle.[51] As we know, it was believed that the she-goat in her nature had a mysterious relationship to the sexual life of women.[52] When the voices of adolescent boys changed, it was said that the boys "were playing the goat."[53] How vitally this relationship between the god and the animal was felt to be can be gauged from the fact that the lush plants which he especially loved have received some of their names from the he-goat. For example, the wild fig tree is called ἐρινεός in Greek,[54] after him, *caprificus* in Latin.[55] In the dialect used in Messenia the tree was actually called τράγος.[56] The same picture recurs in the case of the vine. When one referred to the wild shoots of the vine, one said that it was producing "goat shoots."[57] The oracular response which told the founders of Tarentum to search for a site where a goat dipped his beard into the sea seemed to be fulfilled when they saw a wild fig tree on the sea shore and a vine spread over it, one of whose shoots (ἐπίτραγοι) touched the surface of the sea.[58] It was considered significant that goats like to eat vine shoots (which they unquestionably do). It was supposedly a goat's regular departures from the herd and its later returns in the best of spirits which once made Staphylus, the herdsman of Oineus, aware of the vine.[59]

But the clearest expression of the close association of the animal with the god is found in the names used for the god himself in ritual. He was invoked as the "young kid" in Metapontum.[60] Possibly the name Εἰραφιώτης[61] was also meant to be taken in this way.[62] In myth, too, Dionysus appears in goat form at times. There is the story, for example, that Zeus changed the child Dionysus into a kid (ἔριφος) in order to protect him from Hera's persecutions.[63] In his flight from the terrible Typhon when the other gods also concealed themselves in animal bodies, he himself supposedly assumed the form of a goat.[64]

The he-goat was also favored as a sacrificial victim to Dionysus. It was said that this was his punishment for damaging the vine plants.[65] In Rhodes a kid was sacrificed to Dionysus at the end of the month, Agrianios.[66] In Myconos it was a "kid without blemish" on the twelfth day of Bacchion.[67] In Boeotian Potniai it was believed that the goat sacrificed to the "goat killer" (Αἰγοβόλος) Dionysus was a surrogate for a sacrificial offering of a child in the past.[68]

However, the dark and eerie character of the animal also

leaves its mark in the cult and myth of Dionysus, and it is this duality in its nature which first makes it into a genuine symbol of the two-fold god. Dionysus "of the black goat-skin" (Μελάναιγις) has an epithet here which is used again in the case of the Erinyes (see above, p.114). Plutarch[69] mentions it together with "the nocturnal one" (Νυκτερινός). To his cult, which in Attica was associated with the Apaturia, belonged a legend which obviously referred to the spirit realm beneath the earth.[70] He was also worshipped in Hermione.[71] A figure who was undoubtedly connected with Dionysus Melanaigis was Dionysus Morychos ("the dark one") in Syracuse.[72] The spirit of horror which, according to the myth-making mind, lives in the goatskin is well known to us from the figure of Zeus, who shakes the aegis. The same concept recurs in the Italic cult of Mars.[73] It is precisely out of Italy, moreover, that we get our most explicit evidence for the viewpoint that the he-goat and the she-goat belong to the subterranean world, and to death's realm. The goddess of women, Juno, dresses herself in a goatskin. Thongs from the skin of a sacrificial he-goat serve in the Lupercalia to produce fertility in women. But these animals are so incompatible with the god of heaven, Jupiter, that his priest is not even allowed to speak their names. The Middle Ages, as we know, had a fondness for depicting the spirits of hell in their image. And we must admit that the sensation of the uncanny is not only brought home through their forms, but their movements, too, seem to have something spectral about them—particularly the strange leaps very young kids make. With that we have come back again to the dark and dangerous mystery of the Dionysiac, which also reveals itself in the leaping animals of the god in other ways.

Finally there is the ass, the third of the herbivorous animals which are the favorites of Dionysus. It is not as close to him as the bull and the goat, for none of Dionysus' epithets calls the ass to mind, and Dionysus, himself, never assumed its form. But it does belong to the Bacchic revel rout, as the well-known representations show. On a Berlin cup, an illustration of which appears in Nilsson,[74] the ship of Dionysus has on its bow an ass's head.* The ass appears as the animal the god rides, in the story of how the ass became one of the stars in the constellation of the crab.[75] It was said that it had taught man vine-pruning because of its habit of browsing on vine shoots, and for this reason its image could be seen in Nauplia on a cliff.[76] It was also said to have a fondness for the narthex (which is dear to Dionysus) and ate it without ill effects.[77] It seemed natural for the ass to appear in the circle of Dionysus because of the wild lecherousness for which it was famous,[78] and the vase paintings do not fail to emphasize this characteristic. But the ass was also included in the realm of darkness. The Egyptians, who saw the evil Typhon in it, loathed and feared it intensely.[79] Its irritating, ear-splitting bray probably makes us easily understand why. There is no question that it is more than just a joke when one hears that Dionysus and his attendants appeared in the battle of the giants, mounted on asses, and that the brays of these animals frightened the enemy so that they fled.[80] The Ambracians' dedication of a bronze ass in Delphi was supposedly due to a similar reason.[81]

Thus the same element appears repeatedly in a series of forms which are always new. The spirit of generative moisture and warmth, which reveals itself in the vine and in other plants, also makes a number of animals into attendants and symbols of the god. But these same creations bear witness to the wildness, the unearthliness, and the horror of the Dionysiac life element and remind us that the bloodthirstiest beasts of prey are part of the god's most intimate surroundings.

* See Plate 11.

PLATE 11   Dionysus sailing in a ship with the bow shaped like an ass's head. Detail from a cup (Beazley, *ABFVP*, p. 369, no. 100). From the collection of the Staatliche Museen, Berlin, Antikenabteilung. (Acc. No. 2961)

# 15. *Dionysus and the Women*

Procreation takes place in moisture. But birth also arises from it. Water has always been felt to be the element of women: *Aqua femina*.[1] Goethe, in Part Two of his Faust, with his genuine feeling for primitive ways of thought, has the majestic hymn to water and ocean begin at the moment when Galatea approaches in her conch chariot. Aphrodite rose out of the sea. Hera was brought up in secret by Oceanus and Tethys.

To be sure, the mighty sea has its masculine ruler, and the streams, which flow along full of power, have their male gods. But in the depths of the ocean and on its surface the mermaids and the sea goddesses are more important than the masculine spirits, and Nereus is not surrounded with sons, but with daughters. The springs, the lakes, and the marshy lowlands, however, belong exclusively to female spirits. There, too, lives Artemis, the beautiful maiden, who assists at all births or lets women die in bitter labor. She watches out for the children. And all of the maidens of moisture, to whom the name of *nymphs*, that is, young women or brides, is given, are nurses (the word "nymph" being used in Italy in the form *lympha* to mean "water").

Nymphs also nurture and rear the child Dionysus and accompany the god in his maturity.[2] The women who participate in his mad dances are called "nurses."[3] Certain women are particularly prominent as his foster mothers. Above all, there is Ino, the sister of his mother who died in childbirth, for it is a characteristic of the spirit of this sphere that the mother disappears behind the figure of the foster mother.

Dionysus is always surrounded by women. The nurse becomes the loved one on whose beauty his glances are fixed in drunken rapture. The ideal personification of her is Ariadne.

The divine women of moisture always appear in sisterhoods, and an important myth, whose subsequent influence we encounter in a variety of forms in ancient Italy also,[4] makes them into the nurses of a divinely begotten little boy. Likewise we find sisterhoods in Dionysus' circle, too, and despite the diversity with which the myth speaks of them, we can still clearly see the unity of the basic view. There are almost always three sisters with whom the god comes into contact, and the remarkable story of a little boy who is entrusted to them and is subject to a tragic fate appears again and again in a variety of forms. Semele, herself, has three sisters—Ino, Agave, and Autonoe—who, after her death, take care of the motherless child. In the *Lenai* of Theocritus (26), they appear as the archetypes of the attendants of Dionysus, and the son of Agave falls victim to their madness. Analogous to them are the three daughters of Minyas, who were overcome by the madness of the god in spite of everything they could do to resist it. They, too, have a little boy in their midst, who suffers the most lamentable of deaths.

Much like this is the myth of the three daughters of Proetus, who similarly resisted the god and were driven by him into a state of bacchantic madness.[5] However, there is also a story that it was Hera who had made them mad as a punishment for their want of respect for her divinity.[6] According to Bacchylides, they dared to say that their father far surpassed the queen of heaven in splendor and riches.[7] According to Acusilaus, they made fun of the ancient wooden statue of the goddess.[8] But, current opinion to the contrary,[9] this is by no means an independent form of the myth which has so little to do with the idea of Dionysus that one would have to ask which of the two stories was the older and genuine one. Both have basically the same content. Is not the source of the madness of Dionysus, himself, actually to be traced back to Hera? The goddess of marriage, Hera, more than any other divinity, detests the wild actions of the god and his female band because these actions make a mockery of her entire realm. There is a profound reason, therefore, for the hostility which the women of Dionysus feel toward Hera, and Nonnus hits upon the true sense of the myth when he tells the following story about the maenad, Alcimacheia, which definitely brings the daughters of Proetus to mind: Alcimacheia entered the sanctuary of Hera with the ivy which the goddess hated and struck her statue with the *thyrsus*.[10]

There are also other legends concerning the adoption of the mysterious god in which we meet this circle of sisters again and again. Thus in the cult of Dionysus Melanaigis the story is told of the daughters of Eleuther that they rejected the god when he appeared to them in his black goatskin, and they were driven mad by him as a consequence.[11] The daughters of Semachus, on the other hand, were said to have been immediately friendly to the god when he came.[12] We will have more to say later of the daughters of Erechtheus, whose cult was related to that of Dionysus.[13] But immediately afterward, we will discuss the famous pair of sisters, Procne and Philomela, who also were closely connected with the circle of Dionysus.

Their names already tell us that these groups of sisters who are inseparably connected with the myth of Dionysus are closely related to the bands of sisters found among the spirits of moisture. To the reader of the *Odyssey*, Ino is the well-known sea goddess; Agave and Autonoe show up again in the circle of the Nereids,[14] and much the same is true of others.

The women of the myth are, however, the prototypes of the associations of women who served the cult of Dionysus. Similarly, we see also in the six vestal virgins of Rome the reflection of a mythic band of sisters,[15] and we are all the more justified in thinking of them here particularly because their virginal appearance suggests the nature and the name of the nymphs, and the worship of the phallus is one of the obligations of their service.[16] The legend which deals with the establishment of the Dionysiac women choruses in Magnesia on the Maeander[17] tells how three maenads, who belonged to the lineage of Semele's sister, Ino, had come out of Thebes for this purpose. Just as three women choruses were established in Magnesia, so in a poem by Theocritus (26), Ino, Agave, and Autonoe led three holy bands into the mountains to the festival of Dionysus.[18] The poem, moreover, is called "Lenai," which we recognize as the term used for the orgiastic women of the cult, and, as we know, this is the term which gives its name to the Dionysiac festival of the Lenaea.[19] In addition to the Lenai we know of a large number of other women's societies which had as their function the performance of all sorts of cult practices and the organization of ecstatic dances in the service of the god. On the day of his appearance they evoke the god, who has vanished into the depths or the distance, or they wake up the baby Dionysus, who is sleeping in his cradle. They welcome the wondrous god and are seized and carried away by his passion. In other words, in the *cultus* they take the place of the nymphs, or whatever other name the Dionysiac women have in the myth.

So it is with the thyiads who move to Parnassus for the winter festival. We can get some idea of the wildness of their dances when we hear that they once arrived at Amphissa in complete bewilderment and sank down there in the market place exhausted. At this, the women of the town formed a circle around them as they slept so that the soldiers who were present in the town would not molest them.[20] The group of sixteen women in Elis, who summoned Dionysus with a song whose text we have, is of the same type. Or take the fourteen *gerarai* in Athens, sworn in by the queen who was given in marriage to Dionysus. Perhaps we can recognize them, too, in the Bacchants who mix and ladle out the holy wine before the statue of the god on the so-called Lenaea vases.[21] From occasional references[22] we know the names of other such associations of women whom we characterize, in general, as maenads, although their names change with the places and countries concerned. There are, for example, the Laphystiai, the Dionysiades, the Leucippides, the Bassarai, the Dysmainai, the Klodones, the Mimallones, etc.

Whereas all of the other divinities are accompanied by attendants who are of the same sex as they, women make up the intimate surroundings and retinue of Dionysus. He, himself, has something feminine in his nature. To be sure, he is in no way a weakling but a warrior and a hero who triumphs; and we shall have something to say about that later. But his manhood celebrates its sublimest victory in the arms of the perfect woman. This is why heroism *per se* is foreign to him in spite of his warlike character. In this he is like Paris, the never-to-be-forgotten image of the man who is illuminated by the spirit of Aphrodite. Paris, too, is a virile warrior and yet must of necessity succumb to Menelaus, "the friend of Ares." Likewise Dionysus also is overthrown when he is confronted by tough masculinity. This we already know from the story in the *Iliad* of his encounter with Lycurgus. Moreover, even if he does gain a victory over strong enemies, this occurs characteristically when he has assumed some other form. Thus he overcame the giants as a lion. Or he brings about the fall of a superior opponent with the magic potency of his wine, with which he can overcome even shy huntresses. There are many stories to this effect in Nonnus. Just as the *Iliad* calls Paris γυναιμανής, so a Homeric hymn uses the same term for Dionysus.

In Aeschylus[23] he is called contemptuously "the womanly one" (ὁ γύννις); in Euripides,[24] "the womanly stranger" (θηλύμορφος). At times he is also called "man-womanish" (ἀρσενόθηλυς). The Christians sneer at his effeminacy, to which the strange story of his encounter with Prosymnus can also bear witness.[25] Indeed, there is a tale that Hermes gave the infant Dionysus to Ino with the stipulation that she rear him as a girl.[26]

The feminine aspect of his nature is also revealed in his manner of loving. His whole existence is illuminated and crowned by the love of women. Anacreon's song[27] to him already makes it clear how close Eros and Aphrodite are to him. In it the prayer for love's fulfillment begins with the words "O Lord, whose playfellows are the mighty Eros, and the dark-eyed nymphs and violet Aphrodite!" The goddess of love is called his consort,[28] and she supposedly became the mother of the Charites in Orchomenus by him.[29] Thus many of the nymphs with whom he revels become his mistresses and surprise him one day with a new-born infant boy.[30] However, he is far from being a wanton profligate, and even if he occasionally receives an epithet which sounds obscene to us (like Χοιροψάλας), the high nobility of his spirit is revealed that much more in all representations of him, and the impression they give is emphasized even more by the way in which his actions are contrasted with those of the satyrs, of whose naked lust the god seems to take no notice.[31] Indeed, the one thing which sets him off from all of the truly masculine gods, whose passions are cooled by transient moments of possession, is the fact that his love is ecstatic and binds him to the loved one forever. We see this at its best in the vase paintings.[32] There is good reason for our calling Ariadne the chosen one, for it is quite remarkable how little the myth speaks of any other true love affairs.

This should now prepare us for a proper understanding of the spirit of the love which dwells in the hearts of the women of Dionysus. There is nothing so foreign to the orgiastic dancers of the god as unrestrained erotic sensuality. If an occasional off-color scene shows up among the countless representations of the actions of Dionysus, the remaining scenes demonstrate in a most convincing manner that the maenads are characterized by a stateliness and a haughty aloofness, and their wildness has nothing to do with the lustful excitement found in the half-animal, half-human companions who whirl around them. In the famous messenger speech of the *Bacchae* of Euripides, the modesty of the women in ecstasy is explicitly emphasized in the face of the malicious stories told about them.[33] On vase paintings they brusquely wave off their forward lovers with torches and snakes. According to Nonnus,[34] each has wound a snake around her body beneath her clothes to protect herself from the lustful desires of men even when she is asleep or defenseless. Their love is of a higher type. "The Bacchant pays no attention to the silenus who grabs at her in his lust; the image of Dionysus, whom she loves, stands alive before her soul, and she sees him even though he is far away from her; for the glances of the Bacchant sweep up high into the aether and yet are filled with the spirit of love."[35]

We have found the origin of the Dionysiac women in the element of water, from which the spirits of womanliness rise, together with the magic of beauty, motherliness, music, prophecy, and death. In the final analysis, then, they are representations in the world of the archetype of womanliness. For this reason it would be impossible to think of them as possessed with the same excessive erotic desire found in men. True womanliness reveals itself in the slighter importance of sexual desire, which must, of necessity, vanish before the eternal emotion of a mother's care and concern. These women are mothers and nurses. How eloquent the myth is concerning their infants! In the forests they suckle the young animals with their mothers' milk. On vase paintings one sees nymphs and maenads taking care of male children.[36] But their most famous charge is Dionysus, himself, whom Zeus or his messenger, Hermes, once delivered to the nymphs. This is why the thyiads on Parnassus awaken the sleeping child Dionysus at regular intervals. And the women who hold their revel rout around the mature god are also called "nurses."

This feminine reserve has not the slightest thing to do with what we call morals. It belongs to nature, which has made man and woman so mutually dependent that each must constantly seek the other's company, and yet each is separated from the other by a rift which stems from the primal depths of all that lives. A man, to the degree that he is definitely male, that is to say, created for the passion of reproduction—in the corporeal or the spiritual sense—can forget only too quickly not only the marvelous vision which transports him but the fruit of his love as well. Yet archetypal femininity is such that all beauty, sweetness, and charm must combine their rays into the sun of motherliness that warms and nurtures the most delicate life for all eternity. Mothers and nurses —they are the same here. In sorrow and in pain is revealed the eternal abundance of their existence, of which Goethe once said, "Without being mothers, they must prepare themselves eternally to play the role of nurse."[37] And yet in love for a child the tie with the male returns in a form which is imperishable. We are confronted by an unusually clear picture of this phenomenon, too, in the sphere of the Dionysiac woman. Just as the child Dionysus is himself a member of the male sex, so the children whom we find in the arms of the women are exclusively male. That is highly significant and is unquestionably based on archetypal emotions and viewpoints. In the Tithenidia, too, the "Festival of the Nurse" in Laconia, about which we shall have still more to say later, the nurses bring only male children before the goddess.

As we have said, it would be a great mistake to try to interpret the modest behavior of the women, who are, after all, seized by the wildest excitement, as a form of asceticism. This archetypal world of the feminine knows nothing of the laws and regulations which govern human society, and no breath of the spirit which streams forth from the goddess of marriage, Hera, has touched it. It is a world which conforms completely to nature. To burst the bonds of marital duty and domestic custom in order to follow the torch of the god over the mountain tops and fill the forests with wild shrieks of exultation—this is the purpose for which Dionysus stirs up the women. They are to become like the feminine spirits of a nature which is distant from man—like the nymphs who have nurtured him and who riot and rage with him. This is why Hera hunts down Dionysus from the first moment of his existence, and the women who serve him hate her, as we have already indicated above.

And now there is a repetition here, too, of the horrible darkness which is ready to devour all of the shining brilliance in the realm of Dionysus.

In the most lovable of his creatures—in woman, to whom the secrets of life are intrusted—there are revealed at the same

time not only the splendor and the goodness of Being but
also its terror and destruction. In her madness the mother-
nurse becomes a bloodthirsty beast of prey and tears into
pieces the young life which she loves most dearly. From the
first nurses of Dionysus to the grisly myth of Procne and
Philomela, the picture of the mother who is carried away by
the dark spirit of the god and slaughters her own child in
ghastly fashion is repeated in constantly new forms. This is
followed by bloody pursuit from which, in the myth of Lycurgus, the god, himself, makes his escape into the inaccessible
distance. Such pursuits are not only recounted in the myth.
They also appear as a solemn ceremony of the *cultus*. We
have already discussed all this in detail above, together with
the many forms of the suffering which overtakes all of the
followers of Dionysus without exception—from the mother
of the god, who was consumed by fire without once having
seen the smile of her divine child, to his own tragic destruction.

The dark side, which all of the forms of Dionysus suddenly
turn toward us, demonstrates that they do not originate in
the superficial play of existence but in its depths. Dionysus,
himself, who raises life into the heights of ecstasy, is the suffering god. The raptures which he brings rise from the innermost stirrings of that which lives. But wherever these depths
are agitated, there, along with rapture and birth, rise up also
horror and ruin.

# 16. *Ariadne*

With Ariadne the nature of the Dionysiac woman is exalted to marvelous heights. She is the perfect image of the beauty which, when it is touched by its lover, gives life immortality. And yet, it is a beauty which must pass down a road whose unavoidable termini are sorrow and death.

She is explicitly called the wife of Dionysus.[1] And just as Semele, as mother, may share immortality with the god, so may Ariadne, as loved one—born mortal though she is. For Dionysus' sake, Zeus, as Hesiod says, gave her eternal life and eternal youth. And thus she rides in the chariot of Dionysus toward heaven.[2] In one reference it is also said that he led her to a mountain peak on the island of Naxos, whereupon first he, himself, and then she, disappeared.[3]

She was the daughter of Minos of Crete. So far as we know, she was accorded honors, particularly on the islands (Naxos, Cyprus, Delos, and certainly Crete, too) but, also, in Locris, although it is not definite which territory is actually meant in the sources which have come down to us.

That she is abducted and must experience terrible sorrow is the content of all of her legends. In the version of the story which has become the best known, she is abducted from Crete by Theseus and is falsely deserted on the lonely beach of an island. But in the midst of her broken-hearted laments suddenly the enraptured voices of the Bacchic rout are heard, and Dionysus appears, to raise her up to be the queen of his realm. In the other version of the myth, which is attested to by older and more ancient reports (i.e., older documents with more primeval contents and implications), she was already the loved one of Dionysus when Theseus came to Crete and fled with her in secret. But while she was still in flight, she had to pay for her perfidy with an unhappy ending. Thus the alternation of sorrow and bliss, which, as we shall see, also finds its expression in her cult, is one of the essential concepts underlying her myth, whatever other directions it may take. Each time the figure of Theseus appears (and the myth of Ariadne cannot be imagined without him), a dark destiny enters her life. The divine and the mortal conflict with one another. And the mortal is, so to speak, the reflection of the divine; for just as Dionysus dwells in the depths of the sea with Thetis, so Theseus is a son of the ruler of the sea, Poseidon. On the journey which is to lead him to Ariadne, he dives into the depths of the sea to receive from Amphitrite the crown which he bestows upon Ariadne. Ariadne, herself, is the woman of the sea, at home on the islands, carried away over the sea by the son of Poseidon, Theseus, and taken up by Dionysus into his band like the women of the islands, who are said to have followed him to Argos and were known by the name of "sea women."[4] But she is the queen of the Dionysiac women. She alone is worthy to stand at the side of Dionysus and to become the only one who is raised by him into immortality. This is the reason she wears the crown which the god, in his love, later transported into heaven. She probably received the name Aridela, conferred on her in Crete, because of this crown which shines in the heavens.[5]

She is most closely related to Aphrodite, the divine archetype of bewitching graciousness. In Amathus on Cyprus she was worshipped as Ariadne Aphrodite.[6] She is supposed to

PLATE 12 Dionysus and Ariadne accompanied by satyrs and maenads (VI Century B.C.). A little master band-cup (Beazley, *The Development of Attic Black Figure*, p. 56 and Pl. 24 and 25). From the collection of The Metropolitan Museum of Art, Rogers Fund, 1917. (Acc. No. 17.230.5) Detail of decorative band shown below.

have brought the old carved statue of the goddess from Crete to Delos, and in the famous dance in the Delian festival of Aphrodite (to which we shall return later), her image plays a prominent role. It is also not without significance that a temple of Aphrodite stood in the neighborhood of the sanctuary of Dionysus in Argos, where she was to have been buried.[7] The most important evidence, however, is her name, which, as we have seen, was even associated with that of Aphrodite. Ariadne is a dialectical variant of Ariagne, the form often written on Attic vase paintings.[8] This refers, then, to the one to whom the title of ἁγνή applies to a high degree. Now we know that it was precisely Aphrodite on Delos who was honored with this title.[9] This is usually translated "the most holy." However, the word "holy" can only lead Christian readers into error. The translation "pure," which is just as close, is unsatisfactory because our concept of purity can hardly be separated from its moral connotations. The words "untouched" and "untouchable" get us closest to the real meaning, but by this we must think of the untouchability and untouchableness of a nature which is removed from man and is foreign to his concept of good as well as of evil. This is a nature which is close to the divine, and it is for this reason that the concept of untouchableness is associated simultaneously with that which inspires worship. *Cultus* and the ancient epic award this title only to female deities—in fact, only to those who belong to the mysterious domain of the earth, of the element of moisture, of Becoming, and of death: Artemis, Kore, Demeter, and Aphrodite. Ariadne is close to them all because she is similar to them in nature.

She is maiden and nurse, or mother, at one and the same time, like Artemis, and the dreadful shadows of death play about her figure as they do about that of the goddess. As a dancer, she is also like Artemis. She also seems to be associated intimately with the element of moisture, like this goddess who takes such pleasure in living near seas or lakes and in places rich with water. Theseus, the son of Poseidon, abducts her; Dionysus, who disappears into the watery depths and emerges from them again, becomes her bridegroom. At her festival in Locris the corpse of Hesiod was supposedly washed up on the shore from the sea. It was also not without significance that the honorific in her name shows up again in the name of a nymph of the springs, called Hagno (see below). But the most important of all is the fact that she wears the crown which comes from the sea, for Ariadne's crown is without question none other than that which Theseus received as a gift from Amphitrite in the depths of the sea.[10] It was originally a gift from Aphrodite, who, herself, also wears the golden crown,[11] and in another version of the myth is the immediate bestower of this ornament.[12] The goldsmith who made it was Hephaestus, the accomplished god who once lived with Thetis in the depths of the sea for nine years, fashioning all sorts of precious objects.[13] He had created there a golden amphora for Dionysus, himself, who gave this to Thetis as a gift.[14] So apparent is Ariadne's relationship with the sea and with sea-born Aphrodite.

However, not everything in her nature is accounted for by this. In her Artemis and Aphrodite are reflected, and—as her sad fate and somber cult will show—so is Kore, the goddess of the dead. These elements of multiplicity and paradox point to the fact that she does not belong to the realm of Dionysus because of chance cult migrations and cult associations,[15] (as is generally believed today) but because of her very own essence. She never was the goddess who, one pretends today, could have once walked among the great gods of Greece as one of their peers. As a result of an *a priori* concept of what the cults of the gods mean, should we then carelessly push aside the memorable forms of belief which the myth offers? There is a more profound meaning to the story of the daughter of Minos, who was only raised up to immortality by her association with Dionysus.[16] Ariadne is a mortal Aphrodite. It belongs to the nature of the Dionysiac that life and death, mortality and eternity are mixed up with one another in a miraculous way in those who are near to the god. He, himself, is, after all, the child of a mortal mother, and just as he must endure suffering and death, so the women with whom he is most intimately associated reach a state of glory only by passing through deep sorrow.

That we really should compare Ariadne with Semele is shown us by the myth of her death. Both met destruction through the one they loved. In the *Odyssey*[17] the story is told that Theseus wished to carry Ariadne away with him from Crete to Athens but had to lose her on the island of Dia because Artemis put her to death there at the prompting of Dionysus. The final verse of this account was certainly not added later, as has been suggested,[18] but is absolutely necessary for the completion of the story. As has long been recognized, the analogy of the story of Coronis clears up the meaning of these events. Coronis, too, is put to death by Artemis, and, indeed, it was at Apollo's bidding, because she had become unfaithful to the god. She died at the moment when she was about to bring a child into the world. In other words, Ariadne and Dionysus were lovers. As Epimenides says,[19] Dionysus made the daughter of Minos his own on Crete.[20] The dead Ariadne also rests in the subterranean sanctuary of the "Cretan" Dionysus[21] in Argos. And now we hear that she, too, died while she was pregnant. In Amathus on Cyprus her grave was exhibited in a grove which was designated as belonging to Ariadne Aphrodite. After she was separated from Theseus, she is supposed to have died there in labor without having given birth. Plutarch, who reports this, using Paion of Amathus as his source,[22] tells us, in addition, of a

remarkable cult practice. At her festival, in which sacrifices
were made to her, a young man had to simulate the labor
pains of a woman with the appropriate writhings and screams.
All sorts of opinions have been advanced to explain this custom,[23] but none of them is satisfactory. It sounds much too
unlikely that this is a case of so-called "male confinement" or
some other practice like it to help with childbirth. However, it is significant that the cult practice coincides with the
myth of Semele, who also had to die before she gave birth—
at which point a man (Zeus) miraculously carried the pregnancy through to the end.

A variety of other features of *cultus* and myth still makes
the relationship of Ariadne with the feminine attendants of
Dionysus clearly perceivable. Among these is her fondness
for the dance. In the Homeric description of the shield of
Achilles,[24] it is said that Daedalus made her a χορός (dancing
place) in Cnossus. It is not conceivable that this is meant to
refer to an artistic representation of a choral dance, that was,
according to Wilamowitz,[25] on the crown of Ariadne.[26]
Surely the poet could not have said that the artistic creation
of the god Hephaestus was similar to something made by
Daedalus. On the other hand, it is quite natural for the divine
smith, when he depicts the life of people in the city and in
the country, to picture also a dancing place "like the one
which Daedalus created for the beautiful Ariadne in far-
flung Cnossus." We see from Delian myth and *cultus* how
important the dance was for Ariadne. It was there that Theseus consecrated the statue of Aphrodite which Ariadne had
brought along with her, and then he had the famous Crane
Dance performed for the first time by the fourteen youths
and maidens who had been rescued.[27] This dance is reproduced on the François vase, and the attitude in which Ariadne observes it leads to the conclusion that the dance was
actually to have been held under her supervision or in her

honor. However, in the sources we have, she also appears to be the actual leader of the choral dance of the frenzied women.[28] In Nonnus[29] she also appears together with the maenads—in fact she is clearly in the lead. Specifically, she was supposed to have been one of the women who followed Dionysus to Argos and were put to death by Perseus.[30] Her grave, as we know, was exhibited in Argos (see above).

There is another unusual piece of evidence which establishes the fact that this was the milieu to which Ariadne naturally belonged. Just as it was precisely those nymphs who reared Dionysus as an infant who later make up his revel rout,[31] so Ariadne, too, plays the genuinely feminine role of nursemaid to the divine child. On a vase painting in Palermo[32] the woman to whom Dionysus is given after his birth by Hermes is called Ariagne. This is usually considered to be purely a matter of want of thought on the part of the painter. But to feel this way is to sacrifice a highly valuable source without sufficient reason. It is exactly in this sphere that the nurse is linked to the loved one by a delicate bond. Let us remember that the nymph of the spring, Hagno, who already suggests Ariadne by her name, was supposedly the nurse of Zeus.[33] Ariadne's maternal attributes also seem to show themselves in the myth of the children whom Theseus rescued with her help. She is the one before whom the rescued youths and maidens hold the Crane Dance. She was also remembered in the Athenian festival of the Oschophoria when two boys in girls' clothing carried the ripe grapes, and female δειπνοφόροι were supposed to play the parts of the mothers of the children who had once been marked for destruction.[34]

Thus she shares in the tragic destiny of those who are associated with the god, and, together with the most prominent of them, she is elevated after death. We have already discussed the stories told of her death. But we must still add to

this that there was a myth which said that when she was
abandoned by Theseus, she hanged herself.[35] That reminds us
of the myth of Erigone, which belongs to the Dionysiac
milieu. She, too, hanged herself after her father was killed
because of the wine. However, Artemis, also, is called "the
one who has hanged herself" ("Απαγχομένη) in the cult of
Arcadian Kondylea; and the myth of this cult tells about
children who died violently.[36] Finally, we may think also of
the myth of Charila in Delphi and the ritual in which the
thyiads participated.[37]

All of the versions of her myth bear witness to an alternation of acute ecstasy with heart-rending woe. Her cult in
Naxos was so strikingly paradoxical in nature that one believed there must have been two completely different persons
with the name of Ariadne in question. One part of the cult
was made up of festivals of joy; the other was devoted to
sorrow and lamentation.[38] In this we recognize once again
the duality of all Dionysiac Being. The idea of death is also
expressed in the myth referring to the fact that the corpse
of the murdered Hesiod was once washed up on shore during her festival in Locris.[39] However, the principal versions
of her myth differ when it comes to the motivation behind
her lamentable fate. Either Theseus took her away from the
god, and she had to meet her death at the god's bidding during
their flight, as the *Odyssey* tells the story (this version coincides with those given us by Plutarch,[40] which have her die
on Cyprus or on Naxos shortly after her abduction), or she
experienced the love of Dionysus only after she had been
abandoned. And here the god "who comes," the god whose
epiphany suddenly transforms the world, the deliverer and
comforter, reveals himself to her in the most wonderful
fashion. Shrouded with suffering, she is startled by the exultant shouts of his chorus and wakes, at his bidding, to bliss
in his arms.

# 17. *The Fate of Dionysus*

We have come to know the life element in which Dionysus reveals himself. Again and again it has been confirmed that the life element is at the same time the element of death. This is why Dionysus, himself, goes to his death just as, as the awakener of life, he himself is born.

It is believed today that the myth of gods who are born and die must of necessity have something to do with the change of the seasons and the corresponding changes which occur in plant life.[1] However, the meaning of a true god is never so limited that it could be exhausted by the idea of growth in plants. The primordial force of life which is revealed in Dionysus belongs to a much more profound level of Being than that of the element of growth in the plants on which man depends. This is precisely why he is a god.

With the name "god" we are accustomed to associate the idea of a sovereign lord who is, to be sure, sympathetic with the kingdom he rules but does not himself share its joys, sorrows, and experiences. This idea is foreign to ancient myth. To it, the god, though he appears as a powerful individual, is still, in the final analysis, identical with the spirit and form, that is to say, the essence of the realm in which he is the ruler. The primordial processes which are acted out in it must be consummated in the god himself. If his is a realm of an all-powerful eruptive vitality, then it cannot be otherwise than that he, himself, be born as a child, since birth is the primal phenomenon of his sphere of Being. But if his is a realm of dying and passing away, then he must himself die, must himself taste of the bitterness of a life overwhelmed. Thus Persephone, the queen of the dead, seized suddenly in the midst of the sweetest play of her girlhood and dragged off into the depths, is like every soul which is painfully cut off from the light. As for us, if we wish to have a picture of death, we can think of it only as a skeleton, that is to say, as life which is past.

Dionysus, however, is both life and death, for his spirit reveals itself from out of the immeasurable depths where life and death are intertwined. That is why the myth also has him die.

His grave was in Delphi near "golden Apollo."[2] We learn from Plutarch[3] that in Delphi, where, it was believed, the remains of Dionysus rested near the place where the oracle was, the Hosioi made a secret sacrifice in the temple of Apollo at the very same time when the thyiads were awakening Liknites, the infant Dionysus in the cradle.[4] It is possible that there also was a grave of Dionysus in Thebes.[5] One knew of his death in Argos, too. The subterranean sanctuary in which the coffin of Ariadne was also said to be found seems to refer to this.[6] However, the representation of his death is shown with complete clarity in the ritual in which the Argives regularly called Dionysus out of the depths of the sea. In the process they submerged a lamb as a sacrifice to the "warden of the gates."[7] In short, the god was sealed up in the underworld and must have died. And the myth[8] actually says that Perseus vanquished him and threw him into the sea—that he suffered the same fate, therefore, as his maenads, whose graves were exhibited.

Aside from this isolated reference we possess only one single myth which gives us the story of his destruction. And it is precisely this myth which lets us see clearly that the dying of the god is basic to his nature, since by it Dionysus is plainly associated with the powers of the underworld, and what is done to him is nothing else but what he, himself, does.

This is the meaning of the famous myth of Zagreus, whom the Titans, at Hera's bidding, assault, tear into pieces, and devour.[9] It is well known that the Orphics incorporated this myth into their teachings and found in it a mysterious meaning for the destiny of man. But it is a mistake to maintain that they were the first to claim to see Dionysus in the figure of Zagreus. Zagreus means "great hunter,"[10] and it is this Dionysus whose bloodthirsty hunting the maenads imitate.[11] And just as Dionysus is equated with Hades,[12] so Zagreus is the "chthonic" Dionysus.[13] Aeschylus calls him the son of Hades.[14] The well-known idea that he was the offspring of Zeus and Persephone is already found in Callimachus.[15] And thus he is also called "he who wanders in the night,"[16] as Dionysus is called "the nocturnal one,"[17] and as such had a temple in Megara.[18] Our oldest reference to Zagreus comes out of the *Alcmaeonis*,[19] where he is invoked, together with Ge, as the greatest of all the gods. For Callimachus,[20] Zagreus is only a special name for Dionysus. To be sure, we meet the myth of the rending of Dionysus-Zagreus first in an allusion in a poem which is ascribed to Onomacritus.[21] But K.O. Müller, [22] Welcker,[23] and recently, with reference to Herodotus 8. 27, Weniger[24] have rightly insisted, in opposition to Lobeck,[25] that it must have been much older than this. As a papyrus fragment from the holy books[26] tells us, it belongs to the Dionysiac belief, and it was from this that the Orphics took it over.[27] At the festival of the Lenaea it was remembered in hymns.[28] And it is the Dionysiac belief on which its meaning is based.

The "wild hunter" is himself hunted, the "render" is himself rent. When his destiny overtakes him, he is very like one of his unfortunate victims. Just as the women in Dionysiac madness tear their little boys into pieces, just as the maenads, following his example, tear apart young animals and devour them, so, he himself, as a child, is overcome by the Titans, torn apart, and consumed. It is a fearful struggle, in spite of the superiority of the enemies, for the kingly child assumes the shapes of the most dangerous of the animals, becoming in the end a raging bull. As bull he finally collapses.[29] But the name "Zagreus," which he bears in the myth, shows—as we have said before—that it is the dread god, the merciless destroyer, for whom this horrible end is prepared. One may infer from Firmicus Maternus' rationalistic description[30] that the ritual in Crete in which a living bull was torn into pieces was meant to reproduce this myth ceremonially. For the famous sacrifice on Tenedos was also nothing else but a re-iteration of the horror told in the myth. Here where Palaimon Βρεψοκτόνος was worshipped with child sacrifices,[31] a pregnant cow was reserved for Dionysus, and after it had given birth, it was given post-natal care like a woman who had given birth. But the new-born animal was dressed in *cothurni* and was sacrificed with a stroke of an axe.[32] The *cothurni* clearly suggest Dionysus, himself, who as hunter was accustomed to wear these hunters' boots.[33] Here then, too, we have a representation of a mythical slaughter of the young god. Again there is no question that it is Dionysus, the destroyer, who must suffer this fate; for the cult practice is performed in the service of the "man-render" Dionysus.[34]

The same myth which gave these sacred practices their form and content is unquestionably also the basis for the much discussed Argive ritual.[35] In this ritual the god was called from the dead to his epiphany from out of the depths of the sea. He was, therefore, to enter life anew, to appear as a young god. However, when he was invoked as Βουγενής (and the sources are explicit about this), then this name, which has not been understood up to now, means to infer that the cow has given birth to him in the form of a young bull. This Βουγενής Διόνυσος is none other than "the one who has been born of a cow," to whose fate the sacrificial act in Tenedos refers. In all probability in Argos, too, the dying of the god, which had to precede his reappearance, was thought of as a violent destruction and was possibly represented in this way in cult. Indeed, his death and descent into the lake near Argos was also reported in the variant of the Perseus myth mentioned above.

Finally, it is true that we have no further evidence about the *cultus* to which the well-known invocation hymn of the Elian women belongs.[36] But the fact that the god is asked to come in the form of a bull, and its necessary presupposition that he had disappeared before, almost force us to assume that the determining factor here, too, was the myth of the fall, and, in fact, the violent death of Dionysus. If now, as the hymn says, he was to appear as a raging bull, then we must recognize that the young god, represented on Tenedos as a new-born calf which is sacrificed, cannot have been thought of as weak and defenseless. Rather, he was full of high courage and in possession of tremendous strength. As we know, this is illustrated by the Orphic myth which says that the child Dionysus received the lightning and the throne from Zeus and that as lion, snake, and bull he was an object of dread to his destroyers even in his last hour.

The myth of his reappearance as a young bull is paralleled by the myth of the new-born infant Dionysus, the Liknites, who is awakened by divine women as he lies in his cradle. The thyiads impersonate these women in cult.[37] Unfortunately, we have only Plutarch's single reference[38] for this, and Plutarch has nothing explicit to say about the time when this happened. He only says that, according to Delphic belief, the remains of Dionysus lay near the site of the oracle and that the Hosioi performed a secret sacrifice in the sanctuary of Apollo during the time when the Liknites was awakened by the thyiads. But in another passage[39] the same Plutarch informs us that the Paean of Apollo became silent in Delphi with the beginning of winter, and the dithyramb was sung to Dionysus for three months.

Dadophorios, the name of the first of these three winter months, clearly refers to the torch celebration of the god. At this time of year the thyiads made a biennial trip to Parnassus in order to hold their wild dances there. Because of the bitter cold they were often in danger of their lives and had to be rescued by men who rushed to the scene.[40] When the myth says that the divine nymphs reared the child Dionysus and then formed the retinue of his revel rout, we must conclude that their imitators, the thyiads, began the sacred dance celebration with the discovery and awakening of the infant Dionysus. Certainly the dithyramb was associated with the myth of the birth of Dionysus.[41] If E. Norden's ingenious construction is correct,[42] we can even talk of a specific date, the eighth of November, as the day of the awakening. On the island of Andros the epiphany was celebrated on the Nones of January.[43] The returning god appeared, therefore, at the time when the sunlight was in the process of renewing itself. Since the myth in which the Titans rend Dionysus is likewise associated with Delphi, it stands to reason that the reappearance of the Liknites and his awakening by the women presupposed his violent death. In the fifty-third Orphic hymn it is said, at least, that the "chthonic" Dionysus, who—together with the lovely-haired nymphs—awakens to take part in the trieterical choral dance, has slept in the interim in the house

of Persephone. But in the forty-sixth hymn it says that Dionysus Liknites had been taken to Persephone in accordance
with Zeus' decision and raised there.

The story of his horrible death, which is mirrored in so
many cult practices and is eloquently represented in one myth
we still have, is undeniably like the famous myth of Osiris,
who was put to death by the wicked Set and was cut into
pieces. This has led scholars even very recently to believe that
the myth of Dionysus must be explained as a copy of the
Egyptian myth.[44] As a matter of fact, the comparison of
Dionysus with Osiris, which constitutes a major portion of
Plutarch's essay on Isis and Osiris, is much more meaningful
than the comparison with Thracian, Phrygian, or Minoan
deities. However, the myth of the death of Osiris differs from
that of Dionysus in far too many important points. Isis plays
a significant role in the former, but the Dionysiac myth
knows nothing of a figure comparable to her. Osiris is first
shut up in a coffin and is killed in this way. Later Typhon
tears him into fourteen parts which he scatters far and wide.
Nothing is said about eating the dismembered body. And
finally, Osiris meets his deadly fate when he has reached a
man's estate, after he has ruled for many years filled with
blessings, while Dionysus is a boy when he is overcome by
the Titans. These are not incidental characteristics. On the
contrary, they give the death myth of Dionysus its character
and make the similarities with the Osiris myth appear un-
essential. It is obvious that they get their meaning from the
nature and activity of Dionysus, himself. He is rent apart and
devoured in the first flowering of his youth because he is
himself the render and devourer of young life. Modern theory
which traces this myth back to a so-called sacramental ritual
of killing and eating a deity loses its meaning because it introduces an extraneous concept which is authenticated nowhere

in the sources.[45] The lord of dying and of the dead himself goes through the horror of destruction and, when it is time, must be summoned forth into the light from the abyss of eternal night. However, since in the godhead of Dionysus the interrelationship of life and death is revealed out of the primordial depths, we can say that the power of madness inherent in the destroying creator of existence presents itself to horror as a victim of that destruction.

The mythology of a later period distinguished the Zagreus, who was the child of Zeus and Persephone and who was destroyed by the Titans, as an earlier manifestation of the real Dionysus, the son of Semele, whom Zeus called into life to take the place of Dionysus-Zagreus. This by no means did the old myth an injustice. In it, too, a horrible death precedes the reappearance of the god, and in it the dying god is also related to the powers of the underworld. But in the original conception both are one. The god, with his multiplicity of forms, the lord and first-born child of life and death, is born of Semele as well as of Persephone, and entered Hades as well as Olympus.[46]

But there is not only one way in which the manifold god can come and go. On the one hand he is suddenly there, bursting with joy and wildness into the world of man to which he turns his face—remember the significance of the mask! And on the other hand he disappears just as suddenly again from his raging revel rout. At the festival of the Agrionia the women of Chaeronea searched for some time for Dionysus, who had disappeared, and finally said that he had fled to the Muses and had hidden himself there.[47] At the Agrionia in Orchomenus the women were hunted down with the sword by the priest of Dionysus, and when he could catch them, they were struck down.[48] This corresponds exactly with the *Iliad*'s myth of Lycurgus, who fell upon the women of Dionysus with his fearful ox-goad.[49] In this story the god saved himself by leaping into the sea, where Thetis received him kindly. He disappears in the depth of the sea, where he is at home. And thus he also disappears by going to the Muses. It is said that he suddenly disappeared also on a mountain on Naxos up which he had made his ascent with Ariadne by night, and after he had disappeared, Ariadne disappeared, too.[50]

A long time passed before the one who had vanished appeared again to his followers. The institution of the trieteric festivals of his epiphany (that is, festivals celebrated only once every two years) is unquestionably connected with the concept of his departure or dying and his long absence. Orphic hymn 53 explicitly says that he was sleeping in the interim in the house of Persephone. However, even when he makes a new entrance each year, he comes from a remote, mysterious distance. Nysa, the place where he was reared by the nymphs, was thought to be in the far east. The ancient wine-producing countries lie in the east, while the introduction of the vine into the west is relatively recent. One read already in Eumelus[51] that Dionysus had spent some time with the goddess Rheia in Phrygia, and after he was healed of his madness with her help, he travelled through the entire world. In the distance, too, into which he had vanished, the god who appears with such violence and stormily imposes the intoxicating vitality of his gifts could be thought of in no other way than as a victor and conqueror. It was said he shared in the nature of Ares[52] and was the first *triumphator*.[53] The name Θρίαμβος, which was applied to a Dionysiac hymn and to the god himself (perhaps it is basically identical with Διθύραμβος[54]), is perpetuated, as we know, in the Etrusco-Latin word *triump(h)us*; and in the Roman triumphal procession, which has become historical, it is no accident that the *triumphator*, who took over not only the costume of the image of Jupiter but also its red make-up, reminds us of Dionysus.[55] It has been said of Alexander's victorious procession through India that Dionysus had already preceded him into this land and had forced the people of India to acknowledge his might. His battles and victories are described in detail in Nonnus' poem. Some even maintained that Alexander on his return march through Carmania was imitating the triumphal march of the god.[56] We shall not deal here with what happened to him in history and subsequent legend. But it is obvious that the concept of Dionysus must already have been very familiar to a conqueror of the east. We see, after all, from Euripides' *Bacchae* that long before Alexander the god was believed to have come to Media, Persia, Arabia, and all the way to Bactria.

It is out of a distance such as this that Dionysus appears when his time comes. In the *Bacchae* of Euripides he comes from the region of Lydian Tmolus, and Lydian women make up his retinue, just as in the myth of his encounter with Perseus, the "sea women" are his attendants.

But his approach as it is celebrated by the Ionic cities around the time of the beginning of spring is more mysterious. The one who vanished comes over the sea, the kindred element into which he made his escape, according to the old myth which already appears in the *Iliad*. Whether it is from the east or the west that he comes, he sails silently over the surface of the sea, and at his entry nature quickens. This is why Smyrna (even though it lies on the Asiatic coast) also receives him from the sea.[57] The sign that he comes from there is the ship-cart on which he makes his entrance into the Ionic cities at the Anthesteria festivals. The city Dionysia festival at Athens, instituted by Peisistratus, belongs to the month immediately following. In the same month as the city Diony-

PLATE 13    Dionysus and a satyr. Column krater (ca. 470-460 B.C.)
painted by the Pan painter (Beazley, *ARFVP²*, p. 551, no. 6 [8]).
From the collection of The Metropolitan Museum of Art, Rogers
Fund, 1916. (Acc. No. 16.72)

sia came the Agrionia. They, too, knew of the disappearance of the god, who, however, had not dived into the sea here but had fled to the Muses. Therefore, they, too, must have been celebrating his reappearance. The hymn of Philodamus[58] calls to him to appear "in this holy spring time."[59] Pausanias[60] refers to a spring festival in Laconia in which the miracle of the ripe grape was viewed with wonder. Let us remember also the epithets of Anthios, Antheus given to Dionysus.[61]

In these spring festivals there is no reference to the myth of the birth of the god. He comes out of the distance into which he disappeared.

All of this belongs to the great vision of the epiphany, which is revealed in the myth as well as in the *cultus*. It has nothing at all to do with cult migrations.

It has been felt that several sources which refer to Asia Minor still support the inference that there was a particular form of regular coming and going. In fact, this was the basis for the hypothesis that the religion of Dionysus developed in two different forms and spread to other areas through a variety of routes.[62] For example, there are references to a spring festival in Lydia, too,[63] but unfortunately no details are given about this. Plutarch, on the other hand, informs us that the Phrygians believed that "the god" ($\tau \grave{o} \nu \ \theta \epsilon \acute{o} \nu$) slept in winter and was awake in the summer, and this is the reason why they alternately celebrated orgiastic ($\beta \alpha \kappa \chi \epsilon \acute{v} o \nu \tau \epsilon s$) festivals of Putting to Sleep and Awakening ($\kappa \alpha \tau \epsilon \upsilon \nu \alpha \sigma \mu o \grave{v} s$ and $\dot{\alpha} \nu \epsilon \gamma \acute{\epsilon} \rho \sigma \epsilon \iota s$).[64] But the Paphlagonians say, Plutarch adds, that he is chained and locked up in the winter, but in spring he begins to stir and goes free. The god who is worshipped in this way seems, of course, to have the closest connections with the regular growth and death of plant life, whereas the Dionysus whom we have come to know appears, to be sure, in spring, together with the rising sap and the energy of a newly-awakening nature, yet he does not follow this nature's yearly fate. There are only festivals of awakening in the Dionysiac cult; however, nowhere in it are there any festivals in which the god is put to sleep (κατευνασμοί). Instead, it is precisely in winter, when the sun gets ready to start on its new course, that he makes his most tumultuous entry. He disappears again, moreover, at the same spring festival in which he made his appearance. This the Agrionia and the Lenaea festivals can show us. Must we then really believe that there was still another Dionysus who had continued to be worshipped by the Phrygians and the Paphlagonians? But Plutarch does not say a word about Dionysus' being the god he had in mind. Nor does it follow at all that it is Dionysus because Plutarch speaks of orgiastic festivals and uses the word βακχεύοντες in reference to them.[65] In the same work Plutarch had many significant things to say about Dionysus, and if he had him in mind when he was referring to a Phrygian conception as important as this, it is highly improbable that he would have omitted his name in the very section where he compares Greek and non-Greek practices (after he had previously spoken of Demeter). If we dare make a conjecture, it seems much more obvious to think of the Zeus-like god (διώς) found in the Phrygian inscriptions of imprecation.[66]

Finally, the words of Galen, to which Lobeck[67] referred, may well be true of the cult of Dionysus, who is not specifically named, but they contain nothing more than a reference to an orgiastic custom practiced at the end of spring.

Thus Dionysus presents himself to us in two forms: as the god who vanishes and reappears, and as the god who dies and is born again. The second conception has evolved into the well-known doctrine of numerous rebirths of the god. Basically, however, both conceptions (his vanishing, which is paired with his reappearance, and his death, which is followed by his rebirth) are rooted in the same idea. Both tell of the god with the two faces, the spirit of presence and absence, of the Now and the Then, who is most grippingly symbolized in the mask. With him appears the unfathomable mystery of life and death cemented together into a single entity, and the mystery of the act of creation affected with madness and overshadowed by death. This is why he bears with him not only all of the energy and exuberant joy of a life which is at the height of its activity but also his entire destiny. From his all-too-early birth, from his origin in his mother who perished in flames, sorrow and pain pursue him. His victories become defeats, and from radiant heights a god plunges down into the horrors of destruction. But it is just because of this that the earth also brings forth its most precious fruits through him and for him. Out of the vine, "the wild mother," there erupts for his sake the drink whose magic extends all that is confined and lets a blissful smile blossom forth out of pain. And in the arms of her eternal lover rests Ariadne.

# 18. *Dionysus and Apollo*

One can easily imagine how mystical initiations and doctrines could emanate from the idea of such a god. However, we have no wish to pursue this line of thought further. The mystic aspects and the whole Orphic tradition will not be dealt with here. But, there is a phenomenon that is far more significant to Greek religion as a whole, which still demands our attention.

The idea of Dionysus is alien to Homeric religion even though the poet is acquainted with him and his destinies.[1] Dionysus is different from the true Olympians. As a son of a mortal mother, he seems to belong to the circle of the super-men like Herakles who must first make themselves worthy of admission to heaven. There is, for example, the story that he brought his mother up out of Hades and rose up to heaven together with her.[2] And yet he is different from all those who have had mortal mothers. He was born a second time from the body of Zeus. This is the reason why he is, in a great and complete sense, a god—the god of duality, as the myth of his birth expresses it so beautifully and so truly. As a true god he symbolizes an entire world whose spirit reappears in ever new forms and unites in an eternal unity the sublime with the simple, the human with the animal, the vegetative and the elemental. However, this world is divorced from the realms in which the Olympian gods rule, by its earthly nature, its duality, its close association with death. They have raised their thrones on high in the clear light of day, high above the sphere where the primordial force of the elements rules. Therefore, where they alone rule, there we look for Dionysus in vain.

But the Olympian religion never repudiated or rejected the terrestrial but always acknowledged its sacredness. This is why the most important impulses to vitalize the Dionysiac cult issued from the Apollo of Delphi. What is more, Dionysus, himself, lived in Delphi with Apollo, and it could even seem that he not only enjoyed equal rights with him but was the actual lord of the sacred place.

Apollo shared the Delphic festival year with Dionysus. In the winter months the Dionysiac dithyramb was sung instead of the paean. But Dionysus also received high honors in Delphi in times other than winter. The pediments of the temple of Apollo portray on one side Apollo with Leto, Artemis, and the Muses, and on the other side Dionysus and the thyiads, in short, the raging god.[3] As well-informed a witness as Plutarch[4] states that Dionysus played no smaller role in Delphi than Apollo. One could even maintain that Dionysus had been in Delphi earlier than Apollo.[5] A vase painting of about 400 B.C. shows Apollo and Dionysus in Delphi holding out their hands to one another.[6] Many other examples could be cited for the close association of the two gods. And finally, theological speculation even identified the one with the other.[7]

However, there is a good deal more than this which makes us think that the grave of Dionysus, the myth of whose death was linked to Dephi, was even believed to be in the sanctuary of Apollo.[8] We are confronted by a very similar phenomenon at the Apollonian cult site in Amyclae. There, as it was said, Hyacinthus lay buried in the substructure of the statue of Apollo, and in the festival of the Hyacinthia sacrifices for the dead were offered to him through a bronze door there, before sacrifices were made to Apollo, himself.[9] Now this Hyacinthus, of whom the myth relates that he was the beloved of Apollo, and was killed by him through an unfortunate cast of the discus, is obviously closely related to Dionysus. He, too, was torn away in the bloom of his youth; he, too, rose again,[10] and went up to heaven. On the substructure at Amyclae, Aphrodite, Athena, Artemis, and other divinities were portrayed leading him to Olympus.[11] In addition, one saw there the representations of Dionysus, his mother, Semele, and Ino, who acted as his mother after Semele's death. Hyacinthus, too, was brought up by a foster mother (just like Dionysus). She was Artemis, who was called in Cnidus "Hiakynthotrophos," that is, the nurse of Hyacinthus.[12] She was honored in the festival of the Hiakynthotrophia.[13]

But the similarity extends much farther. Just as Dionysus is always associated with a woman, so Hyacinthus has Periboia at his side. In Amyclae she is called his sister. Like Ariadne and so many of Dionysus' consorts, she, too, died young. And when she is equated with Artemis,[14] who, after all, did nurture Hyacinthus, we are reminded of the fact that the women who accompanied Dionysus and who were loved by him (Ariadne among them) had once been his nurses.[15] But the fact that Periboia is equated with Kore[16] also moves Hyacinthus into Dionysus' vicinity. Periboia's name is found again in the legend of Tennes, the founder of Tenedos. There she is the stepmother who slandered Tennes, as a result of which he was thrown into the sea in a chest together with his sister, Hemithea—much like the infant Dionysus, whom Cadmus locks up in a box with Semele and consigns to the sea.[17] They land on Tenedos, where the cult of the "man-rending" Dionysus is native to the life of the island, and where Palaemon is worshipped with child sacrifices as Βρεψοκτόνος.[18] However, there is not just one woman who accompanies Hyacinthus as Ariadne accompanies Dionysus. Like Dionysus, Hyacinthus has a group of women by his side—women who get their name, Hyacinthides, from him. In them is repeated the same tragic destiny which befell all of the Dionysiac women. They were said to have been slaughtered in Athens for the good of the fatherland. In Apollodorus[19] they are called the daughters of Hyacinthus. According to Phanodemus,[20] they were daughters of Erechtheus,[21] and died on the hill of Hyacinthus. Philochorus testifies that the daughters of Erechtheus were worshipped together with Dionysus.[22] Hyacinthus and the Hyacinthides also die a violent death, like Dionysus and the women associated with him. To this must be added one more point of agreement of a particularly significant nature. We have already mentioned the fact that in the myth of Hyacinthus, as in the myth of Dionysus, the nurse assumes the position of mother. Now, it is precisely on the road from Sparta to Amyclae that the "Festival of the Nurses" (Tithenidia) was celebrated.[23] This was the festival in which Artemis, who had, as we know, nursed Hyacinthus, appeared as Artemis Korythalia and had young children brought to her by their nurses. Insufficient grounds have been advanced to characterize this Artemis as a fertility goddess, and for some strange reason this has produced opposition to the fact that this festival (as our account suggests) charges the nurses, and not the mothers, with the duty of carrying the children (and only the males among them) into the presence of the goddess.[24] These are exactly the characteristics we have come to know and understand in the realm of the Dionysiac. Here, too, the mother disappears behind the nurse whose name (τιθῆναι τροφσί) is borne by all the women attendants of the god. Here, also, it is exclusively male children who are cared for by the nurses. The festival of the Tithenidia, then, does not get its name, as an ancient correspondent suggests, from the human nurses who carry their little boys to the goddess but from the divine "nurses" (τιθῆναι) from whose care the little boy Dionysus was also supposed to have benefitted—or even from the great goddess herself who, as Hyacinthotrophos, took care of Hyacinthus.

Hyacinthus, whom E. Rohde[25] interpreted as an old god who lived beneath the earth,[26] is in reality a figure who stands very close to Dionysus. This seems to emerge, too, from the dual nature of the festival of the Hyacinthia, which, like the Anthesteria, alternated between gravity and frivolity in its three feast days. It is also worth noting that the name of Hyacinthus' sister, who has been equated with Kore (see above), appears again in the name of one of the sisters of Amphiaraus.[27] Moreover, at the Laconian festival of the Hyacinthia, "one wreathed oneself with ivy in accordance with the Bacchic rite."[28] The Hyacinthia were, however, a festival of Apollo and the close association of Apollo with Hyacinthus is encountered again in Tarentum. Here, too, a grave of Hyacinthus was exhibited, and the god worshipped there actually bore the name of Apollo Hyacinthus.[29]

Today it is held as a foregone conclusion that the origin of such cult associations is to be sought in completely external circumstances. Hyacinthus, as the older inhabitant of the cult site, was not forced to yield completely to the newcomer, Apollo, it is true, but he had to retire to a subordinate position. In Delphi, where Apollo was no less closely associated with the Dionysus who reminds us so strikingly of Hyacinthus, the opposite explanation was advanced. Here Apollo is supposed to have been the earlier inhabitant, and it was only his cleverness which let him come to peaceful terms with the wild newcomer, Dionysus.[30] All of this forces us to ask the fundamental question whether the presuppositions used to support this hypothesis and others like it are not much too primitive and superficial. Without the prototype furnished us by the displacement and absorption of pagan worship by the victorious invasions of Christian worship, these presuppositions would hardly have been advanced with such con-

fidence. Where do we have in the Greek sources any indication that one god attempted to drive out or suppress another?
And why should it be Apollo, whose pronouncements from
Delphi insisted upon reverence for the ancient orders of
worship which had preceded him? Did the holiness of the
place where a god was worshipped have so little to do with
his nature that any other god who entered the area had the
desire to win over for himself precisely that site merely because it had already been constituted as a place of worship and
equipped with regulations for festival celebrations? Surely
that is all too reminiscent of the Christian and the modern
way of thinking about a divine being who is not bound to a
particular place or time. Should we not ask whether Apollo
could not have wanted this association for reasons other than
greed and expediency? Could he not have been driven by an
inner necessity to supplement the scope of his own domain by
the proximity of the other—and just this other one—to show
the world that only the two together signify the whole truth?

In Amyclae Apollo was identified so closely with a Dio-
nysiac-like deity that it was suspected that this Hyacinthus
must already have possessed intrinsic Apollonian traits all his
own. In Delphi Dionysus, himself, was not by any means just
tolerated by Apollo. One could say that the thyiads on Parnassus conducted their orgiastic dances for both Dionysus
and Apollo.[31] Thyia, who first is supposed to have served
Dionysus and to have given the thyiads their name, was said
to have been a daughter of the autochthon, Castalios. By her
Apollo fathered Delphos, the eponym of Delphi.[32] The hymn
of Philodamus of Skarpheia tells us of the role Dionysus
played in the Pythian festival, and even as early a hero as Aga-
memnon is said to have made a sacrifice to Dionysus in the
sanctuary of Apollo.[33]

It is improbable that associations of this type were the result
of external encounter and compulsory assimilation. Anyone

who concerns himself with anything more than the simplifica-
tion of hypotheses must certainly be struck by the significance
of an association between Apollo and a god like Dionysus.

The Olympian realm towers above the abyss of the earth-
bound, whose omnipotence it has broken. But the race of its
gods arose itself from these depths and does not disavow its
dark origins. It would not exist if there were no eternal night
before which Zeus, himself, bows;[34] or no maternal womb,
the source of elemental being with all of the forces which
watch over it. Though all of this darkness, this element which
embraces everything with its bounty, this merciless exactor,
this eternal producer and destroyer has transcended itself in
the Olympian metamorphosis, still the light and the spirit
above in heaven must always have beneath them the darkness
and the maternal depths in which all being is grounded.

In Apollo all of the splendor of the Olympic converges
and confronts the realms of eternal becoming and eternal
passing. Apollo with Dionysus, the intoxicated leader of the
choral dance of the terrestrial sphere—that would give the
total world dimension. In this union the Dionysiac earthly
duality would be elevated into a new and higher duality, the
eternal contrast between a restless, whirling life and a still,
far-seeing spirit.

This is what a not merely superficial association of Apollo
with Dionysus would have to tell us. And, if this union actually was consummated, was it brought about only through a
clumsy accident? Is it not more sensible to believe that Apollo
and Dionysus were attracted to one another and sought each
other out—that Apollo had wanted this close association with
his mysterious brother because their realms, though sharply
opposed, were still in reality joined together by an eternal
bond?

And with this marriage, Greek religion, as the sanctification
of objective being, would have reached its noblest heights.

# 19. *Concluding Remarks on Tragedy*

The grandeur of the idea of Dionysus lives on in tragedy. We will not pursue its historical development here. But we must still pose this final basic question: what is the significance of the fact that tragedy developed its universal form within the cult of Dionysus?

That which we generally call "tragic" is not peculiar to tragedy. Its raw material, the heroic myth, is tragic itself. But the tragic element reveals itself so grippingly in the new creation, because of the immediacy of its presentation, that tragedy can claim it for its own. This is the dramatic immediacy through which the life of myth, after it had made its appearance in epic and choral song, rose again in a grand rebirth; this it is in which the Dionysiac spirit and its tremendous excitement make themselves known. No suffering, no ardent desire of the human soul speaks forth from out of this excitement, but the universal truth of Dionysus, the primal phenomenon of duality, the incarnate presence of that which is remote, the shattering encounter with the irrevocable, the fraternal confluence of life and death.

This duality has its symbol in the mask.

True, there have been other masked dances in the past, and there still are today. But what must remain in them as anticipation or as indication, emanates as reality from the depths in which Dionysus holds sway. Here we have not only the spectral presence of demonic beings of nature and the dead.

The whole splendor of that which has been submerged draws imperatively near at the same time that it is lost in eternity. The wearer of the mask is seized by the sublimity and dignity of those who are no more. He is himself and yet someone else. Madness has touched him—something of the mystery of the mad god, something of the spirit of the dual being who lives in the mask and whose most recent descendant is the actor.

This spirit of madness in which the miracle of immediate presence becomes an event was the spirit which breathed new life into the tragic mythos and had it reappear in a form which manifested its high seriousness and majesty more overwhelmingly than any which had come before. And so Dionysus made his appearance at a time of his choosing in the spiritual world of the Greeks, too, and his coming was so shattering that it still affects us today.

# Notes

## I

1. Ulrich von Wilamowitz-Moellendorf, *Der Glaube der Hellenen* (Basel, 1956), Vol.I, pp.159 f.

2. Ibid., Vol.I, pp.9-10.

3. Ibid., Vol.I, p.34.

4. Ibid., Vol.I, p.17.

5. Ibid., Vol.I, p.9.

6. Rudolf Otto, *Das Heilige*[9] (Breslau, 1922). See also the English translation, *The Idea of the Holy*, by John W. Harvey, which appears now in a Galaxy Book, GB 14 (New York, 1958).

7. See, however, Karl Th. Preuss, *Der religiöse Gehalt der Mythen* (Tübingen, 1933).

8. Cf. the custom of the Thargelia, et al. in Jane Harrison, *Prolegomena to the Study of Greek Religion*[3] (Cambridge, 1922), pp.95 ff.; and Martin P. Nilsson, *Griechische Feste von religiöser Bedeutung, mit Ausschluss der Attischen* (Leipzig, 1906), pp.105 ff.

9. Nilsson, p.112.

10. See the detailed description in George T. Basden, *Among the Ibos of Nigeria* (London, 1921), pp.232 f.

11. Paus. 9. 22. 1.

12. Nilsson, pp.392 f.

13 *Il.* 6. 130 ff.

14. Percy A. Talbot, *Some Nigerian Fertility Cults* (London, 1927), pp.47 f.

15. See, in particular, George A. Dorsey, *The Arapahoe Sundance* (Field Columbian Museum 75, Anthropological Series, Vol.IV, Chicago, 1903); Washington Matthews, *The Mountain*

*Chant: A Navajo Ceremony*, U.S. Bureau of American Ethnology, Fifth Annual Report 1883-84, Washington, 1887), pp.379 f. There are many other reports which still await sensible interpretation.

16. Friedrich Schelling, *Philosophie der Mythologie* in *Sämtliche Werke*, Part II, Vol.II (Stuttgart, 1857), p.137.

# II

## 1. *Preface*

1. Georg Hegel, *Phänomenologie des Geistes*, p.45 of the prologue in Vol.II of the *Sämtliche Werke*, H. Glockner, ed. (Stuttgart, 1927).

## 2. *The Birthplace of the Cult of Dionysus*

1. Martin P. Nilsson, *The Minoan-Mycenaean Religion and Its Survival in Greek Religion*² (Lund, 1927), pp.496 ff.

2. Ulrich von Wilamowitz-Moellendorf, *Der Glaube der Hellenen* (Basel, 1956), Vol.II, p.60.

3. Thuc. 2. 15. 4.

4. Ludwig A. Deubner was right about this in his article, "Dionysos und die Anthesterien," *JDAI* 42 (1927), p.189; see also his *Attische Feste* (Berlin, 1932), pp.122 f.

5. See below, Ch.18, p.203.

6. See L. Deubner, *Attische Feste*, p.122.

7. Herod. 1. 150.

8. Wilamowitz, Vol.II, p.60, n.1.

9. Karl O. Müller, *Kleine deutsche Schriften* (Breslau, 1847-1848), Vol.II, pp.28 ff. The review appeared in 1825.

10. Johann H. Voss, *Antisymbolik* (Stuttgart, 1824-1826).

11. *Od.* 9. 196 ff.

12. Hes. *fr.* 120.

13. Eur. *Cyc.* 141 ff.

14. Hes. *Theog.* 941.

15. Hes. *Op.* 614.

16. Hom. *Il.* 6. 136.

17. Hom. *Od.* 24. 73 ff.

18. Nonnus, *Dion.* 19. 120 ff.

19. See Pind. *Pyth.* 3. 9. ff. and 32 ff.; Pherecyd. *fr.* 8; Paus. 2. 26. 6.

20. Plut. *Vit. Thes.* 20. 3.

21. Paus. 10. 4. 2.

22. Erwin Rohde, *Psyche*[10] (Tübingen, 1925), Vol.II, pp.6 ff., 23 ff.

23. Adolf Rapp, *Die Beziehungen des Dionysoskultes zu Thrakien und Kleinasien* (Programm des Karls-Gymnasiums, Stuttgart, 1882).

24. For these Thracians of central Greece, see now also Wilamowitz, Vol.I, pp.50 ff.

25. Otto Gruppe, *Griechische Mythologie und Religionsgeschichte* (Munich, 1906), Vol.I, p.1410.

26. See, for example, Wilamowitz, *Der Glaube der Hellenen*, Vol.II, p.60.

27. Compare, for example, Soph. *Ant.* 956 f.

28. Apollod. *Bibl.* 3. 5. 1.

29. K.O. Müller, *Kleine deutsche Schriften, op. cit.*, Vol.II, p.28.

30. Diod. Sic. 3. 65. 7.

31. Wilamowitz, Vol.II, pp.61-62.

32. See Enno Littmann, *Lydian Inscriptions* in *American Society for the Excavations of Sardis* 6. 1 (Leiden, 1916), pp.38 f.

33. Ulrich von Wilamowitz-Moellendorf, *Pindaros* (Berlin, 1922), p.45.

34. See also M.P. Nilsson, *Minoan-Mycenaean Religion, op. cit.*, p.500.

35. See *Hymn. Hom.* 1. 8; Pind. *fr.* 247 Schröder.

36. See L. Malten, "Der Raub der Kore," *Archiv für Religionswissenschaft* 12 (1909), pp.285 ff.

37. See *Hymn. Hom. Cer.* 17, where I consider the reading of the MSS to be correct in spite of what Malten has said.

38. Paul W. Kretschmer, "Semele und Dionysos," *Aus der Anomia, Archäologische Beiträge Carl Robert dargebracht* (Berlin, 1890), pp.22 ff.

39. *Ath. Mitt.* 14 (1889), Plate 1.

40. Soph. *Ant.* 1131.

41. Eur. *Bacch.* 556.

42. Serv. *Verg. Aen.* 6. 805 ms. D; cf. *Schol. Pers. prol.* 2; also *Schol. Soph. Ant.* 1131.

43. Steph. Byz. Hesych., *Schol. Il.* 2. 508.

44. See L. Malten, pp.288 f.

45. Soph. *Ant.* 1115 f.

46. Cf. Herod. 3. 97. Αἰθίοπες οἱ πρόσουροι Αἰγύπτῳ. . . . ἵ περὶ τε Νύσην τὴν ἱρὴν κατοίκηνται, καὶ τῷ Διονύσῳ ἀνάγουσι τὰς ὁρτάς·

47. Diod. Sic. 3. 65. 7.

48. *Hymn. Hom.* 1. 9. τηλοῦ Φοινίκης σχεδὸν Αἰγύπτοιο ῥοάων·

49. Ap. Rhod. *Argon.* 2. 1214.

50. Xen. *Cyn.* 11. 1; see also Plin. *HN* 5. 74.

51. See also L. Deubner, "Dionysos und die Anthesterien," *JDAI* 42, (1927), 172-192, and *Attische Feste*, p.102.

52. So, for example, Otto Kern, *RE* 5, s.v. *Dionysos*, col.1020 f.; L. Deubner, *op. cit..* Nilsson's quite arbitrary hypothesis on the meaning and origin of the custom can be properly omitted here: M.P. Nilsson, "Die Prozessionstypen im griechischen Kult," *JDAI* 31 (1916), p.334.

53. Wilamowitz, *Der Glaube der Hellenen*, Vol.II, p.61.

54. Paus. 3. 24. 3.

55. Plut. *Mor. De Is. et Os.* 35 (364F).

56. See L. Deubner, *op. cit.*

57. Wilamowitz, *Der Glaube der Hellenen*, Vol.II, p.61, n.2.

## 3. *The Son of Zeus and Semele*

1. Pind. *Pyth.* 3. 86 ff.

2. Pind. *Ol.* 2. 24 ff.

3. For them, see Wilamowitz, *Der Glaube der Hellenen*, Vol.I, pp.400 ff.

4. Pind., *Pyth.* 3. 96 ff.

5. Theoc. *Id.* 26. 1 ff.

6. Eur. *Bacch.* 680 ff.

7. Otto Kern, *Die Inschriften von Magnesia am Maeander* (Berlin, 1900), no. 215.

8. *CIL* 13. 8244.

9. Eur. *Bacch.* 6 ff.

10. Aristides 1, p.72 Keil.

11. See *Fouilles de Delphes*, Théophile Homolle, ed., Vol.III. 1 (Paris, 1929), p.195 and the commentary of Émile Bourguet, pp. 196 ff.

12. Eur. *Bacch.* 11.

13. *Schol. Ar. Ran.* 479.

14. W. Dittenberger, *Sylloge Inscriptionum Graecarum*[2] (Leipzig, 1900), Vol.II, 615.

15. *Hymn. Orph.* 44.

16. Plut. *Mor. Quaest. Graec.* 12 (293 D-F).

17. Ernst Diehl, *Anthologia Lyrica Graeca*[3] (Leipzig, 1942), Vol.VI, p.206.

18. Paus. 2. 37. 5.

19. Paus. 2. 31. 2.

20. Pind. *fr.* 75.

21. Theoc. *Id.* 26.

22. Kern, *Insch. von M., op. cit.*, 214.

23. P. Kretschmer, *Aus der Anomia, op. cit.*, pp.18 ff.

24. Nilsson, *The Minoan-Mycenaean Religion*, pp.495 ff.

25. Wilamowitz, *Der Glaube der Hellenen*, Vol.II, p.60.

26. Apollodorus in Lyd. *De mens.* 4. 38.

27. Diod. Sic. 3. 62. 9.

28. Hom. *Il.* 14. 323.

29. Hes. *Theog.* 940 ff.

30. Pind. *Pyth.* 3. 99.

31. See Apollod. *Bibl.* 3. 5. 3; Diod. Sic. 4. 25. 4; Charax *fr.* 13 (*FHG* 3. 639. 13); "Semele who is called Thyone" is the reading of the Homeric hymn of the Moscow MS.

32. Eur. *Bacch.* 10 f; *Fouilles de Delphes*, Vol.III. 1, p.195; see also Émile Bourguet, p.200, who refers to H. Usener, "Ein Epigramm von Knidos," *RhMus* 29 (1874), pp.35, 49 and *Götternamen*[3] (Frankfurt am Main, 1948), p.287, n.12; also *Schol. Eur. Phoen.* 1751, where the undefiled shrine: σηκὸς ἄβατος, situated in the mountains, is referred to as the τάφος τῆς Σεμέλης: "the tomb of Semele."

33. See Pind. *fr.* 85; Herod. 2. 146; Eur. *Bacch.* 94 ff.; Apollod. *Bibl.* 3. 4. 3, *et al.*

34. Apollod. *Bibl.* 3. 4. 3; Ov. *Fast.* 6. 485; Paus. 3. 24. 4, *et al.*

35. Paus. 3. 23. 8; 3. 24. 4; 3. 26. 1, 4; 4. 34. 4.

36. See Myrsilus: *FHG* 4, p.459, 10.

37. Hom. *Od.* 5. 333.

38. Paus. 3. 24. 4.

39. See Hom. *Il.* 18. 39 ff.; Hes. *Theog.* 240 ff.; Apollod. *Bibl.* 1. 2. 7.

40. Wilamowitz, *Der Glaube der Hellenen*, Vol.I, pp.211 ff.

## 4. The Myths of His Epiphany

1. Friedrich G. Welcker, *Griechische Götterlehre* (Göttingen, 1857-1859), Vol.I, p.445.

2. E. Rohde, *Psyche, op. cit.*, Vol.II, p.41.

3. Sallustius Περὶ Θεῶν 4.9 ταῦτα δὲ ἐγένετο μὲν οὐδέποτε, ἔστι δὲ ἀεί.

4. See, especially, the *Bacchae* of Euripides.

5. Theoc. *Id.* 26.

6. Hom. *Il.* 6. 130 ff.

7. So, too, Wilamowitz, *Der Glaube der Hellenen*, Vol.II, p.60.

8. See Chapter 14.

9. See p.104.

10. *Schol. T. Ilias* 14. 319.

11. Plut. *Mor. Quaest. Graec.* 38 (299F); *Symp. praef.* (717 A).

12. F. G. Welcker, *op. cit.*

## 5. The God Who Comes

1. Plut. *Mor. Symp. praef.* (717 A).

2. See p.77.

3. *Hymn. Orph.* 53.

4. Plut. *Mor. Quaest. Graec.* 36 (299B) αἱ τῶν Ἠλείων γυναῖκες; cf. Plut. *Mor. De mul. vir.* 15 (215 E) αἱ περὶ τὸν Διόνυσον γυναῖκες, ἃς ἑκκαίδεκα καλοῦσιν.

5. See M.P. Nilsson, *Griechische Feste, op. cit.*, p.275; L. Deubner, *Attische Feste, op. cit.*, p.126.

6. Σεμελήιε "Ιακχε Πλουτοδότα: *Schol. Ar. Ran.* 479.

7. See E. Buschor, "Ein choregisches Denkmal," *Ath. Mitt.* 53 (1928), p.101.

8. αἱ τῷ Διονύσῳ ἱερωμέναι γυναῖκες: Harp.

9. *Contr. Neaer.* 73 ff.; Hesychius, s.v. γεραραί et al.

10. Plut. *Mor. De Is. et Os.* 35 (364F).

11. Ibid. (365A). See also Ch.17 below.

12. Soph. *Ant.* 1125.

13. Aesch. *Eum.* 22.

14. See p.62.

15. *Hymn. Orph.* 53.

16. S. Saridakis, F. Hiller v. Gaertringen, "Inschriften von Rhodos," *JÖAI* 7 (1904), p.92; printed also in *Rev. Arch.* 4 (1904), p.459.

17. See also *Hymn. Orph.* 52. 3. No mention will be made of the Orphic tradition of the nurse Hipta and the Dionysus who is amalgamated with Sabazius; cf. O. Kern, *Orphica Fragmenta* (Berlin, 1922), pp.222 f.

18. Soph. *Ant.* 1146 ff.

19. See M.P. Nilsson, "Die Prozessionstypen im griechischen Kult," *JDAI* 31 (1916), p.315.

20. Paus. 2. 75.

21. See Nilsson.

22. See Plut. *Vit. Ant.* 24; *Vell. Pat.* 2. 82. 4.

23. See Nilsson, *op. cit.*, pp.333 ff.; L. Deubner, "Dionysos und die Anthesterien," *JDAI* 42 (1927), pp.174 ff.

24. Paus. 1. 29. 2; Philostr. *VS* 2. 1. 3.

25. See L. Deubner, *Attische Feste* (Berlin, 1932), pp.177 ff., but cf. W. Wrede, "Der Maskengott," *Ath. Mitt.* 53 (1928), pp.92 f.

26. Arist. *Ath. Pol.* 3. 5.

27. *Contr. Neaer.* 73; cf. Hesychius: Διονύσου γάμος.

28. So, for example, Deubner.

29. Herod. 1, 181 f.

30. Wilamowitz, *Der Glaube der Hellenen*, Vol.II, pp.75-76.

31. So O. Gruppe, *Griechische Mythologie, op. cit.*, p.865.


## 6. *The Symbol of the Mask*

1. See below, p.100.

2. August Frickenhaus, *Lenäenvasen* (Berliner Winckelmanns-programm, Berlin, 1912), p.72.

3. Frickenhaus, no. 23.

4. See Eur. *Phoen.* 651 and the scholia; Eur. *Antiope fr.* 203 Nauck.[2]

5. Frickenhaus, no. 1.

6. See Frickenhaus, p.17.

7. Plut. *Mor. Symp.* 5. 3. 1.

8. See also Paus. 2. 2. 7; Kern, *Inschr. von M.*, p.215; Hesychius Ἔνδενδρος, et al.

9. Paus. 8. 15. 3.

10. Walther Wrede, "Der Maskengott," *Ath. Mitt.* 53 (1928), pp.89 ff.

11. Paus. 10. 19. 3.

12. Ath. 3. 78c.

13. Ath. 12. 533c.

14. Wrede, pp.66 ff.

15. Ibid., pp.75 f.

16. See Ernst Tabeling, *Mater Larum* (Frankfurt am Main, 1932), pp.19 ff.

17. So Adolf Furtwängler in Wilhelm H. Roscher, *Ausführliches Lexicon der griechischen und römischen Mythologie* (Leipzig, 1886-1890), Vol.I, 1704 f.

## 7. *Pandemonium and Silence*

1. See Pratinas *fr.* 1; Aesch. *Eum.* 24; Pind. *fr.* 75 Βρόμιον ὃν τ' Ἐριβόαν τε βροτοὶ καλέομεν·

2. *Hymn. Hom.* 7. 56; cf. Anacreon 11, Bergk[4] ἐρίβρομον Δεύνυσον·

3. *Hymn. Hom.* 26. 10.

4. Ἐριβόας, see above.

5. Ov. *Met.* 4. 391 ff.

6. Apollod. *Bibl.* 3. 5. 3.

7. Philostr. *Imag.* 1. 19. 4.

8. Nonnus, *Dion.* 24. 151 ff.

9. Hor. *Carm.* 3. 25. 8 ff.

10. Catull. 64. 60.

11. See Adolf Kiessling, Richard Heinze, edd. 7th ed. (Berlin, 1930) on Horace, *Carm.* 3. 25. 8.

12. See, for example, Suidas: βάκχης τρόπον· ἐπὶ τῶν ἀεὶ στυγνῶν καὶ σιωπηλῶν, παρόσον αἱ βάκχαι σιωπῶσιν·

13. Aesch. *fr.* 57.

## 8. *A World Bewitched*

1. Nonnus, *Dion.* 8. 27 ff.

2. Eur. *Bacch.* 142 ff.

3. Plato, *Ion* 534a.

4. Eur. *Bacch.* 710 ff.

5. Eur. *Bacch.* 699 f.

6. Eur. *Bacch.* 767 ff.

7. Eur. *Bacch.* 743.

8. Eur. *Bacch.* 1109; cf. Hor. *Carm.* 3. 25. 15; for maenads with uprooted tree trunks as *thyrsi*, see Wilhelm Klein, *Die griechischen Vasen mit Meistersignaturen*[2] (Vienna, 1887), p.137.

9. *Hymn. Hom.* 7; there is a similar occurrence on the ship which carries the child Dionysus in a chest to Euboea, as Oppian *Cyneg.* 4. 261 f. tells us.

10. Plut. *Mor. Quaest. Graec.* 38 (299E); Ael. *VH* 3. 42; Ant. Lib. *Met.* 10.

11. Eur. *Bacch.* 443 ff.

12. Apollod. *Bibl.* 3. 5. 1.

13. Eur. *Bacch.* 616 ff.

14. Eur. *Bacch.* 298 ff.

15. Plut. *Mor. Symp.* 7. 10. 2 (716B).

16. Aeschylus in *Schol. Apoll. Rhod.* 1. 636.

17. Diod. Sic. 3. 66. 2.

18. Paus. 6. 26. 1-2; see also Theopomp. in Ath. 1. 34a.

19. Plin. *HN* 2. 231; see also 31. 16.

20. Paus. 6. 26. 2.

21. Steph. Byz. Νάξος.

22. Prop. 3. 17. 27.

23. Cf. Sen. *Oed.* 491 f.

24. Eur. *Phoen.* 226 ff.

25. See also *Schol. Soph. Ant.* 1133.

26. Soph. *Thyestes fr.* 234 (Nauck²).

27. *Schol. Il.* 13. 21 T.

28. Euphorion *fr.* 118 Felix Scheidweiler, *Euphorionis Fragmenta* (Bonn, 1908).

29. ἐν σιωπῇ τεθερισμένον στάχυν: Hippol. *Haer.* 5. 8.

30. See Ferdinand Noack, *Eleusis* (Berlin, 1927), p.233.

31. P. Foucart, *Les Mystères d'Éleusis* (Paris, 1914), p.434.

32. See Washington Matthews, *The Mountain Chant: A Navajo Ceremony, op. cit.*, pp.379 ff., Dance 9.

33. See Frickenhaus, *Lenäenvasen;* L. Deubner, *Attische Feste,*

pp.127 ff., is hardly right when he refers these again to the Lenaea, as did Frickenhaus.

34. See Phanodem. in Ath. 11. 465a; see also p.86 above.

35. See *Contr. Neaer.* 73 ff.

36. M.P. Nilsson, "Die Prozessionstypen im griechischen Kult," *JDAI* 31 (1916), pp.329 ff.; see also E. Buschor, "Ein choregisches Denkmal," *Ath. Mitt.* 53 (1928), p.100.

37. Ar. *Ach.* 1000 f., together with the scholia; Ael. *VH* 2. 41; Ath. 10. 437c.

38. Phanodem. in Ath. 10. 437c.

39. See *Hymn. Hom.* 26; Pherecyd. *fr.* 46.

40. Hom. *Il.* 6. 132; cf. Tryt. *fr.* 1; Soph. *OC* 678 ff. θεαῖς τιθήναις; *Hymn. Orph.* 30. 9, 51. 3, 53. 6; a tragedy of Aeschylus' had the title Διονύσου τροφοί.

41. See Buschor on Furtwängler-Reichhold, Pl. 169, pp.363 ff.

42. Soph. *OT* 1105.

43. Eur. *Bacch.* 754.

44. Nonnus, *Dion.* 45. 294 ff.

45. Eur. *Bacch.* 699 ff.

46. Nonnus, *Dion.* 14. 361, 24. 130, 45. 305.

## 9. *The Somber Madness*

1. Hom. *Il.* 6. 132.

2. Plut. *Mor. Quaest. Graec.* 38 (299F).

3. Paus. 2. 20. 4; 2. 22. 1.

4. Kern, *Inschr. von M., op. cit.*, no. 215.

5. See Ernst Maass, "Die Erigone des Sophokles," *Philologus* 77 (1921), pp.1-25.

6. *Cert. Hom.* 232 f.

7. Paus. 8. 23. 1.

8. So Nilsson, *Griechische Feste*, pp.299 f.

9. See Plut. *Mor. Quaest. Graec.* 38 (299E), Ael. *VH* 3. 42; Ant. Lib. *Met.* 10 from Nicander and Corinna.

10. F.G. Welcker, *Griechische Götterlehre*, Vol.I, pp.445 f.

11. Apollod. *Bibl.* 3. 5. 2, 2. 2. 2. See also Nonnus, *Dion.* 47. 484 ff.

12. Nonnus, *Dion.* 48. 917 ff.

13. Nonnus, *Dion.* 9. 49 ff.

14. Apollod. *Bibl.* 3. 4. 3.

15. Lycophron 229, together with the scholia.

16. Ael. *VH* 3. 42.

17. Porphyr. *Abst.* 2. 55.

18. Ibid.

19. Ael. *NA* 12. 34.

20. So Nilsson, *Griechische Feste*, p.308.

21. See the Tereus of Sophocles and Carl Robert, *Bild und Lied: Archäologische Beiträge zur Geschichte der griechischen Heldensage* (Berlin, 1881), Vol.I, pp.154 ff.

22. Apollod. *Bibl.* 3. 14. 81.

23. Ov. *Met.* 6. 587 ff.; cf. Acc. *trag.* 642.

24. Theoc. *Id.* 26.

25. Eur. *Bacch.* 735 ff.

26. Catull. 64. 257; Lucian, *Bacch.* 2; Nonnus, *Dion.* 43. 40 ff.; *Schol. Ar. Ran.* 357.

27. Eur. *Or.* 1492.

28. Stat. *Theb.* 4. 660.

29. Eur. *Bacch.* 1189 f.

30. Eur. *Bacch.* 138 ff.

31. Eur. *Bacch.* 731.

32. On this see Dilthey, *Arch. Zeit.* 31, p.81; Knapp, *Arch. Zeit.* 36, pp.145 ff.

33. *Mon. d. Ist.* 10. p.23.

34. Eur. *Bacch.* 137.

35. Cf. Apollon. Rhod. *Argon.* 1. 36 θυιάδες ὠμοβόροι; Lucian, *Bacch.* 2 ὠμοφάγοι; *Schol. Ar. Ran.* 357, etc.

36. Plut. *Vit. Them.* 13; *Vit. Pel.* 21; *Vit. Aristides* 9.

37. Cf. Herod. 5. 92. 2; Aesch. *Ag.* 827; *Anth. Pal.* 6. 237.

38. Hom. *Il.* 24. 207.

39. See also the well-known passage in Hom. *Il.* 4. 35.

40. Oppian, *Cynegetica* 3. 78 ff.; 4. 305 ff.

41. Dilthey, *Arch. Zeit.* 31, pp.78 f.

42. Diod. Sic. 4. 5. 2.

43. Plut. *Mor. De E* 9 (389B); cf. F.G. Welcker, *Griechische Götterlehre*, Vol.II, p.575.

44. Eur. *Bacch.* 1017.

45. See Hor. *Carm.* 2. 19. 23.

46. Ant. Lib. *Met.* 10.

47. Nonnus, *Dion.* 6. 169 ff.

48. Ibid. 40. 38 ff.; 36. 291 ff.

49. Ath. 3. 78c; Paus. 2. 2. 5; 2. 7. 6. Cf. Plut. *Mor. De cohibenda ira* 13 (462B).

50. Philostr. *Imag.* 1. 19. 4 (322K).

51. Cf. Oppian, *Cynegetica* 3. 80, et al.

52. Ath. 2. 38e; but see Cornutus *Theol. Graec.* 30.

53. See R. Heinze on Hor. *Carm.* 2. 19. 21.

54. Euphorion (p.30, Scheidweiler).

55. O. Kern, *RE* 5. 1041 s.v. *Dionysos.*

56. Cf. Wilamowitz, *Der Glaube der Hellenen*, Vol.I, p.143.

57. See Verg. *G.* 3. 264; Ov. *Met.* 3. 668; 4. 25; Prop. 3. 17. 8; Pers. 1. 101, together with the scholium.

58. See Alexander W. Mair's edition of Oppian's *Cynegetica* (LCL, London, 1928) on 3. 84, note *a.*

59. Hom. *Il.* 14. 325.

60. Hes. *Op.* 614; Pind. *fr.* 153. 2.

61. *Schol. Ar. Ran.* 479.

62. Hesychius.

63. Ael. *VH* 12. 34.

64. Plut. *Vit. Them.* 13; *Mor. De cohibenda ira* 13 (462B); Ὠμάειος: Porphyr. *Abst.* 2. 55; *Hymn. Orph.* 30. 5, 52. 7.

65. *Hymn. Orph.* 45. 3.

65a. Plut. *Vit. Them.* 13, et al.

66. Porphyr. *Abst.* 2. 55.

67. Hes. *Theog.* 311.

68. Ibid., 300.

69. Philochorus in Ath. 2. 38c.

70. *Schol. Eur. Phoen.* 1031, possibly from the *Antigone* of Euripides; cf. 934.

71. Eur. *Phoen.* 810.

72. See *Schol. Eur. Phoen.* 45.

73. In Athens in connection with the Apaturia: *Schol. Ar. Ach.* 146; cf. Suidas μελαναιγίδα Διόνυσον; in Hermione: Paus. 2. 35. 1.

74. Aesch. *Sept.* 699.

75. Aesch. *Eum.* 500.

76. See also Nonnus, *Dion.* 44. 277.

77. Paus. 8. 34. 1.

78. Eur. *Bacch.* 977 ff.

79. Eur. *HF* 899.

80. Eur. *Hec.* 1077: βάκχαι ″Αιδου·

81. Dilthey, *Arch. Zeit.* 31, pp.78 ff.

82. Diod. Sic. 4. 25. 4; Apollod. *Bibl.* 3. 5. 3; Paus. 2. 31. 2, 2. 37. 5; Plut. *Mor. De Sera* 27 (566A); *Schol. Ar. Ran.* 330; Clem. Al. *Protr.* p.29 P.

83. πλουτοδότης: *Schol. Ar. Ran.* 479.

84. Hes. *Op.* 126; see also *Hymn. Orph.* 73 for the daimon who sends blessings as well as ruin and is similarly called πλουτοδότης; Diehl, *Anth. Lyr. Graec.*, Vol.VI, p.199.

85. Plut. *Mor. Quaest. Rom.* 112 (291A) ὧν τὰ πολλὰ διὰ σκότους δρᾶται; Plut. *Mor. Symp.* 4. 6. 2 (672B); Serv. *Aen.* 4. 303.

86. Paus. 1. 40. 6; Plut. *De E* 9 (389A); Ovid, *Met.* 4. 15; Νυκτερινός: Plut. *Mor. Symp.* 6. 7. 2 (692F).

87. E. Rohde, *Psyche*, Vol.II, p.13, note; p.45, note.

88. Heraclitus, *fr.* 15 Diels, *Vorsokr.*

89. See Wilamowitz, *Der Glaube der Hellenen*, Vol.II, p.207, note 1.

90. Cf. Strabo 10. 468: Βάκχαι Λῆναί τε καὶ Θυῖαι etc.; Heraclitus, *fr.* 14 (Diels); Theoc. *Id.* 26; and the Dionysiac festival of the Lenaea: Nilsson, *Griechische Feste, op. cit.*, p.275, note 2.

91. Nilsson, *Griechische Feste*, p.273.

92. L. Deubner, "Dionysos und die Anthesterien," *JDAI* 42 (1927), p.189.

93. Thuc. 2. 15. 4.

94. See Nilsson, *Griechische Feste*, pp.271 f.

95. Plut. *Mor. Quaest. Graec.* 38 (299E).

96 Plut. *Mor. Symp.* 8, *praef.* (717A).

97. Νεκύσια: Hesychius.

98. Nilsson, *op. cit.*

99. Apollod. *Bibl.* 2. 2. 2.

100. For this distinct possibility, see Nilsson, *op. cit.*


## 10.  *Modern Theories*

1. Karl O. Müller, *Kleine Schriften*, Vol.II, pp.28 ff.

2. K.O. Müller, *Handbuch der Archäologie der Kunst*³ (Breslau, 1848), p.594.

3. E. Rohde, *Psyche*, Vol.II, p.6, note 2.

4. K.O. Müller, *Handbuch*.

5. E. Rohde, Vol.II, note 2 of p.5; p.6.

6. Voigt, W. Roscher, *Lex.* s.v. *Dionysos*.

7. Adolf Rapp, ibid., s.v. *Mainades*.

8. See, for example, M.P. Nilsson, *History of Greek Religion* (Oxford, 1925), pp.205 f.

9. Rapp. *op. cit.*

10. For example, those of L. Weniger, *Archiv für Religionswissenschaft* 9 (1906), pp.234 ff.

11. Voigt, Roscher, *Lex.*, Vol.I, col. 1059.

12. Plut. *Mor. Quaest. Graec.* 36 (299B).

13. Nilsson, *Griechische Feste*, p.292.

14. See Kern, *Orph. frag.*, pp.210 ff.

15. Phot. s.v. νεβρίζειν.

16. Voigt, Roscher, *Lex.*, Vol.I, Col. 1037.

17. Eur. *Cret.* in H. von Arnim, *Supplementum Euripideum* (Bonn, 1913), p.25. See also the ὠμοφάγιον of the Milesian inscription, Wilamowitz, *Der Glaube der Hellenen*, Vol.II, p.367, note 1.

18. Wilamowitz, *Der Glaube der Hellenen*, Vol.II, p.67.

## 11.  *The Mad God*

1. Eur. *Bacch.* 114 ff.

2. See Ael. *VH* 3. 42.

3. Apollod. *Bibl.* 3. 5. 2.

4. Nonnus, *Dion.* 45. 47 ff.; cf. 34. 353 ff.

5. See Diod. Sic. 4. 3. 3.

6. See, for example, *Hymn. Hom.* 26. 7; Soph. *OC* 680.

7. *Hymn. Hom.* 26. 7 ff.

8. Plut. *Mor. De mul. vir.* 13 (249E, F).

9. *Schol. Lycophron* 1237.

10. Plut. *Mor. Quaest. Graec.* 36 (299B): βοέῳ ποδὶ θύων.

11. Hesych.

12. H. von Arnim, *Supplementum Euripideum*, p.47.

13. Eur. *Bacch.* 145 ff.

14. Ibid., 240.

15. Ibid., 135 ff.

16. Oppian, *Cyneg.* 4. 280 ff.

17. See the reproduction in J. Harrison, *Prolegomena to the Study of Greek Religion* (Cambridge, 1922), fig. 137.

18. See page 127 above. *Il.* 6. 132.

19. Clem. Al. *Protr.*, p.11 P.

20. See also Plut. *Mor. De cohib. ira* 13 (462B).

21. ἐλαυνόμενος μανίῃσιν: *Hymn. Orph.* 46. 5; cf. Stat. *Theb.* 5. 92 *insano . . . thyas rapta deo.*

22. Eur. *Cyc.* 3; Pl. *Leg.* 2. 672b; Euphorion *fr.* 13 Scheidweiler; Apollod. *Bibl.* 3. 5. 1. According to Nonnus, who gives us the same information in *Dion.* 32. 98 ff., and describes the madness in 35. 270 ff., he is healed by Hera, herself, by means of her milk: 35. 314 ff.

23. Pl. *Symp.* 218b.

24. Anaximander in Diels, *Vorsokr.*, Vol.I, p.13.

25. Friedrich Schelling, *Ideen zu einer Philosophie der Natur*, *Sämtliche Werke*, Vol.I, 2, p.112.

26. F. Nietzsche, *Geburt der Tragödie.*

## 12. *The Vine*

1. See Pl. *Phdr.* 245; *Leg.* 653, 665.

2. So in Athens: Paus. 1. 2. 5.

3. Paus. 2. 20. 4.

4. Nonnus, *Dion.* 20. 331 f.

5. Hor. *Carm.* 2. 19.

6. See p.79 above.

7. *IG* 5. 46.

8. Philodamus of Skarpheia, 53 ff.

9. See also Diod. Sic. 4. 4. 3.

10. Paus. 5. 14. 10.

11. Plut. *Mor. Symp.* 7. 10. 2 (716B).

12. See also Cornut. 30, p.59 L.

13. Eur. *Bacch.* 298 ff.

14. Liv. 39. 13. 12.

15. Herod. 7. 111.

16. See also Paus. 9. 30. 9; Macrob. *Sat.* 1. 18. 1.

17. Eur. *Hec.* 1267; more on this in Rohde, *Psyche*, Vol.II, p.22, note.

18. *Schol. Pind. Pyth. argum.*

19. Paus. 10. 33. 11. Cf. Wilamowitz, *Der Glaube der Hellenen*, Vol.II, p.74, note 2. Wilamowitz, however, places too little emphasis on the significance of prophecy in the cult of Dionysus.

20. Macrob. *Sat.* 1. 18. 1; cf. Tac. *Ann.* 2. 54.

21. K.O. Müller, *Kleine Schriften*, Vol.II, pp.28 ff.

22. Nilsson, *Griechische Feste*, pp.260, 278, 292, et al.; Kern *Rel. d. Griech.*, p.227.

23. Aesch. *Pers.* 614.

24. Eur. *Alc.* 757.

25. Diod. Sic. 4. 5. 1; πυρίπαις: Oppian, *Cyneg.* 4. 287.

26. Nonnus, *Dion.* 21. 222 et al.

27. Cornut. 30, p.58 L.

28. Archil. *fr.* 77.

29. See Karl Reinhardt, *Poseidonios* (Munich, 1921), p.110 f. on Strabo 628, 268 f., 247; Vitr. 8. 3. 12 f.

30. Cf. Strabo 628.

31. Pl. *Leg.* 2. 666a.

32. See Seneca, *De ira* 2. 19. 5; Reinhardt, *Poseidonios* 111, 324 f.

33. Hor. *Carm.* 3. 21. 2-4.

34. Nonnus, *Dion.* 12. 171: βάκχος ἄναξ δάκρυσε, βροτῶν ἵνα δάκρυα λύσῃ.

35. Nonnus, *Dion.* 7. 367.

36. Hes. *Theog.* 941; *Op.* 614.

37. Alc. 97 D.

38. Hor. *Carm.* 1. 18. 1.

39. Ennius, *Trag.* 124 V.

40. See *Cypria* in Ath. 2. 35c; Pind. *fr.* 124b; Bacchyl. *fr.* 20B; Eur. *Bacch.* 279 ff.; Diphilus in Ath. 2. 35d, et al.

41. Plut. *Mor. Symp.* 7. 10. 2 (716B-C).

42. Eratosthenes in Ath. 2. 36 f.

43. See Alc. 66, 104; Plin. *HN* 14. 141, et al.

44. See Plut. *Mor. Symp.* 1. 1. 2; *Schol. Plat. Symp.* 217e.

45. Nonnus, *Dion.* 7. 7 ff.

46. Gen. 5. 29 with an obvious allusion to 3. 17.

47. Gen. 9. 20.

48. Jeremiah 16. 7; cf. the cup of consolation in Nonnus, *Dion.* 19. 1 ff.

49. Cf. Johann F.H. Gunkel, *Handkommentar zum Alten Testament* (Göttingen, 1922), Genesis 5. 29.

50. Aesch. *Eum.* 728.
51. Hom. *Od.* 21. 295; cf. Callim. *Anth. Pal.* 7. 725; Verg. *Catal.* 11.
52. Hom. *Od.* 9. 196 ff.
53. Hom. *Od.* 21. 295 ff.
54. See, for example, Eubolus in Ath. 2. 36b.
55. Plut. *Mor. De Is. et Os.* 6 (353B); cf. also Plin. *HN* 14. 58.

## 13. Dionysus Revealed in Vegetative Nature

1. See Plut. *Mor. De Is. et Os.* 37 (365E); Ov. *Fast.* 3. 767 ff., et al.
2. *Hymn. Hom.* 26. 1. Also κισσοχαίτης: Ecphantides *fr.* 3; Pratinas *fr.* 1. 43; κισσοψόρος: Pind. *Ol.* 2. 50; Ar. *Thesm.* 988; κισσοθαλής: Pind. *fr.* 75. 11, et al.
3. Cf. W. Wrede, "Der Maskengott," *Ath. Mitt.* 53 (1928), pp.66 ff.
4. Paus. 1. 31. 6.
5. See Plin. *HN* 16. 144; Arr. *Anab.* 5. 1. 6; 5. 2. 5 f., et al.
6. See Plut. *Mor. Quaest. Rom.* 112 (291A); Paus. 7. 20. 2; Arr. *Anab.* 5. 2. 16; Hesych. Βακχᾶν.
7. παράσημον Διονύσου: III Maccab. 2. 29; cf. C.A. Lobeck, *Aglaophamus* (Königsberg, 1829), Vol.I, pp.657 ff.; Wilamowitz, *Der Glaube der Hellenen*, Vol.II, p.372.
8. See Eur. *Phoen.* 65, and scholium.
9. *Hymn. Orph.* 47.
10. Eur. *Antiope fr.* 203 (Nauck²).
11. *Schol. Eur. Phoen.* 651.
12. Plut. *Mor. Amat. narr.* 1 (772B).
13. See Plut. *Mor. Symp.* 3. 5. 2 (653A).
14. Nonnus, *Dion.* 45. 311 ff.
15. Plut. *Mor. Quaest. Rom.* 112 (291A).
16. Plut. *Mor. Symp.* 3. 1. 3 (647A).
17. See Plin. *HN* 24. 75 ff.; Plut. *Mor. Quaest. Rom.* 112 (291A); Tert. *De Corona* 7, et al. For its narcotic qualities, see W. Roscher, Review of L. Weniger, "Altgriechischer Baumkultus," *Berl. Phil. Wochenschrift* 40 (1920), p.198.
18. Arr. *Anab.* 5. 27.
19. Plut., ibid.

20. See G. Hegi, *Illustrierte Flora von Mitteleuropa* (Munich 1936), Vol.V, 2, pp. 924 f.

21. πάσης ὑγρᾶς φύσεως: Plut. *Mor. De Is. et Os.* 35 (365A), cf. 34 (364D); also Varro in Augustine *De civ. D.* 7. 21.

22. Diels, *Vorsokr.*, Vol.I, p.236.

23. Pindar, *fr.* 153.

24. Plut. *Mor. Symp.* 5. 3. 1 (675F).

25. Ἔνδενδρος: Hesych.

26. Diod. Sic. 3. 63. 2; see also Ath. 3. 82d.

27. Kern, *Inschr. von M.*, no. 215.

28. See Ar. *Nub.* 604; Eur. *Ion* 716; *fr.* 752, etc.

29. Paus. 2. 2. 7.

30. Plut. *Mor. Symp.* 5. 3. 1 (676A-B).

31. Plut., ibid.

32. Plut. *Mor. De Is. et Os.* 36 (365B).

33. Hesych.; see also Clem. Al. *Protr.*, p.30 P.

34. Ath. 3. 78 D; Hesych.

35. See *Schol. Ar. Ran.* 330; *Schol. Pind. Isthm.* 3. 88; Dittenberg. *SIG*² 615, et al.

36. Paus. 1. 31. 4.

37. Paus. 7. 21. 6.

38. Ath. 11. 465a; see Euanthes as the son or grandson of Dionysus: Hes. *fr.* 120; *Schol. Ap. Rhod.* 3. 997; Paus. 7. 4. 8.

39. Ov. *Fast.* 5. 345.


## 14. *Dionysus and the Element of Moisture*

1. Hom. *Il.* 14. 201, 246; cf. *Orphic. fr.* 57 K.

2. Arist. *Metaph.* 1. 983 B.

3. See also Plut. *Mor. De Is. et Os.* 34 (364D).

4. Plut. *Mor. De Is. et Os.* 35 (364F).

5. *Schol. Il.* 14. 369 T; cf. Lobeck, *Aglaoph.*, Vol.I, p.574.

6. Nonnus, *Dion.* 20. 325 ff.

7. Paus. 3. 24. 3.

8. Paus. 10. 19. 3.

9. See above p.64.

10. Ath. 1. 27 E.

11. Strabo 8. 363.

12. Paus. 2. 7. 6.

13. Ath. 11. 465 A.

14. Hesych.

15. W. Wrede, "Der Maskengott," *Ath. Mitt.* 53 (1928), p.94.

16. Paus. 2. 23. 1.

17. Paus. 3. 24. 4.

18. Reproduced in Wrede, *op. cit.*, p.89.

19. Paus. 4. 36. 7.

20. Serv. *Verg. Aen.* 1. 720.

21. August. *De civ. D.* 7. 21; see also 7. 2 and 6. 9.

22. Plut. *Mor. De cup. div.* 8 (527D).

23. Heraclitus, *fr.* 15.

24. See Nilsson, *Griechische Feste*, p.281.

25. Dittenberg. *SIG²* 19.

26. Hesych.

27. Paus. 10. 19. 3; see Nilsson, *Griechische Feste*, p. 282.

28. Ath. 1. 30 B, et al.

29. See also the Διόνυσος Ἐνόρχης: Hesych. and *Schol. Lyco-phron.* 212.

30. See the pertinent remarks of E. Buschor, "Ein choregisches Denkmal," *Athen. Mitt.* 53 (1928), p.104.

31. Ar. *Ach.* 263 ff.

32. Hom. *Il.* 21. 237.

33. Compare Wilamowitz, *Der Glaube der Hellenen*, Vol.I, p.147, note 2.

34. See Wrede, *op. cit.*, p.89.

35. Plut. *Mor. De Is. et Os.* 35 (364F).

36. Ath. 2. 38 E.

37. Plut. *Mor. Quaest. Graec.* 36 (299B).

38. Aesch. *Edoni fr.* 57.

39. Eur. *Bacch.* 1017.

40. Ibid., 920.

41. βουκέρως: Soph. *fr.* 874; ταυροκέρως: Eur. *Bacch.* 100; Euphorion, *fr.* 13; Nonnus' poem teems with similar epithets and characterizations; see also Hor. *Carm.* 2. 19. 30; Tib. 2. 1. 3; Prop. 3. 17. 19.

42. Plut. *Mor. De Is. et Os.* 35 (364F).

43. Ath. 11. 476 A.

44. See also *Schol. Lycophron.* 1237.

45. Nonnus, *Dion.* 6. 197 ff.

46. Firm. Mat. *Err. prof. rel.* 6. 5.

47. *Schol. Lycophron.* 1237.

48. Soph. *fr.* 607.

49. Paus. 8. 19. 2.

50. Plut. *Mor. De cup. div.* 8 (527D).

51. Cornut. 30, p.60 L.

52. See Wissowa, *RK*, p.184.

53. τραγίζουσι; Arist. *Hist. An.* 7. 1; the same term was used in Latin: *hirquitallire* and *hirquitallus:* Censorinus, *De die natali* 14. 7; Paul. p.101, 105.

54. From the stem of ἔριφος; see Jacobsohn, Χάριτες *für F. Leo* (Berlin, 1911), p.428.

55. The word *caper* lies hidden in the old festival name of the *Nonae Caprotinae* in which the wild fig is important; see Jacobsohn, ibid.

56. Paus. 4. 20. 2.

57. τραγᾶν; see Victor Hehn, *Kulturpflanzen und Haustiere*[6] (Berlin, 1894), p.537.

58. Dion. Hal. 17. 2.

59. Probus on Verg. *Georg.* 1. 9; cf. C. Robert, *Heldensage* (Berlin, 1920), p.85.

60. Ἐρίφιος: Apollod. in Steph. Byz. s.v. Ἀκρώρεια; in Laconia the term is Ἔριφος: Hesych. s.v. Εἰραφιώτης.

61. *Hymn. Hom.* of the Moscow MS 2, et al.

62. So Porphyr. *Abst.* 3. 17; see Gruppe, *Griech. Mythol.*, p.822, note 4 and Wilamowitz, *Der Glaube der Hellenen*, Vol.II, p.67, note 1.

63. Apollod. *Bibl.* 3. 4. 3; cf. Nonnus, *Dion.* 14. 155 ff.

64. Ant. Lib. 28; Ov. *Met.* 5. 329.

65. Leonidas, *Anth. Pal.* 9. 99; Verg. *Georg.* 2. 380, et al.

66. ἔριφος: Dittenberg. *SIG*[2] 623.

67. χίμαρος καλλιστεύων: Dittenberg. *SIG*[2] 615, 27.

68. Paus. 9. 8. 2.

69. Plut. *Mor. Symp.* 6. 7. 2 (692F).

70. *Schol. Ar. Ach.* 146.

71. Paus. 2. 35. 1.

72. Polemon, *fr.* 73.

73. See Serv. *Aen.* 7. 188 and the Villa Borghese mosaic described by R. Herbig, "Mosaik im Casino der Villa Borghese,"

*Röm. Mitt.* (1925), pp.289 ff., and reproduced in supplement XII.
74. M.P. Nilsson, "Dionysos im Schiff," *Archiv f. Religionswiss.* 11 (1908), p.401.
75. Lactant. *Div. Inst.* 1. 21. 27; *Schol. German. Arat.* p.51 B.
76. Paus. 2. 38. 3; cf. G. Oikonomos, "Bronzen von Pella," *Ath. Mitt.* 51 (1926), pp.83 f.
77. Plin. *HN* 24. 2.
78. See Cornutus 30, p.60 L.
79. See Plut. *Mor. De Is. et Os.* 30 (362F), et al.
80. Ps. Eratosth. (*Cat.*) 11.
81. Paus. 10. 18. 4.

## 15. *Dionysus and the Women*

1. Varro, *Ling.* 5. 61.
2. See *Hymn. Hom.* 26, et al.
3. τιθῆναι: Hom. *Il.* 6. 132, et al.
4. See Ludwig Euing, *Die Sage von Tanaquil* (Frankfurt am Main, 1933), pp.27 ff.
5. Hes. *fr.* 27.
6. Cf. Hes. *fr.* 27 ff.
7. Bacchyl. 11. 50 ff.; cf. Pherecyd. *fr.* 24.
8. Apollod. *Bibl.* 2. 2. 2.
9. See Robert, *Heldensage, op. cit.*, pp.246 f.
10. Nonnus, *Dion.* 30. 195 ff.
11. See Suidas, μελαναιγίδα Διόνυσον.
12. See Philochor. *fr.* 78.
13. Philochor. *fr.* 31.
14. See Hom. *Il.* 18. 39 ff.; Hes. *Theog.* 240 ff.; Apollod. *Bibl.* 1. 2. 7.
15. See L. Euing, *Die Sage von Tanaquil*, pp.33 ff.
16. Plin. *HN* 28, 39.
17. Kern, *Inschr. v. Magnesia* 215.
18. See also Eur. *Bacch.* 680 ff.
19. See Deubner, *Attische Feste*, p.126.
20. Plut. *Mor. De mul. virt.* 13 (249F).
21. Frickenhaus, *Lanäenvasen.*
22. See, for example, Strabo 10. 468.
23. Aesch. *fr.* 61.

24. Eur. *Bacch.* 353.

25. Clem. Al. *Protr.*, p.30 P.

26. Apollod. *Bibl.* 3. 4. 3; cf. Nonnus, *Dion.* 14. 159 ff.

27. Anac. *fr.* 2.

28. *Hymn. Orph.* 55. 7; cf. 46. 3.

29. Serv. *Aen.* 1. 720.

30. Soph. *OT* 1105 ff.

31. See E. Buschor, "Ein choregisches Denkmal," *Ath. Mitt.* 53 (1928), p.104.

32. See Adolf Furtwängler, Karl Reichhold, *Griechische Vasenmalerei* (Munich, 1904-1932), Plates 143-145, with Buschor's comments.

33. Eur. *Bacch.* 686 ff.

34. Nonnus, *Dion.* 14. 363; 15. 80 ff.; 33. 368 f.; 35. 209 ff.

35. Philostr. *Imag.* 2. 17. 7.

36. See Buschor's comments on Plate 149 of Furtwängler-Reichhold.

37. Goethe, *Wahlverwandtschaften* II, 7.

## 16. *Ariadne*

1. Hes. *Theog.* 948; Eur. *Hipp.* 339.

2. Prop. 3. 17. 8; Ov. *Fast.* 3. 510 ff.

3. Diod. Sic. 5. 51. 4.

4. See Paus. 2. 22. 1.

5. Hesych.; see Wilamowitz, *Der Glaube der Hellenen*, Vol.I, p.405.

6. Plut. *Vit. Thes.* 20.

7. Paus. 2. 23. 8.

8. See Paul W. Kretschmer, *Die griechischen Vaseninschriften ihrer Sprache nach untersucht* (Gütersloh, 1894), p.198.

9. ‘Αγνὴ ’Αφροδίτη; see Dittenberg. *SIG*² 769, together with the inscriptions mentioned there in the notes.

10. Bacchyl. 17. 113 ff.; see also Wilamowitz, *Sitz. Berlin* (1925), p.234.

11. See *Hymn. Hom. Ven.* 6. 7.

12. See *Schol. Arat.* 71; Ov. *Fast.* 3. 154.

13. Hom. *Il.* 18. 400 ff.

14. Hom. *Od.* 24. 74 f.

15. See, most recently, Wilamowitz, *Der Glaube der Hellenen*, Vol.I, pp.402 ff.

16. Hes. *Theog.* 947.

17. Hom. *Od.* 11. 324.

18. See, most recently, Wilamowitz, *Der Glaube der Hellenen*, Vol.I, p.404.

19. Diels, *Vorsokr.*, p.498.

20. See *Schol. Ap. Rhod.* 3. 997.

21. Paus. 2. 23. 7-8.

22. Plut. *Vit. Thes.* 20.

23. See Nilsson, *Griech. Feste*, pp.369 ff.

24. Hom. *Il.* 18. 590 ff.

25. Wilamowitz, *Der Glaube der Hellenen*, Vol.I, p.403.

26. See Paus. 9. 40. 2; Welcker, *Gr. Götterlehre, op. cit.*, Vol.II, p.590.

27. Plut. *Vit. Thes.* 21.

28. See Prop. 2. 3. 18.

29. Nonnus, *Dion.* 47. 664 ff.

30. Ibid., 25. 110.

31. See *Hymn. Hom.* 26.

32. *Mon. d. Ist.* II, 17.

33. See Paus. 8. 38. 3 f.; 8. 31. 4; 8. 47. 3.

34. See Plut. *Vit. Thes.* 23, et al.

35. Plut. *Vit. Thes.* 20. 1.

36. Paus. 8. 23. 6.

37. Plut. *Mor. Quaest. Graec.* 12 (293D-F).

38. Plut. *Vit. Thes.* 20.

39. *Certam. Hom.* 234.

40. Plut. *Vit. Thes.* 20.

## 17. *The Fate of Dionysus*

1. See Nilsson, *Minoan-Mycenaean Religion*, pp.461 f.

2. Philochorus, *fr.* 22.

3. Plut. *Mor. De Is. et Os.* 35 (365A).

4. For more on this, see Lobeck, *Aglaophamus*, Vol.I, pp.573 f.

5. See Ps. Clem. *Recogn.* 10. 24; Lobeck, ibid., pp.574 ff.

6. Paus. 2. 23. 8.

7. Plut. *Mor. De Is. et Os.* 35 (364F).

8. See above, pp.77 f.

9. See the reference in Kern, *Orphica fragmenta* 110 and pp. 227 ff.

10. ὁ μεγάλως ἀγρεύων: *Etym. Gud.* 227.

11. See above, p.109.

12. See p.116 above.

13. *Etym. Magn.* 406.

14. Aesch. *fr.* 228; cf. *fr.* 5.

15. Callim. *fr.* 171.

16. Νυκτιπόλος: Eur. *Cret. fr.* 472.

17. Νυκτέλιος: Plut. *Mor. De E.* 9 (389A); Ov. *Met.* 4. 15.

18. Paus. 1. 40. 6.

19. *Alcmaionis fr.* 3.

20. Callim. *fr.* 171.

21. Paus. 8. 37. 5.

22. K.O. Müller, *Prolegomena*, pp.390 ff.

23. Welcker, *Griechische Götterlehre*, Vol.II, p.637.

24. L. Weniger, *ARW* 10, pp.61 ff.

25. Lobeck, *Aglaophamus*, Vol.I, pp.670 ff.

26. Printed in Kern, *Orph. frag.*, pp.101 f.

27. See Wilamowitz, *Der Glaube der Hellenen*, Vol.II, pp.373 ff.

28. *Schol. Clem. Al. Protr.* 4. 4 p.297. 4 Stähl; Deubner, *Attische Feste, op. cit.*, p.126.

29. See Nonnus, *Dion.* 6. 204.

30. Kern, *Orph. frag.*, pp.234 f.

31. Lycophron 229, with scholium.

32. Ael. *NA* 12. 34.

33. See Ar. *Ran.* 47; Paus. 8. 31. 4.

34. Ἀνθρωπορραίστης; see above, pp.107 following.

35. Plut. *Mor. De Is. et Os.* 35 (364F); see above, p.162.

36. See above, p.80.

37. See above, p.80.

38. Plut. *Mor. De Is. et Os.* 35 (364F).

39. Plut. *Mor. De E* 9 (389C).

40. See Plut. *Mor. De prim. frig.* 18 (953D).

41. See Pind. *fr.* 83; Pl. *Leg.*, p.700 B.

42. Eduard Norden, *Die Geburt des Kindes* (Leipzig, 1924), p.36.

43. See above, p.98.
44. Wilamowitz, *Der Glaube der Hellenen*, Vol.II, pp.372 f.
45. See above, pp.130 f.
46. Cf. Plut. *Mor. De sera* 27 (566A); Hor. *Carm.* 3. 3. 13, et al.
47. Plut. *Mor. Quaest. conv.* 8. *praef.* (717A).
48. See above, p.103.
49. *Il.* 6. 132 ff.
50. Diod. Sic. 5. 51. 4.
51. Eumelus, *fr.* 10 K.
52. Eur. *Bacch.* 302; Plut. *Vit. Demetr.* 2; Macrob. *Sat.* 1. 19. 1, et al.
53. Diod. Sic. 4. 5. 2; Arr. *Anab.* 6. 28. 2; Lactant. *Inst.* 1. 10. 8; Tert. *De Corona* 7. 12.
54. See Wilamowitz, *Der Glaube der Hellenen*, Vol.II, p.78, note 2.
55. See the wooden statues of Dionysus with their red paint: Paus. 2. 2. 6 and also Paus. 7. 26. 11; 8. 39. 6.
56. Arr. *Anab.* 6. 28; Plut. *Vit. Alex.* 67.
57. See above, p.64.
58. Diehl, *Anth. Lyr. Graec.* 6, p. 252.
59. See also Pindar's dithyramb for the City Dionysia, *fr.* 75.
60. Paus. 3. 22. 2.
61. Paus. 1. 31. 4; 7. 21. 6.
62. Nilsson, *Minoan-Mycenaean Religion*, pp.496 ff.
63. See Himer. *Orat.* 3. 6.
64. Plut. *Mor. De Is. et Os.* 69 (378F).
65. This in spite of Wilamowitz, *Der Glaube der Hellenen*, Vol.II, p.63.
66. See Kretschmer, *Aus der Anomia*, p. 19.
67. Lobeck, *Aglaophamus*, Vol.I, p.271, note; cf. Nilsson, *Griech. Feste*, p. 262.

## 18. *Dionysus and Apollo*

1. See above, pp.53.
2. See Apollod. *Bibl.* 3. 5. 3; *Schol. Ar. Ran.* 330; Horace has him enter there, after a life filled with fame, in his tiger chariot: *Carm.* 3. 3. 13.
3. Paus. 10. 19. 4.

4. Plut. *Mor. De E.* 9 (388E).

5. *Schol. Pind. Argum. Pyth.;* see E. Rohde, *Psyche*, Vol.II, p.54, note 2.

6. *Compte-rendu de la commission archéol. de St. Pétersbourg* (1861), Plate 4. See M.P. Nilsson, *Geschichte der griechischen Religion* (Munich, 1955), Plate 38.

7. See Macrob. *Sat.* 1. 18. 1 ff., et al.

8. See above, p.190.

9. Paus. 3. 19. 3.

10. Nonnus, *Dion.* 19. 104.

11. Paus. *op. cit.*

12. See *GDI* 3502, 3512; *Arch. Anz.* (1905), p.11.

13. See Nilsson, *Griech. Feste*, p. 241.

14. Hesychius.

15. See above, p.187.

16. Hesychius, see below, p.206.

17. See pp.162 f.

18. See p.106.

19. Apollod. *Bibl.* 3. 15. 8.

20. Phanodemus, *fr.* 3.

21. See also Ps. Demosthenes, *Epitaph.* 27.

22. Philochorus, *fr.* 31.

23. See Polemon in Athen. 4. 139 A.

24. Nilsson, *Griech. Feste*, pp.188 f.

25. E. Rohde, *Psyche*, Vol.I, p.140.

26. So also Samson Eitrem, *RE* 9, col. 14 f., s.v. Ὑάκινθος.

27. Diod. Sic. 4. 68. 6.

28. Macrob. *Sat.* 1. 18. 2.

29. Polyb. 8. 28; see also Apollo Hyakinthios in Nonnus, *Dion.* 11. 330.

30. See Wilamowitz, *Der Glaube der Hellenen*, Vol.II, p.73, et al.

31. Paus. 10. 32. 7; cf. Nonnus, *Dion.* 27. 259 f.; Luc. 5. 72 ff.

32. Paus. 10. 6. 4.

33. *Schol. Lycophron.* 209.

34. Cf. *Il.* 14. 261.

# Index

Agave, 66, 67, 172, 174

Agrionia, Agriania, Agrania (festival), 44, 77, 79, 103, 105, 118-119, 196, 199, 200; as festival of the dead, 103; as days of the dead, 118-119; time of, 119

Aigai, "one-day vines" at, 99

Anthesteria (festival), 80, 100, 159, 163, 198, 206; time of, 119; festival of the dead in Athens, 117; at Smyrna, 53; Thucydides on, 53

Aphrodite, 161, 171, 184; associated with Ariadne, 182-183; with Dionysus, 176

Apollo, 185; the nature of his world, 142; opposition of, to Dionysus questioned, 207; relationship of, to Dionysus, ch. 18 passim; in Amyclae, 203; in Delphi, 203; in Tarentum, 206

Archon Basileus, wife of, 80, 83, 84, 85, 100

Ariadne, 57, 98, 164, 172, 177, ch. 16 passim; associated with Aphrodite, 182-183, 185; with Kore, 184; with moisture, 184; with Semele, 185, 186; compared to a maenad, 94; crown of, 184; and the dance, 183, 186-187; death of, 57, 188; dies in labor, 185; disappearance of, 197; duality of, 188; grave of, 104, 187; hangs herself, 188; immortality of, 181-182; in Argos, 185; in Crete, 181; in Cyprus, 181, 185, 186; in Delos, 181, 183, 186; in Locris, 104, 181, 184; in Naxos, 181; meets Dionysus, 188; as nursemaid to Dionysus, 187; as the wife of Dionysus, 181; as woman of the sea, 182; Plate 12

Ariagne (dialectical variant of Ariadne), 183, 187

Aridela (name for Ariadne), 182

Artemis, 57, 171, 204; as the Lady of Clamours, 92; associated with Ariadne, 183-184; kills Ariadne, 185; kills Coronis, 185; Apagchomenē, 188; Korythalia, 205; Orthia, 104, 113

Ass, associated with Dionysus, 111, 170; in Delphi, 170; in Egypt, 170; head of, on bow of Dionysus' ship, 170; Plate 11

Autonoe, 66, 67, 172, 174

Bakchai, 134

Bacchanalia, 144

Bakchos, as Lydian equivalent for Dionysus, 60

Bassarai, 175

Birth, arises from moisture, 171; related to death, 138

Blood sacrifice, origins of, 20-21

Bull, associated with Dionysus (see also Dionysus in animal form), 110, 165; as victim of

Bull—*Cont.*
  maenads, 96; represents duality
  of Dionysus, 166; statue of, in
  Greece, 166
Buskins, *see Cothurnus*

Charites, associated with Diony-
  sus, 144, 164, 176
Choes (festival), 63, 86, 104
Christians, attitude toward Dionysus, 176
City Dionysia (festival in Athens), 83, 164, 198
Claros, Apollonian seers in, 144
Coronis, 57, 185
*Cothurnus, cothurni*, 83, 107, 192
Crane Dance, 186, 187
Creativity, relationship to deity,
  25, 31
Cult patterns, as a reflection of
  myth, 16
*Cultus*, definition of, 4; nature of,
  21, 22; its forms determined by
  the proximity of deity, 20; as a
  new creation, 12; as a creation
  of the human spirit, 18; criti-
  cism of, as an imitation of myth,
  18; relationship to myth in religion of Dionysus, 44-45; as a
  sacred language, 19; as presupposing myth, 16; origins of, 18;
  origins of, arising from an encounter with deity, 27; Wilamowitz on the purpose of, 14

Dance, and Dionysus, 143; associated with Ariadne, 186-187
Death, relationship to life in Dionysus, 137-142
Deity, imminence of, used to explain origins of *cultus*, 34; as
  the origin of creativity, 29-31
Dionysiades, 175
Dionyso, 88
Dionysus, as alien to Homeric
  religion, 202-203; his aloofness,
  165; in animal form, as boar,
  110; as bull, 110, 134, 166, 193,
  as goat, 168; as lion, 110, 176,

193; as snake, 110, 193; and
  Apollo, ch. 18 *passim;* marries
  wife of Archon Basileus, 83, 84,
  85, 117; early appearance in
  Greece, 58; appears to Ariadne,
  182, 188; appears in spring, 163,
  199; Argive festival of, 63-64;
  associated with the sea, 198; his
  birthplace, ch. 2 *passim;* bloodthirstiness of (*see* also Dionysus
  Omēstēs), 135; as conqueror, 77,
  197-198; linked with death, ch.
  17 *passim;* as the "delight of
  mortals," 55; as deliverer (*see*
  Dionysus Lyaios), 97; devoured,
  192, 195; dismemberment of, by
  the Titans, 107; diversity of, 50;
  dual birth of, 65; the duality of,
  121, 169, 200-201, 202; as "the
  god of two forms" (dimor-
  phos), 110; as "the eater of raw
  flesh" (*see* Dionysus Omēstēs),
  109; his entry into Greece, 52;
  the myths of his epiphany, ch.
  4 *passim;* the fate of, ch. 17
  *passim;* his femininity, 175, 176;
  grave of, in Argos, 190; in Delphi, 103-104, 190, 203; in Thebes,
  190; Homeric epic on, 53; as
  hunter, 109; as Iakchos, 82; as
  the god of imminence, ch. 5
  *passim;* as "the joyful," 56; as
  Liknites, 81, 82, 190, 193-194,
  194; as Lord of Souls, 49, 117;
  as the "loud shouter," 93; as the
  mad god, ch. 11 *passim;* associated with madness, ch. 9 *passim;*
  madness of, caused by Hera,
  173; symbol of mask of, explained, ch. 6 *passim;* depicted
  as mask on a column, 86; as lord
  and bearer of moisture, 156; and
  the element of moisture, ch. 14
  *passim* (166 ff.); multiplicity of,
  196; myth of death of, compared with that of Osiris, 195;
  origins of, in Asia Minor, questioned, 60; possible origins in
  Thrace, 52; in Lydia, 52; in

Phrygia, 52; origin of name of, 61; as god accompanied by pandemonium and silence, ch. 7 *passim;* as spirit of paradox, 136; compared to Paris, 175-176; and the pirates, 93, 96, 111; associated with prophecy, 97, 144; description of the ship of, 93; ship-cart of, 53, 198; the death-like silence which accompanies him, 93-94; as son of Zeus and Semele, ch. 3 *passim;* as suffering god, 103; relationship to Thetis, 56-57; and his relationship to tragedy, ch. 19 *passim;* in underworld, 79; brings back Semele from the underworld, 115; associated with the underworld, 115, 169, 190, 191; as god of vegetation, 49-50; revealed in vegetative nature, ch. 13 *passim;* as tree, 110; as god of wine, ch. 12 *passim;* and women, 142; associated with women, ch. 15 *passim;* womanly epithets of, 176; the women of, persecuted by Lycurgus, 16; as Zagreus, 105, 107; associated with Zagreus, 191-192

Dionysus Aigobolus, 168; Aktaios, 163; Anthios (antheus), 159, 199; Anthrōporrhaistēs, 105, 107, 113; Bakcheus, masks of, on Naxos, 88; Bougenēs, 162, 166, 193; Bromios, 93, 133; Dandritēs, 157; Eiraphiōtēs, 168; Eleuthereus, image of, at City Dionysia, 83; Eriphios, 167 (note 60); Euanthēs, 159; Kadmeios, 67; Kissokomēs, 153; Limnagenēs, 163; Limnaios, 163; Lysios, Lyaios, 97, 113; Lysios, 106; Mainomenos (*see* also Dionysiac madness), 127, 135; Mainolēs, 135; Meilichios, masks of, on Naxos, 88; Melanaigis, 114, 169, 173; Morychos, 169; Melpomenos, 143; Mousagetēs, 144; Nuktelios, 116, 191 (note 17); Omadios,

107; Orthos, 114; Palagios, 163; Perikionios, 153; Phallen, mask of, on Lesbos, 88; Ploutodotēs ("giver of riches"), 103, 113; Polygēthēs ("the joyful one"), 103, 113, 148; Pyrigenēs, 146; Pyroeis, 146; Thriambos, 197; Thyonidas, 71, 134 (note 11), 165; Zukites, 158

Dionysus, at Aigai, 99; in Amphicleia, 144; at Andros, 98, 194; in Arcadia (Alea), 104; in Arcadia (Cynaitha), 167; in Argos, 80, 104, 106, 118-119, 143, 162, 166, 183, 190, 192-193; in Athens (*see* also Lenaea), 175; in Attica, 169; in Boeotia, 58, 119, 157, in Boeotia (Chaeronea), 119, 196; in Boeotia (Orchomenus), 103, 118, 176, 196; in Boeotia (Potnai), 168; in Chios, 107, 163; on Cithaeron, 167; in Corinth, 157; in Crete, 167; in Cyzicus, 166; in Delos, 164; at Delphi, 53, 99, 190, 203; in Elis, 98, 131, 166, 175, 193; in Euboea, 163; in Hermione, 169; in Icaria, 153, 163; in India, 93, 198; in Laconia (Brasiai), 162, 163, 199; in Lesbos (Methymna), 163; in Lydia, 52, 199; in Magnesia on the Maeander, 174; in Megara, 191; in Messenia (Cyparission), 164; in Metapontum, 168; in Myconos, 168; on Naxos, 98, 144, 197; in Olympia, 144; in Pagasae, 163; in Paphlagonia (?), 199; on Parnassus, 174, 207; in Phocis, 58; in Phrygia, 52, 59-60, 197, 199; in Rhodes, 134, 168; on Samos, 111; on Sicyon, 163; in Smyrna, 198; in Sparta, 163; in Syracuse, 169; in Tenedos, 107, 132, 192, 204-205; in Teos, 97; at Thebes, 153; in Thrace, 58-59

Dithyramb, 194, 203; associated with myths of birth of Dionysus, 194

Divination, *see* prophecy
Dolphin, 155
Dysmainai, 175

Epidemic, dancing, 125; religious, 124-125
Erechtheus, daughters of, 173, 205
Erigone (daughter of Icarius), 104, 157, 188
Erinyes, relationship to Dionysus, 114, 143; worshipped as Maniai, 114
Eros, associated with Dionysus, 176
Exekias, 63, 163; Plate 10

Fig tree, associated with Dionysus, 158, 167-168; symbol for sexual intercourse, 158
Flute, excites madness, 94
François vase, picture of Dionysus on, 90; Crane Dance on, 186
Frickenhaus, 86, 100
Fruit, under the care of Dionysus, 157

*Gerarai*, 80, 100, 175
Goat, 111; as sacrificial victim to Dionysus, 168; associated with Dionysus, 167-169; with the underworld, 169; characteristics of, 168; "playing the goat," 167; gives its name to trees, 167-168
Grotto, associated with Dionysus, 163-164; Plate 5
Hades, 158; relationship to Dionysus, 116, 143
Hagnē, definition of, 183
Hera, 135, 168, 171, 172, 173, 179
Heraclitus, on identification of Dionysus with Hades, 116-117
Hermes, 106, 176, 178; characteristics of, 9; festival of, at Tanagra, 41-43; gives Dionysus to nurses, 102, 187; Plate 7
Hiaknythotrophia (festival), 204
Honey, flows from the earth at appearance of Dionysus, 96
Horns, as characteristic of Diony-sus, 134, 166; worn by Laphys-tian maenads, 167
Hosioi, 190, 194
Hyacinthia (festival), 203, 206
Hyacinthides, 205
Hyacinthus, relationship to Apol-lo, 203-204; similarity to Diony-sus, 204-207

*Iliad*, on Dionysus, 54, 57-58; on Dionysus as wine-god, 55-56
Ino (nurse of Dionysus), 63, 66, 72-73, 106, 163, 172, 174, 176; as mortal woman, 73; *Odyssey* on, 73; throws herself into sea, 162-163
Insanity, ascribed to nymphs, 162
Inspiration, relationship to deity, 25-26
Ivy, 86, 87; as antidote to intoxica-tion, 155; appears at birth of Dionysus, 153; associated with death, 155, 157; with Diony-sus, 152-157; warded off earth-quakes, 153; used to decorate graves, 155; grew first in Achar-nian deme, 153; growth pattern analyzed, 154; causes madness, 156; in Nysa (India) on Mt. Meros, 153; compared to snakes, 154; can cause sterility, 155; as "twice born," 154; and vine compared, 155-156; and vine as siblings, 153

Katagogia (festivals of the return of the god), in Ionia, 83
Kid, 155, 168
Klodones, 175
Kore (goddess of the dead), 184, 204

Lamb, as sacrifice to Dionysus, 162
Laphystiai, 134, 167, 175
Lenaea (festival), 67, 80, 174, 175, 200
Lenai, 80, 174
Leopard, 112, 113; Plate 6

Laurel, associated with Apollo, 153

Leucippides, 175

Leucothea (*see* Ino), 73

Lions (*see* also Dionysus in animal form), 109-110, 111-114; young of, suckled by maenads, 102; Nemaean, 113

Lycurgus, 16, 54, 59, 76, 103, 119, 162, 175, 180, 196-197; story of, in *Iliad*, 44

*Lympha, see* nymph

Lynx, 111, 112, 113

Madness, Dionysiac, origins and nature of, discussed, ch. 9 *passim;* origin of, in vegetative magic, criticized, 129-130; the nature of, 143; divine, meaning of, in Dionysus, 136-142

Maenad, maenads (*maenades*), 93-94, 175; origin of name, 94; aloofness of, 177; bloodthirstiness of, 135; bring forth liquids from the earth, 96; evocative of the spirits of the dead, 114-115; nature of ecstasy of, 177; as nurses, 102; coupled with adjective, "ōmophagos," 109; in speechless trance, 94, 115; suckle young of wild beasts, 96, 102; tear apart young of wild beasts, 106, 108-109; *see also* Plates 1-3, 9, 12

Magic, nature of, 35-36

Mana, 11

Mania, *see* madness, Dionysiac

Maron (called Euanthes), as descendant, son of Dionysus, 55

Mask, 209-210; as pure confrontation, 91; of Gorgo, Silene, Achelous, 88; at sanctuary of Artemis Orthia, 87; significance of, 89; as symbol of Dionysus, ch. 6 *passim;* wreathed in ivy, 153

Melikertes (son of Ino), 106

Milk, flows from earth at appearance of Dionysus, 96

Mimallones, 175

Minyas, daughters of, 74, 93, 96-97, 105, 110, 111, 133-134, 172

Moisture, Aristotle on, 161; associated with Ariadne, 184; with birth, 171; with Dionysus, 156, ch. 14 *passim* (160 ff.); Thales on, 161

Morbidity, its relationship to Dionysiac madness discussed, 124

Müller, K. O., 55; on Dionysus in Thrace, 59; on Dionysiac madness, 122, 127, 133; argues against early association of wine with Dionysus, 145

Muses, association of, with Dionysus, 144

Music, relationship to Dionysus, 144

Myrtle, associated with the dead, 158; favorite of Dionysus, 158; used as a surrogate for Semele, 158

Myth, aetiological in nature, 17; origins of, 17, 22-23; as poetry, 13-16; as a product of cult practices, 17; Greek, the nature of, 23, 120

Narthex, associated with Dionysus, 170

Nietzsche, F., 122, 136

Nilsson, M. P., on Dionysus' appearance in festival of the dead, 117; views on birthplace of Dionysus, 52

Nymph, nymphs, 171; as nurses of Dionysus, 171; on Nysa (Parnassus), 81

Nysa (birthplace and home of Dionysus), 59, 61-63; as fairyland, 61; location of, in Arabia, 62, 63; in Egypt, 63; in Ethiopia, 62; in Euboea, 62; on Helicon, 62; in India, 61, 63; in the Land of the Sun, 62; in Lydia, 62; on Parnassus, 62; in Syria, 63; in Thrace, 59, 62

Nysa (nurse of Dionysus), as daughter of Aristaius, 61

Nyseion, 59

Oracles, associated with Dionysus in Amphicleia, 144; in Delphi, 144; in Thrace, 144
Osiris, myth of death of, compared with that of Dionysus, 195

Palaimon, *see* Melikertes
Panther, 110, 111-112, 114, 155; Plate 8
Paris, and Dionysus compared, 175
Parnassus, 194; "one-day vine" at, 98-99
Peisistratus, 198
Pentheus, 66, 74, 76, 108, 109, 110, 114, 157, 166
Periboia, 204
Persephone, 61, 115, 190, 195, 197
Perseus, 74, 77, 104, 162, 193
Phallus, 158, 164-165, 174; as friend of the god, Dionysus, 165
Pharmakos ritual, 39-40
Philomela, 11, 173, 180
Pine, associated with the vine, 157-158; sacred to Dionysus, 157
Plato, on fire and wine, 146-147; on the madness of the philosopher, 136
Priapus, 158; identified with Dionysus, 165
Primaeval, nature of, 120
Procne, 108, 173, 180
Proetus, daughters of, 119, 172-173
Prosymnus, 176
Puberty, rites of, explained, 138

Religion, Greek, anthropological approach to origins of, 7; evolutionary approach to origins of, 8, 9, 10; philological approach to origins of, 7, 8; utility thesis of origins of, 7, 14, 21, 37-38
Rohde, E., on Dionysus as "Lord of Souls," 117; on Dionysiac

madness, 122-123, 126, 127-128; on historical truth in myth, 75; on Hyacinthus, 206; on migration of Dionysus from Thrace, 58

Sacrifice, human, in cult of Dionysus, 113; sacramental, 131; theory of sacramental, criticized, 131-132
Satyrs, as attendants of Dionysus, 165, 176; *see* also Plates 12, 13
Semachus, daughters of, 173
Semele (Thyone), 148, 172, ch. 3 *passim;* accorded cultic honors, 67; as daughter of Cadmus, 66; her desire to dance, 96; as Ge, 69; as Phrygian earth goddess, 60; as mortal woman, 70, 72; holy precinct of, 67; worshipped in Thebes, 71; Plate 4
Ship-cart, 63, 85, 117, 163
Silene, 88
Silenus, 177
Sisterhoods, of Dionysus, 172; in Magnesia on the Maeander, 174
Snake, snakes, 154, 155, 177; associated with Dionysus and maenads, 94, 96, 177; becoming ivy, 155
Sperm, associated with Dionysus, 164
Sphinx, 113-114; as maenad, 114; relationship to Dionysus, 143
Spirit, Greek, as mirrored in religion, 23
Spring, created by Dionysus, 164
Sterility, associated with the ivy, 155
Superstition, nature of, 37

Tattooing, of ivy leaf on initiates of Dionysus, 153
Theseus, 184; abducts Ariadne, 181; relationship to Ariadne, 182
Thetis, 182; relationship to Dionysus, 54, 56
*Thiasos,* 66

Thyia (daughter of Castalios), 207

Thyia (festival), 98

Thyiad, thyiads (*thyiades*), 44, 57, 81, 82, 129, 134, 193, 194, 207; on Parnassus, 174-175, 178

Thyone (*see* Semele), 134; meaning of this title of Semele, 70-71

*Thyrsus*, 96, 157; *see* also Plates 1, 2, 3, 4, 6, 7

Titans, 107, 131; tear apart Zagreus, 131, 192

Tithenidia (festival), 179

Tree-Dionysus, 87

Trees, associated with Dionysus, 157

*Triumphator*, associated with Dionysus, 197-198

Truth, in wine, 149

Vegetation magic, 129

Vegetative nature, and Dionysus, 128; ch. 13 *passim*

Vine, vines, Alcaeus on, 148; Ennius on, 148; Horace on, 148; and ivy as siblings, 153; "oneday," 97, 98-99, 146

Voigt, F. A., on ecstasy, 129; on the rites at Tenedos, 132; on the tearing of animals into pieces, 130

Water, as a Dionysiac element, 162; as dwelling place of the mysteries of life, 161; as the element of women, 171; released with the appearance of Dionysus, 96

Wilamowitz-Moellendorf, U. von, on Ariadne and the choral dance, 186; on Dionysus' arrival in Greece, 53, 59, 60; theory of, on historical formation of the gods, 8-10; philological approach to Greek religion, 8 ff.; on sacramental sacrifice in cult of Dionysus, 132

Wine, at Anthesteria, 100; early association of, with Dionysus, 145; as a conqueror, 150; as a deliverer, 148, 149; its duality, 151; used to produce ecstasy, 145; its fiery nature examined, 146-147; flows from earth at appearance of Dionysus, 96; as gift of Dionysus, 146; Horace on, 148, 149; as metaphor for Dionysus, 146; miraculous appearance of, at festivals of Dionysus, 98; mixing of, before Dionysus (Plate 2), 100; its mysterious nature analyzed 147; on pirate ship, 96; as producer of madness, 150-151; relationship to Dionysus, ch. 12 *passim*

Women, bloodthirstiness of, 180; associated with Dionysus, ch. 15 *passim;* with springs, 171; with water, 171; nature of ecstasy of, 179-180; their relation to Dionysiac ecstasy, 126-127; seized by Dionysiac madness, 134

Zagreus, 131, 191-192; antiquity of myth of, 191; as bull, 167, 192; associated with Dionysus, 196; as chthonic Dionysus, 191; torn to pieces by Titans, 192